G. (George) Eugène-Fasnacht

The student's comparative grammar of the French language; with an historical sketch of the formation of French

For the use of public schools

G. (George) Eugène-Fasnacht

The student's comparative grammar of the French language; with an historical sketch of the formation of French
For the use of public schools

ISBN/EAN: 9783337085612

Printed in Europe, USA, Canada, Australia, Japan

Cover: Foto ©Paul-Georg Meister /pixelio.de

More available books at **www.hansebooks.com**

THE STUDENT'S COMPARATIVE GRAMMAR

OF THE

FRENCH LANGUAGE

WITH AN HISTORICAL SKETCH OF THE FORMATION OF FRENCH.

FOR THE USE OF PUBLIC SCHOOLS.

BY

G. EUGÈNE-FASNACHT.

TWELFTH EDITION.
THOROUGHLY REVISED.

WILLIAMS & NORGATE,
14, HENRIETTA STREET, COVENT GARDEN, LONDON;
AND 20, SOUTH FREDERICK STREET, EDINBURGH.
1890.

PREFACE TO THE FIRST EDITION.

> Une langue nous deviendrait plus vivante encore, si nous pouvions associer à son étude celle de l'idiome dont elle dérive. A. VINET.

My object in compiling this new French Grammar has been to provide an elementary manual of moderate size drawn up on a plan calculated to stimulate a practical application of the student's knowledge of the dead languages (especially of Latin) and thus to bring his reflective powers into active exercise.

It is not my intention to enter into a discussion of the merits or demerits of the comparative method of studying languages, but it is my firm opinion that, in the very lowest forms, a judicious reference to cognate idioms and a careful comparison with them, so far from confusing the youthful mind, will invest the dry subject of grammar with an interest which cannot fail to prove most beneficial to the student's progress.

The essential points in which this Grammar differs from others with regard to practical utility and which, upon unprejudiced inspection, will, I trust, justify its appearance in print, are briefly these:

Constant reference to Latin, (see especially §§ 27—38, the Feminine of Adjectives); §§ 90—99, Irregular Verbs; §§ 134—151, Syntax of Moods and Tenses; § 243, Adverbs of Negation, etc.)

New arrangement of the paradigms of Pronouns on the plan adopted in Latin Grammars, — the only way of bringing light and order into this most difficult part of French Accidence.

In the paradigms of the Conjugation of Regular Verbs the Tenses of the Subjunctive and Conditional stand opposite to the Tenses of the Indicative from which they are respectively derived.

In the treatment of Irregular Verbs, instead of the usual alphabetical lists to be mastered by sheer strength of memory without the student even learning wherein the Irregularities consist and how to account for them, I have introduced an altogether new classification, which attempts to combine scientific accuracy with practical utility. All the irregularities stand out in bold print and are briefly explained by reference to Latin.

a*

In the Syntax a separate chapter has been devoted to the *Infinitive* mood, which, strange to say, is entirely neglected or only incidentally alluded to in even the better grammars now in use. The absurdity of the attempt to write even the easiest piece of French Prose composition without a fair knowledge of the uses of this mood is too obvious to require demonstration (see especially § 152).

With regard to the vexed question of the Place of Adjectives before or after the Substantive, a fundamental theory is presented in § 174.

PREFACE TO THE SECOND EDITION.

The clearer arrangement of paradigms (§§ 49—64, 78—79, 187—195), the introduction of a complete Verbal Index and of a separate chapter for the Syntax of Cases on a plan similar to that adopted in Latin Grammars, and the careful revision of the text throughout, will, it is hoped, bear ample testimony to the author's anxiety to render this second edition more worthy of the eminent Public Schools in which the first edition has been introduced, notwithstanding its many defects.

I need hardly add that I have again carefully consulted the most recent labours in the field of modern philology and derived invaluable assistance from the standard works of Littré, Diez, Maetzner, Max Müller, Ampère and Brachet. To these my obligations have been continuous throughout the book.

PREFACE TO THE ELEVENTH EDITION.

I gladly avail myself of the demand for a new edition to make a few further alterations in points of detail. The general plan of the book remains unaltered.

My hearty thanks are due to several of my colleagues for many valuable suggestions.

November 1887. G. Eugène-Fasnacht,
Late Assistant Master, St. Peter's College, Westminster.

CONTENTS.

INTRODUCTION: PAGE

Historical Sketch of the Formation of the French language XI

ACCIDENCE.

THE ALPHABET:
- §§ 1-4. Vowels, Consonants 1
- §§ 5-7. Accents, Orthographical Signs 2

ARTICLES:
- §§ 8-12. Definite, Partitive, Indefinite 4

SUBSTANTIVES:
- §§ 13-21. Declension, and Formation of the Plural 5
- § 22. Plural of Compound Substantives 7
- § 23. Genders of Substantives 9
- §§ 24-26. Formation of the Feminine 10

ADJECTIVES:
- §§ 27-38. Formation of the Feminine 13
- §§ 39-41. Comparison (regular and irregular) 16

NUMERALS:
- §§ 42-48. Cardinal, Ordinal, Fractional, Collective, Proportional, Adverbial 17

PRONOUNS:
- §§ 49-52. A. *Personal Pronouns*, Conjunctive, Reflective, Disjunctive 21
- §§ 53-55. B. *Possessive Pronouns*, Possessive Adjectives and Possessive Pronouns proper 23
- §§ 56-61. C. *Demonstrative Pronouns,* { Demonstrative Adjectives / Demonstrative Pronouns proper } 24
- §§ 62-64. D. *Relative Pronouns* 25
- §§ 65-66. E. *Interrogative Pronouns* { used Adjectively / — Substantively } 26
- § 67. *Periphrastic Interrogation* 27
- §§ 68-71. *Indefinite Pronouns* { used Adjectively / — Substantively / — both Adjectively and Substantively } 29

CONTENTS.

VERBS:

PAGE

§§ 72-76. **Auxiliary** Verbs, **Avoir**, **Être**, Affirmatively 29
        —   -   -   -   - Interrogatively, Negatively 32

Regular Verbs.

§§ 77-79. Conjugations, Principal Parts, **Derivation of** Tenses 34
- 80-83. A. Active Voice. Paradigms **of the Four** Conjugations:
        Aimer, Finir, Recevoir, Vendre... 36
§ 84. Remarks on Peculiarities 44
- 85. B. **Passive Voice**... 46
§§ 86-87. C. **Intransitive** Verbs....................................... 47
§ 88. D. Reflective Verbs.. 48
§§ 89-90. E. Impersonal Verbs... 50
        F. Strong **and Anomalous Verbs:**
§ 91. General Remarks 51
- 92. *First* Conjugation 52
      Second Conjugation:... 54
- 93. I. Verbs which **in the** Pres. Indic. contract their endings.
    (A.) Verbs **which drop** their Stem Consonant **in** the Sing.
        Pres. Ind.
    (B.) Verbs **which do not** alter their stem.
    (C.)   -   -   alter the Vowel of their Stem.
- 94. II. **Verbs** which **follow** the 1st Conjugation—
    (A.) In the **Present Tense** (Past Part. -ert).
    (B.) In the **Present**, Future and Conditional.
Third Conjugation: 58
- 95. I. Verbs the stems of which end in **V**
- 96. II. -   - - - - - - **L**
- 97. III. - which cannot be classified.
Fourth Conjugation:... 60
- 98. I. Verbs the Stems of which end in *a Vowel*,
    (A.) Pret.: **s-is**, Past Part.: **i-t**,
    (B.) -   **s**,   -   - **i-t**,
    (C.) -   **us**,   -   - **u.**
- 99. II. Verbs the Stems **of** which end in *a Consonant*
    (A.) Inf.: nd-re, Pres. Part.: gn-ant, Past Part.: **-nt**,
    (B.) - ou-d-re,   -   - s (l, lv)-ant, - - -u,
    (C.) - ît-re,   -   - iss-ant,   -   - -u.
§§ 100-103. Defective Verbs 68

ADVERBS:

§§ 104-106. Formation and Comparison of Adverbs 70
§ 108. Adverbs of Place; Time; Order, Manner, Degree, Quantity;
     Affirmation and Negation 72

PREPOSITIONS:

§ 109. Simple and Compound Prepositions 74

CONTENTS. VII

CONJUNCTIONS: PAGE
§ 110. I. Coordinate Conjunctions 76
II. Subordinate Conjunctions, requiring
  a) The Indicative.
  b) The Subjunctive.
  c) The Indicative or Subjunctive
  d) The Infinitive.

APPENDIX I. *Gender of Substantives:*
§§ 112-114. Gender ascertained by *Meaning, Termination, Derivation* 78
§ 115. Substantives of either Gender according to the Meaning 84

Plural of Substantives:
- 116. Substantives with a different meaning in the Singular and the Plural 85
- 117. Substantives not used in the Singular 86

SYNTAX.

CONSTRUCTION:
§§ 118-124. Logical, Inverted and Periphrastic Construction 86

THE VERB:
§§ 125-128. *Concord* 88

Government of Verbs:
§ 129. The Accusative 89
§§ 130-131. The Dative 90
- 132-133. The Genitive 92

Moods and Tenses:
§§ 134-140. *Indicative Mood.* Present, Imperfect, Preterite, Indefinite, Pluperfect, Anterior, Future 94
§ 141. *Conditional Mood* 97
§§ 142-150. *Subjunctive Mood* after Verbs and Conjunctions expressing—
  a) Wish, Command, Necessity
  b) Doubt Ignorance, Uncertainty
  c) Affection of the Mind
  d) Purpose, Result, Concession, Supposition
  98
  The Subjunctive in *Relative* and *Principal* Clauses 100
§ 151. Sequence of Tenses 102

Infinitive Mood:
- 152. The Infinitive instead of the Indicative and Subjunctive 103
- 153.   "   "   without Prepositions .... —
- 154.   "   "   after **Faire** 104
- 155-156. The Infinitive preceded by **de**, by **à** 104

Participles:
- 157-159. The Present Participle and the Verbal Adjective 106
- 160-164. The Past Participle 107

CONTENTS.

ARTICLES AND SUBSTANTIVES:

		PAGE
§ 165.	*Definite* Article used in French, but not in English..	110
- 166.	- - - instead of the Indef. Art. in English	111
- 167.	- - omitted in French, but not in English	—
- 168.	*Indefinite* Article - - - - - - -	—
- 169.	Repetition of the Article	—
- 170.	*Partitive* Article	112

ADJECTIVES:

§§ 171-174.	*Place of Adjectives*	112
- 175-176.	*Adjectives of different meanings* before or after the Substantive	114
§§ 177-180.	Agreement of Adjectives	115
§ 181.	Government of Adjectives	—
§§ 182-186.	Degrees of Comparison. Dimensions	116

PERSONAL PRONOUNS:

§§ 187-195.	a) *Conjunctive* **Personal** Pronouns; their Position; **le, la, les, en, y**	118
- 196-199.	b) *Disjunctive* Personal Pronouns	123

POSSESSIVE PRONOUNS:

§§ 200-203		124

DEMONSTRATIVE PRONOUNS:

§§ 204-208.	Ceci, cela; ce; même	125

RELATIVE PRONOUNS:

§§ 209-218.	Qui, lequel, dont, **quoi, ce qui,** où	**127**

INTERROGATIVE PRONOUNS:

§§ 219-224.	Qui? que? **lequel? quel?** quoi?	129

INDEFINITE PRONOUNS:

§ 225.	Quelqu'un; personne, **aucun,** nul, pas un; autre, autrui; tout, tous; chaque, **chacun;** qui que, quelque que, quel que, quiconque; on, l'on	131

ADVERBS:

§§ 238-242.	*Place of Adverbs; Adverbs of Quantity;* Plus que and davantage; plus tôt and plutôt; comme and comment	133
- 243-252.	*Adverbs of Negation:* ne; ne pas, ne point; pas instead of point; omission of pas and point; ne after Verbs of fearing and preventing	134

PREPOSITIONS:

§§ 253-266.	à; de; dans and en; dans and à; avant and devant; entre and parmi; chez; près de, auprès de, proche; sur and au-dessus de; sous and au-dessous de; envers and vers; de and par; par, à travers, au travers de; d'après, selon, suivant	137

CONTENTS.

CONJUNCTIONS:

	PAGE
§§ 267-275. **Que; si; par ce que** and **parce que; quoi que** and **quoique; pendant que** and **tandis que**	140

APPENDIX II. *Observations, Exceptions, Alphabetical Lists, Supplementary Notes* to the following paragraphs:

to §§ 129-132. Alphabetical list of Verbs which govern the Accusative, Dative or Genitive 143

to § 133. Verbs with different constructions 144

- 153. Verbs which require the Infinitive without preposition .... —
- 155, 156. Verbs which require the Infinitive preceded by **de**, by **à** 145
- 159. Verbs the Pres. Part. of which differs from the Adjective derived from them .... —
- 165, 167. The *Definite* Article *used* or *omitted* in French 146
- 168. The *Indefinite* Article *omitted* in French.............................. —
- 170. **De** instead of **du, des** etc. .... —
- 178, 180. *Agreement* of Adjectives; **feu**; 184, French Superlat. = English Comparat. 147
- 191. *Personal* Pronouns repeated; 197, **ce l'est, ce les sont** .... —
- 200. *Possessive* - - .... —
- 201. **De** after **changer, redoubler; le mien**, etc., equivalent to **my own** etc. 148
- 204. **Cela** referring to Persons; 205, **ce** before **devoir**, etc.; 206, **qui** for **celui qui**; 216, **quoi** idiomatically; 217, **qui** for **ce qui**; 221, **que?** for **pourquoi?** .... —
- 226. **Ne** suppressed; 228, **autre** emphatically; 230, **tout** (Adverb) agreeing in Gender and Number.. —
- 233. **Qui que ce soit, quoi que ce soit** = **personne, rien; quelque** = about .... —
- 239. **Bien, mieux, mal** used adjectively; Adverbs **requiring prepositions** 149
- 240. **Plus que** and **plus de; plus ... plus; ni ... non plus; au moins** and **du moins** .... —
- 249. **Pas** and **point** omitted .... —
- 250-252. **Ne** after **craindre, empêcher, douter** .... —
- 270. **Que** in adverbial expressions; **que si**; 272, **quand même, si ce n'est** .... —

INTRODUCTION.

A SKETCH OF THE HISTORY OF THE FORMATION OF THE FRENCH LANGUAGE.

§ 1. Every student, who has mastered his „Commentarii de Bello Gallico", is aware that, at the period when Cæsar appeared in Gaul, three different nations were distinguished among the inhabitants of that country: the *Aquitanians,* the *Belgians* and the *Gauls.* The idioms spoken by the Gauls and Belgians differed so little from each other that they may be considered as dialects of the same language, *the Celtic.*

No monument of this Celtic language has been handed down to us, for the plain reason that the Druids, who were the only men capable of writing it, were forbidden to record anything relating to their religion, laws, and customs. The only relics of it which have reached us, consist of a few isolated words, especially names of places, provinces, rivers, mountains, terms relating to matters of domestic and rural life, the meaning of which can only be elucidated by the help of the still existing dialects of the Celtic family of languages: the *Welsh, Irish, Gaelic* and *Breton.*

From the time of the Roman conquest the Latin language was gradually introduced into all Gaul; for the policy of the Romans was to assimilate to themselves the conquered nations and to subject them not only to their own laws and institutions, but also to imbue them with their own ideas; and to that end the language of Rome was imposed as the official language; all acts and decrees concerning matters of legislation, administration, justice, etc. being issued in Latin.[1])

1) „Toutes les Gaules jusqu'au Rhin parlaient la langue latine; la religion parlait latin, la loi parlait latin, la guerre parlait latin; partout

It is a general historical fact that, in the case of the amalgamation of two nations, that language is pretty sure to prevail in the long run which is spoken by the more civilized people. This was the case with the Greeks under the Romans, and again with the Gauls. The latter, although an essentially warlike nation, who had once brought Rome to the verge of ruin, were, in intellectual culture, no match for their masters, and the necessary consequence was, that the Latin language rapidly spread and finally prevailed in the conquered provinces of Gaul.[1])

§ 2. It would, however, be a great mistake to suppose that all Romans spoke the language of Cicero, Cæsar, and Virgil. The elegance of style, the intricacies of construction and the discriminate choice of words which we admire in the historians, orators, and poets of the Golden Age of Roman literature, had nothing in common with the language of the illiterate people. The lower classes in the cities, the country-people, the soldiers, the sailors had then, as they still have in some degree, a dialect of their own, known by the name of *lingua rustica, sermo plebeius*, or *castrense verbum*.[2]) It is this dialect then, and not Literary Latin, that the great majority of the Gauls, who were brought in contact almost entirely with

le latin était la langue que le vainqueur imposait au vaincu. Pour traiter avec lui, pour lui demander grâce, pour obtenir la remise de l'impôt, pour prier dans le temple, toujours il fallait la langue latine." Villemain.

1) „Une langue riche, savante, fixée par de grandes œuvres littéraires, puissante expression d'une société constituée, d'une administration qui réglait les destinées du monde, la langue du peuple-roi, était entrée en lutte contre un idiome traditionnel, sans écriture, sans monuments." Pellissier.
„Ce succès prodigieux d'une langue sur tant d'autres fut dû à la supériorité de la civilisation romaine, à l'attrait qu'elle inspira et à la longue durée de sa domination." Littré.

2) Already as far back as the Second Punic War this gap between the Sermo plebeius and Literary Latin had gradually begun to widen, especially when after the complete subjection of Greece, the Roman Aristocracy became acquainted with the superior culture of their Greek subjects whose arts, sciences and literature soon became a matter of fashion among the Upper Ten Thousand in the mighty Republic. But the new words thus introduced into the Latin Vocabulary remained altogether as alien to the common people as in our days such terms as for instance Protoplasm, Rococo and the —ologies, are to the great masses in our manufacturing towns and in our rural districts.

soldiers and settlers, heard spoken in their daily intercourse and which they consequently adopted. It can easily be imagined that, in the mouths of the Gauls, the pronunciation of this already deteriorated idiom was not improved. The literary documents we still possess of those times bear ample testimony to the fact that on account of the inability of the Gauls to understand the true meaning and force of foreign inflections, the further process of decay of Rustic Latin was much hastened.

This important fact alone will account for the derivations of a great many French words, the origin of which must offer an insolvable riddle to any one not acquainted with it.

Thus for instance, the words—
   cheval, bataille, voyage, feu, chat, semaine,
which have no analogy whatever with their Latin equivalents
   equus, pugna, iter, ignis, felis, hebdomas,
if traced back to their parents in the Popular Speech—
   caballus, batalia, viaticum, focus, catus, septimana,
will not only teach us to what quarters we must apply in our etymological researches, but they will also serve fully to bear out the correctness of the fact stated above.

In proportion as the decrepit Roman Empire was tottering to ruin and the whole fabric of society fast verging towards utter dissolution, it was the popular idiom which more and more prevailed at the expense of the literary language, until the latter altogether ceased to exist as a *spoken* language. This happened when, in the fifth century of the Christian era, the Teutonic nations after a struggle of several centuries, at last inundated the whole Western Roman Empire and gave it the finishing blow.

§ 3. But though the invading Franks, Burgundians, Goths, etc., in overthrowing the Empire, gave the *coup de grâce* to literary Latin, they in their turn had to submit to that law mentioned above (see § 1.) according to which, when two nations coalesce, the language of the more civilized people gets the upper hand. Add to this that the Franks who occupied the Eastern, Central and Northern Part of Gaul were proportionately in such small numbers that they were, **so to** say, drowned among the millions **of** Gallo-Romans.¹)

The language of these Franks was one of the many dialects of the Teutonic family, of which Anglo-Saxon, and consequently English, forms a branch. Although this infusion **of a** new element did not materially affect the *lingua rustica*, it **was only natural** that many terms for which the Gallo-Romans had no, or only approximate, **equivalents** should find their way into the predominating language. This was especially the case with words relating to warfare, weapons, feudal institutions, and with **proper nouns.**

Note to § 3.

To **show how little chance the Teutonic** dialects of the invading **Franks,** Burgundians, Goths, etc. had **of supplanting** the language of the Gallo-Romans, a distinguished French Scholar, M. Ampère, **has** very pointedly observed that many Teutonic words were indeed **adopted** by the Gauls, who however seem to have employed many of them **with a very bad grace**; **thus, to** the present day, several words derived **from** German are used **as** terms **of** contempt or disparagement, as:

lande (from land), *heath, barren moors*, **rosse** (from ross) *a jade*, **un pauvre hère** (from Herr) *a poor devil*, **bouquin** (from buch) *an old book.*

In **this** respect the Normans, though they did not succeed in imposing their Norman French on the conquered Anglo-Saxons, fared considerably better; for many terms of their vocabulary, so far from being used disparagingly, got the better **of** the corresponding Anglo-Saxon words, as all who have read Ivanhoe must be aware:

(Ivanhoe, chapt. I.):

„And *Swine* is good Saxon, **said the jester, but how call you the sow** „when she is flayed, and drawn, **and quartered,** and hung **up by the heels** „like a traitor?

„**Pork,** answered the Swineherd . . .

„. . . said Wamba: And **Pork is** good Norman French, and so when „the **brute** lives, and is in charge of a Saxon slave she goes by her **Saxon** „name, **but** becomes a **Norman** and is called pork when she is carried to „the castle-hall to feast among the nobles . . .

„There is old Alderman **Ox** continues to hold his Saxon epithet while he is under the charge of serfs, but becomes **Beef,** a fiery French gallant, when he arrives before the worshipful jaws that are destined to consume him. Mynheer **Calf,** too, becomes Monsieur de **Veau in** the like manner; etc."

1) „The same thing which happened to the Frank conquerors of Gaul and the Norman conquerors of Neustria happened again **to** the Norman conquerors of England — they had to acquire the language of their conquered subjects." Max Müller.

Thus were introduced among others the Old High German words—

marahscalh, alod, scepeno, siniscalh, etc.

which latinised assumed the form of—

mariscallus, alodium, skabinus, siniscallus, etc.

These latter forms in their turn, sharing the fate of all words of the Great Latin stock among which they had obtained a citizenship, had to undergo successive modifications until they became what they now are: *Maréchal, alleu, échevin, sénéchal* ...

The number of words thus introduced amounts to about five hundred, and, as has been mentioned before, merely constituted an addition to the vocabulary without modifying the structure of the language any more than the incomparably stronger admixture of foreign elements affected the Syntax of English.

It would be impossible to assign a definite date for the period when Latin, after passing through successive stages of decay, so far lost its characteristic features as to justify the use of a new name for an offshoot of it, which after all is still Latin and nothing but Latin.[1]) This would be as unwarrantable as to fix an arbitrary date for the epoch when Anglo-Saxon, after consecutive alterations, may appropriately be called English.

§ 4. We have evidence that in the ninth century the Franks no longer knew the language spoken by their ancestors, the conquerors of Gaul: after the breaking up of the Frankish Empire founded by Charlemagne, his grandsons Charles le Chauve, to whom the Western part (Gaul) had been apportioned, and Louis le Germanique, thus called because he inherited the German provinces east of the Rhine, united against their Imperial brother Lothair, and conquered him in the battle of Fontenoy (841 A. D.) To secure the advantages obtained by this victory they concluded, a year after, a treaty which they confirmed by a solemn oath taken in the presence of their respective armies. Charles, the king of the Western kingdom, pronounced that oath in German in order to be understood by the soldiers of his brother Louis. The latter, on the other

---

1) „Le français est une langue latine; les mots celtiques y sont restés, les mots germaniques y sont venus; les mots latins sont la langue elle-même, ils la constituent." J. J. Ampère.

hand, for the purpose of making his words intelligible to the Western Franks, who, as mentioned above, no longer understood German, expressed himself in their own language, the *lingua Francica*, as it was then called.

This oath known under the name of *Serment de Strasbourg* is the earliest monument we possess of French. Inasmuch as it offers some interest, we give it here together with a literal translation:

Pro deo amur et pro christian
- dei amore - - christiano
poplo et nostro commun salvament,
populo - - communi salvamento,
dist di on avant, in quant Deus
de-isto die in-ab-ante, - quantum -
savir et podir me dunat, si salvara
sapere - posse - donat, sic salvare
jeo cist meon fradre Karlo
ego ecc'istum meum fratrem Carolum,
et in ajudha et in cadhuna cosa,
- - adjutu - - quâque-unâ causâ,
si com om per dreit son
sic quomodo homo - directum suum
fradra salvar dist, in o quid
fratrem salvare debitus est, - illo -
mi altre si fazet, et ab Ludher
mihi alterum sic faciet, - - Lothario
nul plaid nunquam prindrai,
nullum placitum - prehendere-habeo,
qui meon vol cist meon
quod meâ voluntate ecc'isti meo
fradre Karle in damno sit.
fratri Carolo - - -

Pour (de) Dieu amour et pour (du) chrétien, et peuple notre commun salut, de ce jour en avant, en tant que Dieu savoir et pouvoir me donne, ainsi sauverai-je celui mon frère Charles, et en aide et en chaque chose, ainsi comme on, par droit, son frère sauver doit, en ce que il à moi de même fasse; et avec Lothaire nul accord jamais prendrai, qui à mon vouloir, à celui-ci mon frère en dommage soit.

Such were the beginnings of the rising language as spoken in the Frankish kingdom, such was the state of an idiom destined to shine before long with great splendour under the name of *French*, and it is to that period that we may trace back the final establishment of the French as a nation, for a nation may be considered as such from the time only when it possesses a language of its own.

§ 5. At that critical transition period, however, Latin was branching off into the various ramifications in which it, to the present day, survives under the names of *Italian, Portuguese, Spanish* and *French;* but, just as in Italy and Spain the current of the rising language was not flowing in a single channel, so in France it bifurcated into two principal dialects; in other words, two languages corresponding to two nationalities sprang from the ruins of Latin:—

In Southern Gaul, under the influence of a climate and a civilisation similar to those of Italy, its offshoot was the *Provençal*, an idiom energetic, supple, and melodious in its character, which subsequently owed its perfection and celebrity to the songs of the *Troubadours,* the predecessors of Chaucer and of the German Minnesingers.

In Northern Gaul, i. e. north of the Loire, Latin, affected by a much stronger infusion of Germanic elements and by a less genial climate, produced a widely different language, inferior to the former both in harmony and regularity, with harsher and more nasal sounds. *This neo-Latin idiom of Northern Gaul alone, and not the Provençal, is the earliest form of Modern French.*[1])

§ 6. But the *langue d'oïl* itself was subdivided and, in fact (as far as the *Patois,* still *spoken* to the present day, are concerned) may still be subdivided into four different dialects, namely, those of *Picardy, Normandy, Burgundy, and Isle de France* (centre of France, round Paris).[2]) All these were nearly equal in importance

---

1) The two languages which thus simultaneously grew up on the soil of France, are also called *Langue d'oc* (whence the still existing name of the province Languedoc) instead of Provençal, and *Langue d'oïl,* from the habit prevailing in the Middle ages of calling languages after their particles of affirmation. *Oc* is the Provençal, and *oïl* (pronounced exactly like *oui*) the old French, term for *yes.*

2) „Un mot latin qui, examiné en Italie, en Espagne, en Provence et en France, subit quatre transformations primitives, subit, sous le chef français, des transformations secondaires, quand on l'examine en Bourgogne, dans l'Ile de France, en Normandie, en Picardie et dans le pays wallon. Le mot latin est comme une plante exotique qui, soumise à des conditions de climat de plus en plus différentes, subit des modifications de plus en plus grandes, mais toujours enchaînées l'une à l'autre."

Littré, Hist. de la langue française. VII.

at first, and were **not only spoken by the people, but also written
by the** contemporary **Poets** (*Trouvères*) and Chroniclers in these
respective provinces, **none of them being as yet considered as the**
standard national tongue.

At this stage of scission, the old French language is the true
and faithful reflection of the political condition of **France**, the soil
of which, during the period of the Feudal system, **was** parcelled
out among several chiefs. Among these, several dukes and counts,
the dukes of Normandy for instance, owned larger **and** wealthier
dominions than even the kings of France.

§ 7. Now **comes** the question how it came to pass that *one*
among those four equally influential dialects gradually rose to
eminence **and** at last completely prevailed **as** the only literary
language **to** the exclusion of the three others?

Towards the middle of the thirteenth century the kings of **the**
Capet dynasty had considerably extended their **dominions at** the
expense of their once all powerful vassals; thus *Berry* (in 1101),
Touraine (in 1203), *Normandy* (in 1204), **had** successively been
added to the royal possessions. In proportion as the political preponderance of the rising dynasty increased, the dialect spoken in
their hereditary lands and in their capital, Paris, was **gaining a**
commensurate supremacy, and soon became the only *written* **language**;
whilst the other dialects, no longer written, **soon** ceased **to be con**sidered **as languages and were** reduced **to the** condition of *Patois*.[1]

§ 8. But still, **to the great** detriment of the phonetic **regularity**
of the French Vocabulary, **many** words of these neglected dialects
kept their ground side **by** side with words **of the** same Latin root,
but diversely modified in the predominating dialect. A few words
which **exist in** a double form in modern French will illustrate this
interesting fact:

The modern French words *champ* (field), and *camp* (camp) are
both derived from the **same** Latin word *campus;* the first found its
way into French through **the** medium of the dialect of *Isle de France*
(Paris), the **other** through that of *Picardy*, and the difference in

---

[1] Thus **in** England, the kings of Wessex having obtained the supremacy, the dialect of the West-Saxons became the literary language and is the one in which **all** the chief Anglo-Saxon works have come down to us. (See Marsh, Lect. on the Engl. lang. II.)

their initial consonant arises from the fact that the Latin hard *c* was invariably modified into *ch* in the former, whilst it remained *c* hard in the latter; thus—

the Latin *causa* becomes *chose* in **Isle de France**, but *cause* in Picardy
- *carta* - *charte* - - *carte* - .

§ 9. If we cast a retrospective glance over this period (extending over more than a thousand years) of the formation of a new language and draw up our résumé, we find—

(1) That *Popular Latin*, introduced into Gaul by the Roman conquest and adopted by the Teutonic tribes who settled in Gaul, gradually developing the germs of decay already perceptible in Latin long before that conquest, assumes there towards the 9th century the shape of two new languages— the Langue d'oïl in the North and the the Langue d'oc in the South;

(2) That the *langue d'oc* or Provençal is superseded by its northern sister-tongue and ceases to exist as a literary language;

(3) That of the four dialects which constituted the *langue d'oïl*, the one spoken in *Isle de France* (with Paris for its capital) preponderates in proportion as that Province, the nucleus of the rising kingdom, obtains the political ascendency.

§ 10. It now remains to examine the characteristic features of this *langue d'oïl*, and to point out the most important alterations in the structure of its parent language, which impart to it the character of a distinct idiom:—

Loss of four cases out of six. In adopting the language of Rome, the illiterate **Gauls and Teutons**, unable to comprehend the delicate shades of meaning conveyed by the six Latin cases, dropped four of them, retaining only the Nominative and Accusative. These remained till about the end of the *fourteenth* century, when the distinction between them altogether disappeared, and the *Accusative*, not the Nominative, obtained to the exclusion of all other cases.

The necessary consequence of this loss of cases was the *introduction of the Articles*, both definite and indefinite, the former derived from the Latin demonstrative pronoun *ille, illa*, the latter from the numeral adjective *unus, una*.[1]

[1] Compare the English and German, in which languages both articles: *the*, der, die, das; *an*, ein, etc. are derived from the demonstrative pronoun and from the numerical adjective respectively.

§ 11. The *neuter gender disappears* and is chiefly absorbed by the Masculine Gender.

Yielding to the impulse of the analytic tendency in modern languages the Latin synthetic method of forming the *Degrees of Comparison* is abandoned, and the inflectional particles are superseded by the use of *plus*.

The Latin particle *ter* used for the *Formation of Adverbs*, being unaccented (see § 15) was lost in the process of contraction and mutilation which all Latin words had to undergo, and the deficiency is made up by another word:— *ment*, from the Lat. *mente*, abl. of *mens*.¹)

The whole *passive* voice is formed by means of the *Past Participle* and the Auxiliary Verb *être*.

And finally the *Future and Conditional* are reconstructed by means of affixing the *present* and *imperfect* of the Verb *avoir* to the Infinitive. ²)

§ 12. Towards the close of the twelfth century this process of *organic* formation of French may be considered to be completed; for all words subsequently introduced into the language from Latin, Greek, Italian, Spanish, Arabic, German, English, etc., are merely additions to the Vocabulary. In their passage into French these latter words are not, like the former, moulded into French according to the laws which, previous to that period, invariably regulated the process of formation. To exhibit the nature of these important laws will form the subject of the following chapter.

1) Comp. the English *wise* in like*wise*, etc.; and the German *weise* in folgender*weise*

2) "The Roman had no suspicion that *amabo* was a compound; but it can be proved to contain an auxiliary Verb as clearly as the French future. The Latin future was destroyed by means of phonetic corruption. When the final letters lost their distinct pronunciation, it became impossible to keep the Imperfect *amabam* separate from future *amabo*. The future was then replaced by dialectical regeneration, for the use of *habeo* with an Infinitive is found in Latin, in such expressions as *habeo dicere*, I have to say, which would imperceptibly glide into— I shall say ..."

Max Müller, Science of Lang. II. 6th lect.

LAWS OF FORMATION.

§ 13. If we compare any two French words which happen to be derived from the same Latin word, but one of which is of *primary* and the other of *modern* formation, the characteristic features of these laws become easily discernible. The subjoined list of words will render our meaning more intelligible:

Latin.	French.	
	Organic (Primary) Formation.	*Inorganic* (Modern) Formation.
ministérium	métier	ministère
rígidus	roide	rigide
redémptionem	rançon	rédemption
blásphemum	blâme	blasphème
pórticus	porche	portique
natívus	naïf	natif
natális	noël	natal.

Before entering into these laws we must once more insist upon the important fact that the whole Vocabulary of French consists of words of either *organic* or *inorganic* formation:—

We call words of *organic* formation, those which up to the twelfth century were spontaneously, and, as it were, instinctively moulded by the nation at large according to the peculiarities of their organs of Speech.

We call words of *inorganic* formation, those which after that period, when all sense of the spoken popular Latin was extinct, were merely engrafted upon the already existing stock by scholars who, totally ignorant of the laws which had regulated the growth of popular words, merely adapted them approximately in their terminations. It is only to words of *organic* formation, then, that these laws apply:

§ 14. (a) In all words of *organic* formation *the tonic accent*[1]) *of the Latin word is retained*— whilst words in which this law is violated are of *inorganic* formation:—

[1]) To prevent misunderstandings we must observe once for all that the modern French accents (aigu, grave, circonflexe) have nothing whatever to do with the Latin *tonic* accent (arsis), which in French is either on the *last* syllable when it contains no *e mute*, as, maisŏn; or on the *last but one* when the last contains an *e mute*, as, malăde.

	Latin.	*Organic.*	*Inorganic.*
as,	frágilis	frêle (frail)	fragíle
	rígidus	roíde (stiff)	rigíde
	móbilis	meúble (furniture)	mobíle.

§ 15. (b) The last or last but one syllable, if unaccented (atonic) disappears or becomes mute in French :—

fidélis	feál	(fidèle)
víncĕre	vaíncre	
dícĕre	dire	
amámus	aimóns	

§ 16. (c) The unaccented (atonic) vowel— *immediately* preceding the accented (tonic) syllable—

remains in French — if long :—
    ornāméntum   ornement

but disappears — **if short** :—

| carĭtátem | chertó | charité |
| sepăráre | sevrér | séparer. |

Words in which, as in the third column, this law is violated are of **modern** (inorganic) formation.

§ 17. (d) The unaccented vowel, *not immediately* preceding the accented syllable, is retained in French :—

| advocátus | avoué | avocat |
| communicare | communier | communiquer. |

If we bear in mind that popular French is derived from popular Latin, and literary French from literary Latin, and that already in this popular Latin of the classic period we see this process of contraction in full operation, we can easily account for the principle of this second law.

§ 18. All words in which the intermediate (medial) consonant (between two vowels) is dropped, are of **popular** origin. In words of erudite origin it is retained : as,

redemptionem	rançon	rédemption
fidelis	féal	fidèle
regalis	royal	régal
natalis	noël	natal

nativus   naïf   **natif**
parabola   parole   **parabole.**[1]

§ 19. We cannot conclude this sketch without briefly touching upon another important fact, we mean the adoption of the letter *s* for the formation of the plural, because that process involves a peculiar feature of the whole system of formation of French words.

It has already been mentioned (§ 10) that the Six Latin cases were first reduced to two, the Subjective and Objective, as will be seen from the following paradigm:

	Sing.	*Plural.*
Nom.	li murs (muru*s*),	li mur (muri),
Acc.	le mur (murum),	les murs (muro*s*).

In the 14th century this last remnant of the Latin system of declension gradually wore away, so that there was only one case left for each number. But which of these two still existing cases was now most likely to obtain? Surely the one most in use, and this was the Accusative, being the representative of the previously suppressed Genitive, Dative and Ablative. Henceforth therefore the old French Accusative (le mur, *sing.*, les murs, *plur.*) became the exclusive forms for each number.

§ 20. On the same principle we may account for the fact that nouns ending in *-al* form their plural in *-aux*, and those ending in *eau, eu,* etc. by adding *x:* as,

chevaux, châteaux, cheveux, etc.;

[1] "What happened in French happened in Latin. As the French are no longer aware that their *paysan*, a peasant, and *païen*, a pagan, were originally but slight dialectic varieties of the same Latin word *paganus*, a villager, the citizen of Rome used the two words *luna*, moon, and *Lucina*, the goddess, without being aware that both were derived from the same root. In *luna* the c belonging to the root *lucere*, to shine, is elided; not by caprice or accident, but according to a general phonetic rule which sanctions the omission of a guttural before a liquid. Thus *lumen*, light, stands for *lucmen*, *examen* for *exagmen; flamma* for *flagma* (from *flagrare*) etc. This is in fact the same phonetic rule which, if applied to the Teutonic languages, accounts for the German *Nagel* into *nail*, *Hagel* into *hail*, *Regen* into *rain*, *Segel* into *sail*, and which, if applied to Greek and Latin, helps us to discover the identity of the Greek *láchnē*, wool, and Latin *lâna;* of Greek 'aráchnē, a spider, and Latin *aránea*." Max Müller, Science of Lang. II, 6th lect.

for *x* and *z* in old French spelling were equivalent to *s*, this *x* being generally added to words originally ending in *l*. Now *l*, conformably to its tendency to become vocalized in French when followed by a consonant, was softened into *u*: as,

	Sing.	*Plural.*
Nom.	chevals,	cheval,
Acc.	cheval,	chevals, (chevaus, chevaux).

Compare: falsus = faux; altus = haut; capillus = cheveu; mollis = mou; melius = mieux, etc.

By means of this change of *l* into *u* and *s* into *x* we can also explain how the Prepositions *de* and *à* contracted with *le* and *les* became *du, des, au, aux,* respectively.

FORMATION OF PERSONS AND TENSES.

§ 21. **A. Comparative** table of Latin and French Personal suffixes:

First Conjugation.		Second Conjugation.				Third & Fourth Conjugation.	
		(a) Inceptive:		(b) Non Inceptive:			
Latin (I).	French.	Latin (III).	French.	Lat. (IV).	French.	Lat. (II).	French.
-o	-e	-isco (esco)	-is	-io	-s	-oo	-s
-as	-es	-iscis	-is	-is	-s	-es	-s
-at	-e	-iscit	-it	-it	-t	-et	-t
-ámus	-ons	-iscimus	-issons	-imus	-ons	-émus	-ons
-átis	-es	-iscitis	-issez	-ítis	-es	-ótis	-es
-ant	-ent	-escunt	-issent	-iunt	-ent	-ent	-ent

NB. For a complete table of all tenses consult Maetzner's French Gr. p. 204.

A comparison of French Personal endings with Latin shows that—

(1) the *s* of 1st p. sing. is inorganic, having been irrationally added in the 14th century by way of assimilating the 1st p. with the 2d. Therefore the student who meets with such forms as—

je voi, je croi, je die, etc. in the works of Corneille, Molière, Racine and even of Victor Hugo should not allow himself to be mislead by ignorant annotators into the belief that these forms are arbitrarily clipped merely for the sake of the rhyme;

(2) the organic *t* of the 3d p. sing. has disappeared in the Pres. and Preterite Indic. of the 1st Conj., and in the Future and Subj Pres. of all Conjugations.

Obs. This *t* reappears, however, and does service for the sake of euphony in inverted constructions:—

a-t-il? aime-t-il? parla-t-il? finira-t-il? etc.

(See also, § 4. Serment of Strasbourg, the form 'dunat'.)

(3) not only final consonants, but also unaccented vowels have fallen **away** or become mute, according **to** § 15 (b):— amám(u)s = aimons; amat(i)s = aimez[1]); **amant** = **aiment** ('-ent' mute) ame(m) = aime; etc.

B. Formation **of** Tenses:—

(1) The Pres. Indicat., Subj., **Imperative** and Infinitive, from the corresponding Latin tenses. (See **A.**)

(2) **The** Imperfect Indicat. **from the Lat. Imperfect:**— -ábam = oie, see § 18; -oie = ois, see A. **(1)**; **and ois** = **ais** in the 18th century, see Brachet's Hist. Grammar.

(3) The Preterite from the Lat. Perfect:—

cant-ávi = chant-ai, by the elision of *v*, see § 18.
cant-ávimus = chant-âmes,[2]) see §§ 14, 15 & 18.

Chantas, chantâtes, chantèrent, from the contracted forms **cantasti, cantastis, cantárunt.**

(4) The Imperfect. **Subj. from the Lat.** Imperf. Subj. (contracted form):— cantássem = **chantasse,** according to §§ 14, 15 & 21. A, (3).

(5) The Pres. **Part. from the Lat.** Participle, Accusative Case, (see § 19):— amántem = **aimant,** according to §§ 14 & **15.**

(6) The Past **Part. from the** Supine:—

amátum = aimé,
finitum = fini, etc.

For the strong forms consult Brachet's Historical Gr., Section III.

The **Formation of** the Future, Conditional and Passive Voice is explained § **11.**

1) For *s* = *z*, **see** § 20.
2) O. **Fr.** chantasmes; the *s* **is** inorganic like **A.** (1).

The Alphabet.

§ 1. The French Alphabet consists of 25 letters, being the same as the Latin, or the English without W:

	A,	B,	C,	D,	E,	F,	G,	H,	I,	J,	K,	L,	M,
Named:	ah,	bay,	say,	day,	ay,	f,	zhay,	ash,	ee,	zhee,	kah,	l,	m,

	N,	O,	P,	Q,	R,	S,	T,	U,	V,	X,	Y,	Z.
„	n,	o,	pay,	küh,	airr,	s,	tay,	ü,	vay,	eex,	eegrek,	z.

Obs. 1. W occurs only in words derived from foreign languages.

ACCENTS AND ORTHOGRAPHICAL SIGNS.

§ 2. There are in French three Accents which serve to mark the peculiar pronunciation of certain vowels; or as the distinctive mark of words spelt alike, but of different meaning, or again, to indicate the suppression of letters.

§ 3. I. The *acute* **accent**, l'accent aigu, (´) is placed over the vowel **e**, when it has a close and short sound (*e fermé*): as,

témérité, été.

II. The *grave* accent, l'accent grave, (`) is placed over the vowel **e**, when it has a broad or open sound (*e ouvert*): as,

première, zèle.

Obs. The grave accent also serves to distinguish words spelt alike: as,

où, *where*; ou, *or*.   la, *the, her*; là, *there*.
à, *to, at*; a, *has*.   dès, *since*, des, *of the*.

III. The *circumflex*, l'accent circonflexe, (ˆ) is placed over vowels with a broad or open sound: as, **grâce**, and generally marks the suppression (elision) of one or more letters: as,

âne (Lat. asinus); âme (anima); sûr (securus); gaîment, instead of gaiement; vous aimâtes (amastis); qu'il aimât (amasset); croître (crescere).

Obs. Like the grave accent, the circumflex also serves to distinguish two words spelt alike: as, tû, *Perf. Part. of* taire; tu, *thou*.
dû, - - - devoir; du, *of the*.

§ 4. I. The *Apostrophe*, l'apostrophe, indicates the elision of **a final a, e** or **i** before a word beginning with a **vowel** or **silent h**: as,

l'âme, l'homme, *instead of* la âme, le homme.

This elision occurs in the following words: le; la; je, me, te, se; ce; de; ne; que; jusque; except je, ce, le, la, when they stand after the Verb: as,

j'aime, *but*, suis-je aimé; c'est vrai, *but*, est-ce elle?

Eugène, French Grammar.

Obs. 1. The elision of **i** only takes place in **si** before **il, ils**: as,
s'il(s), *but*, si elle(s), si on; etc.

The **e** of presque is elided only in presqu'île (peninsula);
of entre only in compound words: as, entr'acte, entr'ouvert.
of jusque only before à, au(x), en, ici, où, alors.
of lorsque, puisque, quoique, only before il(s), elle(s), on; un(e): as, puisqu'elle, quoiqu'une.
of quelque only before un and autre.

Obs. 2. Before the following words the vowel is not elided, huit, onze, oui: as, le huit, le huitième, le onze, le onzième, le oui.

II. The **cedilla, la cédille** (,) placed under **c** before **a, o, u** indicates that **ç** is pronounced like ss, and not like k; as,
il commença, le garçon, aperçu; see p. 44.

III. The **diaeresis, le tréma** (¨), indicates that the **vowel** over which it stands is pronounced distinctly from the vowel before or after it: as, naïf, Noël, héroïne, ambiguë.

Obs. In words terminating in -guë, the diaeresis indicates that **u** is pronounced, though ë is not, whereas in -gue without diaeresis, both u and e are mute: as, aiguë (u sounded), but langue (ue mute).

IV. The **hyphen, le trait d'union** (tiret) (-) marks the connection of two or more words: as, arc-en-ciel; donne-moi (§ 74); lui-même; vingt-huit; sur-le-champ; peut-être.

SOUNDS.
§ 5. SIMPLE VOWEL SOUNDS.

a (*long*): château, nation, char, lard, cable, etc. | **a** (*short*): la, mal, patte, parler, amour, oracle

Obs. a before liquid il(ill) must be pronounced = ä (not = ai); bataille, = bätä-ye, etc.

e (*surd*): je, me, te, le, se, que, etc.; pomme, table, île, venir, remarque, secour, appeler, aiment, etc.

The letter **e** *is silent* in ach(e)ter, gai(e)ment, gai(e)té, lou(e)rais.

e *close* (fermé): né, été, célérité, régénéré, armée, etc.; et, charmer, donnez, couperai (-ais exceptionally in saïs, s, t).

e *open* (ouvert), *long*: dès, mère, poète, tête, être, même, miel, sel, sec, es, est, les, inquiet, elle, fer, ver, vers, vert, caresse, chrétienne, peine, aile, chaîne, chaise, aime.

i (*long*) lie, amie, mourir, dites; **i** (*short*): ici, écrit, vis, six, lys, lyre.

o *close* (*long*): chose, dôme, nôtre, etc.; (*short*) · mot, joli, notre, cause, autre, veau, etc.

SOUNDS.

o *open* (*long*): or, sort, tort, **aurore, Maure**; (*short*): **ordre,** Rome, **Paul,** mauvais, post-scriptum.

u (*long*): sûr, mûr, écriture, ruse, **eu, eûmes, eûtes, eurent**; (*short*): **sur,** cuit, lucre, nul, etc.

Obs. The letter u is silent after **g or q,** being only a phonetic sign that the guttural is hard. (See §§ 30, 3.)

eu *close* (*long*): bleu(e), jeûne, vœu, œufs, bœufs; (*short*): feu, jeune, œil.

eu *open* (*long*): **peur,** heure, **cœur,** etc.; (*short*): **neuf, seul,** œuf, bœuf, orgueil.

ou (*long*): **cour**(t), jour, jalouse, joue, etc.; (*short*): fou, **clou,** choux.

Obs. ua = a after g or q, as q(u)and, q(u)art, etc. Except in-quarto, etc.

§ 6. DIPHTHONGS.

aï: aïeul, Bayonette, Bayeux, fayence, etc.
oi (= oua): soir, croire, ivoire, moi, soi, roi, toile, poêle, moelle, etc.
oy (= oua-yi): royal, envoyer, tutoyer.
ouï: Louis, jouir, enfouir.
uy (= u-yi): essuyer, tutoyer.
ia: social, fiacre, etc.
ié: moitié, plier, riez, etc.

ay (= è-yi): pays, paysage, payant, etc.
ui: sui, suif, cuit, fuyant, pluie (See note to u above.)
iai: liaison.
iè: fermière, pierre, ciel.
ieu: lieu, yeux, cieux.
io, iau, violon, bestiaux.

§ 7. NASAL AND LIQUID SOUNDS.

(1) **an** (or **en, am, em,** etc.): as—l'an, enfant, en, vent.

Notice that tan, tan(t), tem(ps), ta(o)n, are pronounced exactly alike; **thus** chan(t) = cham(ps).

(2) **in** (or **ain, ein, im, yn, ym**): as—**fin,** sain, sein, peint, syntaxe, intact, imbu.
(3) **on** (or **om**): as—ton, tombeau, lon(g), on(t), ron(d).
(4) **un** (or **eun, um**): as—un, brun, parfum, à jeun.
(5) **ian** (or medial **ien**): as—friand, patience.
(6) **éen** (or final **ien**): as—chaldéen, le sien, tiens, **ancien.**
(7) **ion**: as—passion, travaillions.
(8) **oin**: as—coin, coin(g).
(9) **uin**: as—juin.

Obs. A vowel immediately after **n** or **m** removes the nasal sound:
    intact (nasal),   inutile (not nasal).
    impur   ,,   image   ,,

(10) Final **-il** and *medial* -ill-, sounded approximately like **yi** in Paris (with audible l—as recommended by Littré—in Central France and French Switzerland): as—péril, bétail, conseil, soleil, œil, recueil, bouvreuil, fenouil, fille, échantillon, bataille, corbeille, feuille, gargouille.

(11) **-gn-,** sounded approximately like -ny(e)- as—campagne, campagnard, règne, ligne, besogne, brugnon.

The Article (L'Article).

§ 8. Three kinds of Articles are distinguished in French: The **Definite**, the **Partitive** and the **Indefinite**.

§ 9. THE DEFINITE ARTICLE.

	Sing.			Plur.	
Masc.	**le;**	**l'**	before a vowel	**les,**	*the.*
Fem.	**la;**	**l'**	or silent h.	**les,**	*the.*

§ 10. With the Prepositions **de**, *of*, and **à**, *to*, the Def. Art. **le** and **les** form the following contractions:

de le = **du** *of the*	**de les** = **des** *of the*	(*See Introduct.* § 20).
à le = **au** *to the*	**à les** = **aux** *to the*	

§ 11. THE PARTITIVE ARTICLE.

Equivalent to the English **some**, **any** (*expressed or understood*).
The Partitive Art. is supplied by the Genitive of the Definite Art.: as,

	Sing.			Plur.	
Masc.	**du;**	**de l'**	before a vowel	**des,**	*some, any.*
Fem.	**de la;**	**de l'**	or silent h.	**des,**	*some, any.*

le vin *the wine*	**du vin** *some (any) wine,*	or *wine.*
la viande *the meat*	**de la viande** *some (any) meat,*	or *meat.*
l'eau *the water*	**de l'eau** *some (any) water,*	or *water.*
les livres *the books*	**des livres** *some (any) books,*	or *books.*

§ 12. THE INDEFINITE ARTICLE.

Masc.	Nom. and Acc.	**un**	*Fem.*	**une,**	*a, an.*
	Genitive	**d'un**		**d'une,**	*of (from) a.*
	Dative	**à un**		**à une,**	*to (at) a.*

Obs. Le, la, les are derived from the Lat. Demonstrative Pronouns **ille, illa, illos, illas**; as in English and German the Def. Art. is derived from Demonstratives.

The Indef. Art. **un** (une) is derived from the Lat. Numerical Adj. **unus** (una). Compare the Engl. **an, a,** as derived from **one**, and the German **ein, eine, ein**. See also Introduct. § 10.

The Substantive (Le Substantif).

§ 13. There are no Declensions proper in French (Introd. § 30.); the want of case inflections is partly supplied by Prepositions: **de** (*of, from*) for the Genitive (Abl.), and **à** (*to, at*) for the Dative: as,

N. & Acc.	Guillaume	*William*	Athènes	*Athens.*
Gen.	de Guillaume	{ *William's* / *of (from) William*	d'Athènes	*of (from) Athens.*
Dat.	à Guillaume	*to William*	à Athènes	*to (at, in) Athens.*

MASC.

Sing. — *Plural.*

N. & Acc.	le frère	*the brother*	les frères	*the brothers.*
Gen.	du frère	{ *the brother's* / *of (from) the brother*	des frères	*of (from) the brothers.*
Dat.	au frère	*to the brother*	aux frères	*to the brothers.*

FEM.

N. & Acc.	la sœur	*the sister*	les sœurs	*the sister.*
Gen.	de la sœur	{ *the sister's* / *of (from) the sister*	des sœurs	*of (from) the sisters.*
Dat.	à la sœur	*to the sister*	aux sœurs	*to the sisters.*

MASC. & FEM.

N. & Acc.	l'ami	(amie, f.) *the friend*	les amis (amies)	*the friends.*
Gen.	de l'ami	{ *the friend's* / *of (from) the friend*	des amis	*of (from) the friends.*
Dat.	à l'ami	*to the friend*	aux amis	*to the friends.*

§ 14. **Substantives taken in a Partitive Sense are** declined thus:

N. & Acc.	du fer	*(some, any) iron*	de l'eau	*(some, any) water.*
Gen.	de fer	*of (from) iron*	d'eau	*of water.*
Dat.	à du fer	*to iron*	à de l'eau	*to water.*
N. & Acc.	de la viande	*(some, any) meat*	des livres	*(some, any) books.*
Gen.	de viande	*of meat*	de livres	*of books.*
Dat.	à de la viande	*to meat*	à des livres	*to books.*

Obs. If the Substantive is preceded by an Adjective, **de** alone is used without the Article: as,

de bon fer; de bonne viande; de bonne eau; de bons livres.

§ 15. After **Substantives** and **Adverbs** of **measure, quantity** and **negation, de** is used without the Article: as,

une tasse de lait; un peu de viande; **assez** d'eau; une quantité (beaucoup) de livres; **point** d'argent; etc.

THE FORMATION OF THE PLURAL OF SUBSTANTIVES.

(Introd. §§ 19-20.)

§ 16. General Rule. An **s** is added to the Singular:

el rère, les frères, *the brothers.* | l'homme, les hommes, *the men.*
a maison, les maisons, *the houses.* | l'histoire, les histoires, *the stories.*

§ 17. Special Rules. Substantives ending in **s, x, z** (sibilants) remain **unaltered**: as,

le temps, les temps, *the times.* | la voix, les voix, *the voices.*
l'excès, les excès, *the excesses.* | le nez, les nez, *the noses.*

§ 18. An **x** is added to nouns ending in **au** and **eu**:

le château, les châteaux, *the castles.* | le feu, les feux, *the fires.*
le noyau, les noyaux, *the kernels.* | le vœu, les vœux, *the vows.*

The following seven substantives in **-ou** also take **x**:

le bijou, les bijoux, *the jewels.* | le genou, *the knee.*
le caillou, *the pebble.* | le hibou, *the owl.*
le chou, *the cabbage.* | le pou, *the louse.*
le joujou, *the plaything.*

All other Substantives in ou follow the General Rule: le fou, les fous, etc.

§ 19. Nouns in al change this al into aux (Introd. § 20): **as**,

l'amiral, les amiraux, *the admirals.* | le cheval, les chevaux, *the horses.*

Exceptions. Some Substantives **in al** follow the **General Rule**; as,

le bal, *the ball,* les bals. | les carnavals, *the carnivals.*
les chacals, *the jackals.* | les régals, *the entertainments.*
les narvals, *the swordfishes.* | les servals, *the tiger cats, etc.*

§ 20. The following in **ail** change this **ail into aux**:

le travail, les travaux, *the works.* | le soupirail, *the airhole.*
le bail, les baux, *the leases.* | le vantail, *the folding-door, leaf.*
le corail, les coraux, *the corals.* | le vitrail, *the stained-glass windows.*
l'émail, les émaux, *the enamel.* | les bestiaux, *the cattle.*

All other Substantives in **ail** follow the General Rule: **as**,

le détail, les détails, *the details.* | l'éventail, les éventails, *the fans,* etc.

§ 21. The following Substantives have a double plural:

	Irregular:	Regular:
l'aïeul *the grandfather*,	les aïeux *the ancestors*,	les aïeuls *grandfathers*.
le ciel *the sky, heaven*,	les cieux *the heavens, skies*,	les ciels *skies in pictures, climate, bed-testers*.
l'œil *the eye*,	**les yeux *the eyes*,**	les œils (œils-de-bœuf) *oval windows*.
l'appât *the bait*,	les appas *the charms*,	les appâts *baits*.
le travail *the work*,	les travaux *the works*,	les travails **reports** (*of a minister*).

Obs. 1. **Proper Nouns** remain unaltered in the Plural: as, les deux Corneille; les Soliman.

Except the names of some dynasties and families: as, les Horaces, les Curiaces, les Gracques, les Césars, les Macchabées, les Bourbons, les Stuarts.

Obs. 2. **Words of Foreign Origin** do not take the Sign of the Plural: as, les fac-simile, les Te-Deum, les in-folio, les post-scriptum, etc.

Except those which have been quite assimilated by constant use: as, les échos *the echoes*; les pensums *the tasks*; les numéros *the numbers*, etc

§ 22. PLURAL OF COMPOUND SUBSTANTIVES.

Only the **declinable components**, i. e. **Substantives** and **Adjectives**, can take the sign of the plural.

Accordingly the sign of the plural is added

(a) to **both** words, if the Compound be formed of two *Nouns*, — Substantive or Adjective —: (Except when a Preposition is suppressed, see b).

le chef-lieu	les chefs-lieux	*the chief towns.*
le chou-fleur	les choux-fleurs	*the cauliflowers.*
le beau-frère	les beaux-frères	*the brothers in law.*
le gentilhomme	les gentilshommes	*the noblemen.*
le bonhomme	les bonshommes	*easy-going men.*
monsieur	messieurs	*gentlemen.*
madame	mesdames	*ladies.*
mademoiselle	mesdemoiselles	*young ladies.*
monseigneur	messeigneurs (nosseigneurs, obsol.)	*lordships.* *noble lords.*

(b) to the **first** word only, if the Compound be formed of two **Nouns**, *linked by a Preposition* (expressed or implied):

l'arc-en-ciel	les **arcs**-en-ciel	*the rainbows.*
le chef-d'œuvre	les **chefs**-d'œuvre	*the masterpieces.*
le ver-à-soie	les **vers**-à-soie	*the silkworms.*
le timbre-poste	les **timbres**-poste	*the postage-stamps.*
l'hôtel-dieu	les **hôtels**-dieu	*the hospitals.*

(c) to the **last** word only, if the first be a *Verb*, *Preposition* or any *indeclinable prefix*:

le porte-manteau	les porte-**manteaux**	*the portmanteaus.*
l'avant-coureur	les avant-**coureurs**	*the forerunners.*
le vice-roi	les vice-**rois**	*the viceroys.*

(d) to **neither,** if both form a Compound used as an epithet **to** another word **understood**, and which—if expressed—would take the sign of the plural:

l'abat-jour, les abat-jour (= des **fenêtres** qui abattent le jour), *lamp-shades ;* le réveille-matin, les réveille-matin (= des **horloges** qui réveillent à une heure fixe du matin), *alarums.*

Thus—
les coq-à-lâne, *cock and bull stories.* les tête-à-tête.
les pied-à-terre, *occasional lodgings.* les pot-au-feu, *boiled beef and broth.*

Obs. 1. If the second word expresses plurality it takes the plural inflection in both Sing. and Plur. of the Compound :

un or des cure-dents (= **un instrument pour curer les dents**), *toothpicks.*
un or des essuie-mains (= **un linge pour essuyer les mains**), *towels.*

Obs. 2. When **garde** in compounds signifies a **person** (*keeper, nurse, etc.*), it takes **s,** but remains unchanged when it is a **Verb :**

la garde-malade, les gardes-malades, *the sick-nurses.*
le garde-manger, les garde-manger, *the pantries, larders.*

Obs. 3. If the component parts have entirely coalesced, the Compound Noun is treated as a Simple Noun :

le parapluie, les parapluies, *the umbrellas.*
le chevau-léger, les chevau-légers, *the light horsemen.*
Thus also la grand'mère, les grand'mères, *the grandmothers.*

For lists of Substantives with different meaning in the Sing. and Plural, **and** of Substantives not used in the Sing. see Appendix I. §§ 116 and 117.

The Genders of Substantives.

(The Rules for ascertaining the Genders of Substantives are collected in the Appendix I. §§ 112—114).

§. 23. SUBSTANTIVES OF BOTH GENDERS.

1. **Amour,** *love;* **orgue,** *organ;* **délice,** *delight;* (see § 114. Except. 2.)
Masculine in the Sing. | *Feminine* in the Plur.

2. **Gens,** people, is *masc.* but **an** Adjective qualifying **gens**

is *Masculine* when it stands **after:**	*Feminine* when it immediately precedes gens:*
Des gens résolus.	De vieilles gens. Quelles sottes gens!

*Except **tous** which takes the feminine form only when it **immediately** precedes another adjective with a distinctive feminine inflection:

Tous ces honnêtes gens. | Toutes ces sottes gens.

(Ceci est dû à une lutte entre le genre propre de gens qui est féminin (Lat. gentes) et le genre de l'idée qu'il exprime (hommes, individus) qui est masculin. *Littré*).

Obs. **Gens** in compound words is always Masc.: Gens de lettres, Gens d'honneur, etc.

3. **Pâques,** *Easter.*

Masc. Sing. as a general rule:	*Feminine* in the expression—
à Pâques prochain, *Next Easter.*	Faire de bonnes Pâques, *To receive the sacrament.*
	Pâques fleuries, **Palm-Sunday.**

Pâque, *Passover,* is *Fem.*

4. **Œuvre,** *work.*

| *Masc.* = the works of an engraver or musician; le grand œuvre, *the philosopher's stone.* | *Feminine* = work, action, in general. |

5. **Personne,** *person.*

| *Masc.* when used as an **Indef. Pronoun:** Personne (*no one*) n'est parfaitement heureux. | *Fem.* when used as a **Substantive:** Cette jeune personne n'est pas heureuse. |

6. **Chose,** *thing.*

| *Masc.* when used as an Indef. Pron. Quelque chose est **arrivé,** *Something has happened.* | *Fem.* as a Substantive: **la chose.** Quelque chose que, *whatever,* is fem.: quelque chose qu'il ait **faite.** |

7. Couple, *couple.*

Masc.: two (to match). A male or female.
Un couple d'amis. Un heureux couple.

Fem.: two (of a sort), **a brace**:
Une couple d'œufs.

8. Enfant, *child* (always *Masc.* in the Plur.).

Masc.: a boy

Fem. sing.: a girl.

9. Foudre, *lightning, thunderbolt.*

Masc. in the figurative sense only:
Un foudre de guerre, *a great warrior.*

Feminine in the literal sense of *lightning.*

For a complete list of Substantives of both genders according to their meaning, see App. I. § 115.

FORMATION OF THE FEMININE OF SUBSTANTIVES.

§ 24. The Rules are the same as those for the Formation of the Feminine of Adjectives, see §§ 28—37: as,

un Français, une Française ; un fermier, une fermière ; le chat, la chatte.
un baron, une baronne ; un élève, une élève ; un époux, une épouse.

Exceptions.

§ 25. Many in e *mute* take -sse: as,

l'abbé	*the abbot,*	l'abbesse.	l'ogre,	*the ogre,*	l'ogresse.
l'âne	*the ass,*	l'ânesse.	le prêtre,	*the priest,*	la prêtresse.
le chanoine,	*the canon,*	chanoinesse.	le prince,	*the prince,*	la princesse.
le diable,	*the devil,*	la diablesse.	le pauvre,	*the beggar,*	la pauvresse.
le comte,	*the earl,*	la comtesse.	le prophète,	*the prophet,*	la prophétesse.
l'hôte,	*the host,*	l'hôtesse.	le Suisse,	*the Swiss,*	la Suissesse.
le maître,	*the master,*	la maîtresse.	le tigre,	*the tiger,*	la tigresse.
le nègre,	*the negro,*	la négresse.	le traître,	*the traitor,*	la traîtresse.

Obs. The following change their termination -eur into -eresse :

le chasseur,	*the hunter*	la chasseresse, *in poetical style ; otherwise* chasseuse.
le défendeur,	**the** *defendant* (Law),	la défenderesse.
le demandeur,	**the** *plaintiff* (Law),	la demanderesse (la demandeuse, *the beggar*).
l'enchanteur,	*the enchanter,*	l'enchanteresse.
le pécheur,	*the sinner,*	la pécheresse (le pêcheur, *the fisherman,* la pêcheuse).
le vendeur,	*the seller* (Law),	la venderesse (l. vendeuse, *the seller* in general).
likewise : le devin, *soothsayer,*		la devineresse.

FEMININE OF SUBSTANTIVES. 11

§ 26. Nouns the **Feminine** form of which, though of the same root, differs more or less from the **Masculine** form:

l'ambassadeur,	the *ambassador,*	l'ambassadrice.
le canard,	the *duck,*	la canne.
le caneton,	the *duckling,*	la canette.
le chameau,	the *camel,*	la chamelle.
le chanteur,	the **singer,**	{ la cantatrice, *the professional singer.* { la chanteuse, *the amateur singer.*
le cheval,	the *horse,*	la cavale.
le chevreuil,	the *roe,*	la chevrette.
le cochon,	the *pig,*	la coche.
le compagnon,	the *companion,*	la compagne.
le daim,	the *fallow deer,*	la daine.
le dieu,	the *god,*	la déesse.
le dindon,	the *turkey,*	la dinde.
le doge,	the *doge,*	la dogaresse.
le duc,	the *duke,*	la duchesse.
l'empereur,	the *emperor,*	l'impératrice.
le fils,	the *son,*	la fille.
le gouverneur,	the *governor,*	la gouvernante.
le héros (h aspirate),	the *hero,*	l'héroïne (h mute).
le loup,	the *wolf,*	la louve.
le mulet,	the *mule,*	la mule.
le neveu,	the *nephew,*	la nièce.
le nourricier,	the *foster father,*	la nourrice.
le roi,	the *king,*	la reine.
le serviteur,	the *servant,*	la servante.

Obs. Many Substantives denoting professions almost exclusively followed by men remain unaltered, if applied to women: as,

l'auteur, *the author, authoress.*	le peintre, *the painter.*
le docteur, *the doctor.*	le témoin, *the witness,* etc.

§ 26 (a). **Masculine** names of living beings the **Feminine** of which is of a different root:

le bélier,	*ram,*	la brebis.	le mari,	*husband,*	la femme.
le bouc,	**he-goat,**	la chèvre.	le sieur,	*a Mr.*	la dame.
le bœuf,	*ox,*	la vache.	monsieur,	*Mr., Sir,*	madame.
le cerf,	*stag, hart,*	la biche.	l'oncle,	*uncle,*	la tante.
l'étalon,	*the stallion,*	la jument.	papa,	*papa,*	maman.
le coq,	*cock,*	la poule.	le parrain,	*godfather,*	la marraine.
le frère,	*brother,*	la sœur.	le père,	*father,*	la mère.
le garçon,	*boy,*	la fille.	le sanglier,	*wild boar,*	la laie.
le gendre,	*son-in-law,*	la bru (*obsol.*)	le singe,	*ape,*	la guenon.
l'homme,	*man,*	la femme.	le taureau,	*bull,*	la génisse.
le jars,	*gander,*	l'oie.	le verrat,	**boar,**	la truie.
le lièvre,	*hare,*	**la hase.**			

The Adjective (L'adjectif).

§ 27. FORMATION OF THE FEMININE OF ADJECTIVES.

Adjectives are either of **one** termination for both genders, **two** terminations (one for each gender), or **three** terminations (two for the masc. and one for the fem.)

§ 28. *Adjectives of one Termination:*

Adjectives ending in e mute in the masc. remain unaltered in the **Fem.:** as,

  utile, *masc. and fem., useful;* **fidèle,** *masc. and fem., faithful.*

  Obs. Compare the Latin adjectives: utilis, (m. and f.) fidelis, (masc. and fem.) etc.

§ 29. *Adjectives of two Terminations:*

Preliminary Remark. In most Adjectives derived from Latin, the Latin stem-consonant, altered or dropped in the *Masc.* of the French adjective, reappears in the *Feminine:* as,

	Masc.	Fem.	Lat.
French	vif,	vive,	vivus.
"	bénin,	bénigne,	benignus.

§ 30. General Rule. The Feminine is formed by adding **e mute** to the masc. termination; as,

Masc.	Fem.		Masc.	Fem.	
petit,	petite,	**small.**	appliqué,	appliquée,	*diligent.*
joli,	jolie,	**pretty.**	meilleur,	meilleure,	*better.*

Obs. 1. When the final consonant is preceded by an **e**, this e takes in the *fem.* a grave accent: as,

  m. léger, *fem.* légère, *light;* secret, secrète, *secret.*

Obs. 2. Adjectives ending in gu take ë in the feminine (§ 7. Obs.): as, *masc.* aigu, *fem.* aiguë, *acute; masc.* ambigu, *fem.* ambiguë, *ambiguous.*

Obs. 3. **Long** and **oblong** insert **u** before **e** (to preserve the hard sound of **g**): as,

  longue, oblongue.

ADJECTIVE.

§ 31. Special Rules. Adjectives ending in **el, ell, en** and **on** double their final consonant and add **e** mute: as,

Masc.	Fem.		Masc.	Fem.	
cruel	cruelle,	*cruel.*	européen	européenne,	*European.*
pareil	pareille,	*like.*	bon,	bonne,	*good.*
chrétien	chrétienne,	*christian.*	*also* gentil*	gentille,	*pretty, gentle.*

*The other Adjectives in -il follow the General Rule.

§ 32. Adjectives ending in **s** or **t** form their Feminine according to § 29, i. e. according to the corresponding Latin adjective, and consequently,

either, (a) **double their final consonant: as,**

Masc.	Fem.		Masc.	Fem.	
bas (*low*, Lat. bassus)	basse,	*low.*	exprès (expressus)	expresse,	*express.*
gras (crassus)	grasse,	*fat.*	gros (grossus)	grosse,	*thick.*
las (lassus)	lasse,	*tired.*	net (nitidus)	nette,	*neat, clear.*
épais (spissus)	épaisse,	*thick.*	sujet (subjectus)	sujette,	*subject.*

Obs. The following also double their final consonant:

brunet, brunette, *dark;* sot, sotte, *foolish;* coquet, coquette, *coquettish;* doucet, *demure;* vieillot, *oldish,* etc.

or (b) **simply add e mute,** (see General Rule § 30. Obs. 1): as,

ras	(rasus)	rase,	*level.*	inquiet	(inquietus)	inquiète,	*uneasy*
obtus	(obtusus)	obtuse,	*obtuse.*	secret	(secretus)	secrète,	*secret.*
complet	(completus)	complète,	*complete.*	prêt	(præstus)	prête,	*ready.*
concret	(concretus)	concrète,	*concrete.*	dévot	(devotus)	dévote,	*devout.*
discret	(discretus)	discrète,	*discreet.*	idiot	(idiota)	idiote,	*idiotic, silly.*

or (c) **change their final consonant: as,**

absous	(absolutus)	absoute,	*absolved.*	tiers	(tertius)	tierce,	*third.*
dissous	(dissolutus)	dissoute,	*dissolved.*				

Irregular: Frais (Old. Germ. *frisc*) **fraîche,** *fresh.*

§ 33. Adjectives ending in **f** or **x** change their final consonant, according to § 29, into **ve** and **se** respectively: as,

actif	(activus)	active,	*active.*	glorieux	(gloriosus)	glorieuse,	*glorious.*
neuf	(novus)	neuve,	*new.*	jaloux	(zelosus)	jalouse,	*jealous.*

Obs. bref (brevis) brève *short,* according to Obs. 1 to § 30.

§ 34. The following adjectives also form their Feminine according to § 29:

doux (dulcis) douce, *sweet*.
faux (falsus) fausse, *false*.
roux (russus) rousse, *red, sandy*.

bénin (benignus) bénigne, *benign*.
malin (malignus) maligne, *malignant*.
favori (favoritus) favorite, *favorite*.

§ 35. Adjectives ending in **c** change this **c** either into **que** (to preserve the hard sound of c) or into **che**: as,

caduc (caducus) caduque, *decrepit*.
public (publicus) publique, *public*.
turc turque, *Turkish*.
grec (græcus) grecque, *Greek*.

sec (siccus) sèche*, *dry*.
blanc (old Germ. blanch) blanche, *white*.
franc (old Germ. franco) franche, *free, frank*.
(franque *frankish*, as, langue franque).

***Obs.** From Lat. sicca; thus in a great many cases the Lat. **c** followed by **a** is softened in French into **ch**: as,

casa = chez; catena = chaine, etc.; see Introd. § 8.

§ 36. Adjectives ending in **-eur** form their Feminine either in **-eure, -euse, -rice**, or **-eresse**:

(a) in **-eure**, those derived from Latin comparatives (comprising all in -érieur): as,

meilleur, meilleure, (melior) *better*; supérieur, supérieure (superior) *superior*.

(b) in **-euse**, those which are formed from a Present Participle by changing **-ant** into **-eur**: as,

    flatt-eur (from flatt-ant) flatt-euse, *flattering*
    tromp-eur („ tromp-ant) tromp-euse, *deceitful*.

(c) in **-trice**, those in **-teur** derived from Lat. Adjectives in **-tor** f. **trix**: as,

créateur, créatrice, *creating*; consolateur, consolatrice, *comforting*, **consoling**.

(d) in **-eresse**, the two following (see § 25. Obs.):

vengeur, vengeresse, *avenging*; enchanteur, enchanteresse, *charming*.

Obs. A few adjectives have no Feminine terminations: as, châtain, *nut-brown*; hébreu, *Hebrew* fat, *foppish*, etc.

Adjectives of Three Terminations.

§ 37. The following *five* **adjectives**, which have **a second masculine termination when standing before a** *masc. Noun Sing.* **beginning with a** *vowel* **or** *silent h*, **form their Feminine from this latter form by doubling the final consonant and adding e mute (see § 29); as,**

Masculine:			*Feminine:*	
before a Consonant:	before a Vowel or silent h:		before both Consonants and Vowels:	
beau,	bel	(bellus),	belle,	*fine, beautiful.*
fou,	fol	(follis),	folle,	*foolish.*
mou,	mol	(mollis),	molle,	*soft.*
nouveau,	nouvel	(novellus),	nouvelle,	*new.*
vieux,	vieil	(vetulus),	vieille,	*old.*

Obs. **vieux** is sometimes used before nouns beginning with a vowel or silent h: as,
 un vieux ami, un vieux homme; *but*, le vieil homme, in the scriptural sense of *sinner*.

§ 38. FORMATION OF THE PLURAL OF ADJECTIVES.

In the Formation of the Plural Adjectives follow **the same** rules as the Substantive (see §§ 16—19): **as,**

(1) **Principal Rule**: by adding **s**: grand, grands; grande, grandes.
 Except: tout, *all*, pl. tous.

(2) Adjectives in **s, x,** do not change: bas, *pl.* bas; heureux *pl.* heureux.

(3) Adjectives in **au** take **x**: beau, *pl.* beaux.
 Those in ou or eu take s: fou, *pl.* fous; bleu, *pl.* bleus.

(4) Adjectives in **al** change this into **aux**: général, *pl.* généraux.

Obs. 1. In the fem. pl. all these adjectives follow the Principal Rule: as, basse, basses; belle, belles; toute, toutes, générale, générales, etc.

Obs. 2. For reasons of euphony, the *masc. pl.* form of many adjectives in -al is very unsettled; a few hardly ever used in the *masc. pl.* take s: fatals, frugals, glacials, natals, navals, pénals; with many others the use of the *masc. plur.* is altogether avoided: déloyal, labial, mental, total, etc.

Obs. 3. Compound Adjectives denoting **colour**, and simple Adjectives derived from Substantives denoting colour, do not take the Sign of the Plural: as, châtain-clair, *light brown;* paille, *strawcoloured,* etc.

N.B.—For the *fem. plural* of Compound Adjectives, see p. 85.

§ 39.   COMPARISON OF ADJECTIVES.

Obs. The Principal Rule for forming the Degrees of Comparison in French is analogous to the Exceptional Latin Rule for adjectives which have a vowel before the termination **us**: as, noxius, magis noxius, maxime noxius.

§ 40. The **Comparative** is formed by placing the adverb **plus**, *more*, before the Adjective, and **the Superlative** by placing the *Def. Art.* or a *Possess. Adj.* before the Comparative: as,

Positive.	Comparative.	Superlative.
beau belle } *fine*, beaux	plus beau plus belle } *finer*, plus beaux	le plus beau la plus belle } *the finest*. les plus beaux

mon plus beau
ma plus belle
mes plus beaux (belles) } *my most beautiful.*

Obs. When the Superlative Adjective follows **the** Noun, the Definite **Article** must be placed both before the Substantive **and** the Adjective: as,

La femme **la** plus modeste.   **Les** femmes **les** plus modestes.

§ 41.   IRREGULAR COMPARISON.

	Positive.	Comparative.	Superlative.
bon,	*good*,	meilleur (melior), *better*,	**le** meilleur, *the best*.
mauvais,	{ *wicked*, { *bad*,	pire (pejor), *more wicked*, plus mauvais, *worse*,	le pire, *the most wicked*. le plus mauvais, *the worst*.
petit,	*small*,	{ moindre (minor), *less*, { plus petit, *smaller*,	le moindre, *the least*. le plus petit, *the smallest*.

Obs. 1. **Mauvais** in the sense of *bad* (*physically*), **petit** in the sense of *small* (in size), are compared regularly: as,

plus mauvais, le plus mauvais; plus petit, etc.

Obs. 2. **For** Comparatives in **-érieur,** see § 36 (a).

The superl. inflection *-issime* (from Latin *-issimus*) is used in the familiar style with a few adjectives: grandissime, richissime, sénérissime, etc.

Notice the following idiomatic forms of comparison:

Un mets tout ce qu'il y a de plus recherché.
Ce palais est tout ce qu'on peut imaginer de splendide.
Une dame on ne saurait plus aimable.
Le Saint des Saints (scriptural).   Le brave des braves.

Numerals. (Adjectifs numéraux.)

§ 42.   A   CARDINAL NUMBERS. (CARDINAUX.)

1	un, f. une	21	vingt **et** un
2	deux	22	vingt-deux
3	trois	30	trente
4	quatre	31	trente **et** un
5	cinq	40	quarante
6	**six**	50	cinquante
7	sept	60	soixante (x pronounced as ss)
8	huit	70	soixante-dix (soixante et dix, etc.)
9	neuf	71	soixante-onze
10	dix	72	soixante-douze, etc.
11	onze	80	quatre-vingt**s**
12	douze	81	quatre-vingt-un
13	treize	82	quatre-vingt-deux
14	**quatorze**	90	quatre-vingt-dix
15	**quinze**	91	quatre-vingt-onze
16	**seize**	99	quatre-vingt-dix-neuf
17	**dix-sept**	100	cent
18	**dix-huit**	101	cent un, etc.
19	**dix-neuf**	200	deux cent**s**
20	**vingt**	250	deux cent cinquante, etc.

1000 mille,   100,000 cent mille,   2,000 deux mille (*no* s),
1,000,000 un million,   2,000,000 deux millions,
1871 mil huit **cent soixante-onze**,   1,000,000,000 un milliard.

Obs. The old (more consistent) forms **septante** (70), **octante** (80), **nonante** (90), survive only as provincialisms. Notice also La Version des Septante.

Pronunciation. 1. The final consonant of cinq, sept, huit, is sounded before a vowel or silent h, or when the numeral is standing alone: as, cinq‿arbres; six‿hommes; il y en a sept; *but* cinq (*pron.* cin) maisons.

2. Six, dix, neuf, are pronounced = siss, diss, neuf, if used substantively; il y en a six; nous sommes dix; chapitre neuf; = **siz, diz, neuv,** if used **adjectively** before **a vowel or silent h**: six arbres = si-zarbres;

Eugène, French Grammar.

dix heures = di-zeures; neuf hommes = neu-vommes; = si, di, neu, if used **adjectively** before a consonant: si jours; di commandements; neu muses.

3. Though h in **huit** is silent, and **onze** has no h at all, we say:
'**e** huit, **le** onze, instead of l'huit, l'onze; thus: le huitième, etc.

Obs. 1. Quatre-vingt, and cent in the plur. only take an **s** when not followed by another Numeral: as,

quatre-vingts soldats; **deux** cents hommes; *but* quatre-vingt-douze soldats, deux cent quatre-vingt-dix hommes.

2. If used as ordinal numbers, **cent** and **quatre-vingt** never take **s**: as, page quatre-vingt, chapitre deux cent.

3. **Mille** is written **mil** in dates (of the Christian era) if followed by another Numeral, and not preceded by another: as,

mil huit cent; *but* l'an mille, l'an deux mille.

4. Mille, *thousand*, never **takes s**: as, dix mille, *ten thousand*.
but dix milles, *ten miles*.

5. As in English, we may say—onze cent(s) (1100), douze cent(s) (1200), etc.

§ 43. *B.* ORDINAL NUMERALS. (NOMBRES ORDINAUX.)

Ordinal Numbers are formed by affixing -**ième** (from Lat. -**imus**) to a Cardinal Number (except *the first* and *last*): as,
le premier, la première (primarius), *the first,*
le second, (secundus) ⎫
le deuxième, ⎭ *the second,*
le troisième, *the third,*
le cinquième, *the fifth,* (u is inserted after q,)
le neuvième, *the ninth,* (f is changed into v,)
le trentième, *the thirtieth,* (Card. Numb. ending in e drop this e,)
le millième, *the thousandth,*
le dernier, *the last.*

Obs. **unième** is used only when connected with another numeral: as, vingt et unième, trente et unième, etc.

§ 44. Instead of **Ordinal Numbers** (as in English and Lat.) **Cardinal** Numb. are used in French

(a) in apposition to **names of Sovereigns** (*except* premier, *and sometimes* second): as,

Louis quatorze; *but* François premier; Frédéric second; Henri deux.

Obs. Exceptionally: Charles-Quint and Sixte-Quint (Lat. **quintus**), for the Emperor Charles **V.** and Pope Sixtus **V.**

(b) for the **days of the month** (*except* le premier): as,

le cinq novembre, le dix-huit brumaire; le onze juillet, le huit octobre, *but* le premier janvier, le premier courant.

Obs. 1. In Quotations, *Cardinal Numbers* may also be used instead of Ordinals (*except* le premier): as,

Chapitre treize. Page cent vingt et un.

Obs. 2. prime (primus) is used exceptionally in: de **prime** abord, *at first sight*; **tiers**, f. **tierce** (tertius), only in a few terms, as le **tiers-état**, *the Commons* (French History).

§ 45. *C.* FRACTIONAL NUMERALS. (NOMBRES FRACTIONNAIRES.)

un demi,	(dimidium)	} *half,*
une moitié,	(medietatem)	
un tiers,	(tertius)	*third,*
un quart,	(quartus)	*fourth.*

un cinquième, *a fifth,*
cinq sixièmes, ⁵/₆,

From *five* upwards Ordinal Numbers **are** used. (*Comp. Latin.*)

§ 46. *D.* COLLECTIVE NUMERALS. (NOMBRES COLLECTIFS.)

These are formed by affixing **-aine** (*Lat. suffix*-ana) to the Cardinal Numb. (those **in -e** drop this e); only the following are used:

une huitaine,	*about eight,*	une trentaine,	*about* 30,
une dixaine,	- *ten,*	une quarantaine,	- 40,
une douzaine,	*a dozen,*	une cinquantaine	- 50,
une quinzaine,	*about fifteen,*	une soixantaine,	- 60,
une vingtaine,	*a score,*	une centaine,	- 100,

un **millier,** *about* 1000.

§ 47. *E*. PROPORTIONAL NUMERALS. (NOMBRES PROPORTIONNELS.)

simple	(Lat. simplus)	*simple,*	sextuple	*sixfold,*
double	(duplus)	*double,*	septuple (septuplus)	*sevenfold,*
triple	(triplus)	*treble,*	octuple	*eightfold,*
quadruple	(quadruplus)	*fourfold,*	décuple	*tenfold,*
quintuple	**(quintuplus)**	*fivefold,*	centuple	*hundredfold.*

All others are formed thus: vingt **fois autant,** etc.

§ 48. *F*. NUMERAL ADVERBS. (ADVERBES NUMÉRAUX.)

These denote the number of times that anything occurs, as:

une fois, (Lat. vices) *once,*   dix fois, *ten times,*
deux fois, *twice.*   cent **fois,** *a hundred times,* etc.

The Pronouns (Les Pronoms).

A. PERSONAL PRONOUNS (PRONOMS PERSONNELS).

§ 49. Personal Pronouns in French are either

(a) **Conjunctive**; i. e. connected with a Verb as Subject or Object (proclitic or enclitic):

je	I,	nous	we,
tu	thou,	vous	you,
il	he,	ils	they, m.
elle	she,	elles	they, f.

Je loue, **I** am *praising*.
Elle le loue, *She praises* him.

(b) **Disjunctive**, i. e. employed by themselves or governed by a Preposition:

moi	I, me,	nous	we, us.
toi	thou, thee,	vous	you.
lui	he, him,	eux	they, them, m.
elle	she, her	elles	they, them, f.

Qui est là? moi, *Who is there?* **I**.
Elle parle de lui, *She is speaking of* **him**.

§ 50. A. CONJUNCTIVE PERSONAL PRONOUNS.

SINGULAR.

	First Person.	Second Person.	Third Person.
Subj. or Nom.	je, *I.*	tu, *thou.*	il, elle, *he, she, it.*
Dir. Obj. or Acc.	me, *me.*	te, *thee.*	le, la, *him, her, it.*
Ind. Obj. or Dat.	me, *to me.*	te, *to thee.*	lui, (y) *to him, to her, to it.*

PLURAL.

Subj. or Nom.	nous, *we.*	vous, *you.*	ils, elles, *they.*
Dir. Obj. or Acc.	nous, *us.*	vous, *you.*	les, *them.*
Ind. Obj. or Dat.	nous, *to us.*	vous, *to you.*	leur (y) *to them.*

See also §§ 187—191.

Obs. e and a in je, me, te, se, le, la are elided before a verb beginning with a vowel or silent h. (see § 7). The Genitive Sing. and Plur. are wanting and are supplied by the Gen. of the Disjunctive Pron. (See § 52.); as,

Il parle de moi. Nous nous souvenons de lui.

The Genitive and Dative of the third Person, both masc. and fem., Sing. and Plur., are also expressed by the Pronominal Adverbs **en** and **y**; especially with reference to things, (see §§ 193—195):—

en, *of* or *from him, her, it, them,* as:
Je t'en donnerai. *I will give you some of* **it**.
J'en ai plusieurs. *I have several of* them.

y, *to* or *at him, her, it, them,* as:
Nous y consentons. *We agree* **to it** (*or* to them),

§ 51. The **Reflective** Pronouns of the First and Second Pers. are the same as the Accusative of the Conjunctive **Pronoun** (see Reflexive Verbs, pp. 48, 49): as,

me, *myself,*   te, *thyself,*   se, *himself, herself, itself.*
nous, *ourselves,*   vous, *yourselves,*   se, *themselves.*
(se is the third Pers. *m.* and *f.*, Sing. and Plur.)
soi, *one's self.*

The same Pronouns are also **used** to express *one another, each other.*

§ 52.   B. DISJUNCTIVE PERSONAL PRONOUNS.

SINGULAR.

	First Person.	Second Person.	Third Person.
Subj. & Object.	moi, *I;*	toi, *thou;*	lui, elle, *he, she.*
Genitive.	de moi	de toi	de lui, d'elle (en).
Ind. Obj. or Dat.	à moi	à toi	à lui, à elle, (y).

PLURAL.

Subj. & Object.	nous, *we;*	vous, *you;*	eux, elles, *they.*
Gen.	de nous	de vous	d'eux, d'elles (en).
Dat.	à nous	à vous	à eux, à elles (y).

See also §§ 196—199.

Soi, *one's self, itself,* is the Refl. Disjunctive Pronoun for the third Person.

Obs. Disjunctive Pronouns are strengthened by affixing même (Lat. *semetipsissimus*): as,

moi-même, *I myself,* toi-même, lui-même, elle-même, soi-même. nous-mêmes, *we ourselves,* vous-mêmes, eux-mêmes, elles-mêmes, (Compare Latin: egomet, mihimet ipsi etc.)

B. POSSESSIVE PRONOUNS (PRONOMS POSSESSIFS.)

§ 53. These are employed either (a) **adjectively**, i. e. as Adjectives modifying a Substantive, **or** (b) as **Pronouns proper**, i. e. instead of a Substantive:

§ 54. (A) POSSESSIVE ADJECTIVES.

	Sing.			Plur.	
masc. **mon,**	*fem.* **ma,**	*m. & f.* **mes,**	*my.*
„ **ton,**	„ **ta,**	„ **tes,**	*thy.*
„ **son,**	„ **sa,**	„ **ses,**	*his, her, its.*
m. & f. **notre,**		„ **nos,**	*our.*
„ **votre,**		„ **vos,**	*your.*
„ **leur,**		„ **leurs,**	*their.*

(Comp. mon, ton, son with the Lat. Poss. Pron. in the Acc. meum, tuum, suum, etc., see also Introduct. § 19.)

mon, ton, son are used instead of **ma, ta, sa,** for the sake of euphony, before fem. nouns beginning with a vowel or silent h, as: mon‿âme, ton‿humeur, son‿ardente dévotion.

§ 55. (B) POSSESSIVE PRONOUNS.

SING.		PLUR.		
Masc.	*Fem.*	*Masc.*	*Fem.*	
le mien,	la mienne,	**les miens,**	les miennes,	*mine.*
le tien,	la tienne,	**les tiens,**	les tiennes,	*thine.*
le sien,	la sienne,	**les siens,**	les siennes,	*his, hers, its.*
le nôtre,	la nôtre,	**les nôtres,**	les nôtres,	*ours.*
le vôtre,	la vôtre,	**les vôtres,**	les vôtres,	*yours.*
le leur,	la leur,	**les leurs,**	les leurs,	*theirs.*

See also §§ 200—203.

Obs. Another Form of the Poss. Pronoun is found in the Disjunctive **Personal Pronoun** preceded by the Preposition **à**: as,
à moi, *mine;* à toi, *thine;* à nous, *ours;* etc. (Comp. Lat. Est mihi liber).

C. DEMONSTRATIVE PRONOUNS. (PRONOMS DÉMONSTRATIFS.)

§ 56. These are employed either, (a) **adjectively** before a Substantive (Demonstrative **Adjectives**), *or* (b) as **Pronouns proper**, instead of a Substantive (Demonstrative **Pronouns**).

(A) DEMONSTRATIVE ADJECTIVES.

	Sing.			Plur.
masc. { **ce,**	before a consonant	} *this, that;*	*masc. & fem.*	
{ **cet,**	before a vowel or silent h		**ces,** *these, those.*	
fem. **cette,**				

Ce livre, cet ami, cet homme. | Ces livres, ces amis, ces hommes.
Cette femme, cette amie, cette humeur. | Ces femmes, ces amies, ces humeurs.

§ 57. The distinction between **this** and **that**, **these** and **those**, is expressed in French by affixing the particles
 -ci to the nearer object,
 -là to the remoter object; (*Comp. Latin:* hic *and* ille) as,

ce livre-ci,   cette maison-ci, *this*,   ces hommes-ci, *these men.*
ce livre-là,   cette maison-là, *that*,   ces hommes-là, *those men.*

Obs. tel, telle, *pl.* tels, telles, (talis) *such,*
même, *pl.* mêmes, *same.*

§ 58. (B) DEMONSTRATIVE PRONOUNS. (See also § 201—8.)

SING. *[one* PLUR.

m. **celui,** *f.* **celle,** *that, he, the* | m. **ceux,** *f.* **celles,** *those, they*
m. **celui-ci,** *f.* **celle-ci,** *this one* | m. **ceux-ci** *f.* **celles-ci,** *these*
m. **celui-là,** *f.* **celle-là,** *that one* | m. **ceux-là,** **celles-là** *those*
neutral. **ce,** *that, it,* (§ 207)
 „ **ceci,** *this,*
 „ **cela,** (ça in fam. style) *that,* } *no plural*

m. **le même,** *f.* **la même,** | les mêmes, *the same.*
m. **un tel,** *f.* **une telle,** *such a one,* | de tels, *f.* de telles, *such ones.*

Obs. celui, celle, are derived from Latin **ecce** in connection with **ille, illa.**

§ 59. **celui, celle, ceux, celles** are used

(1) before a relative sentence: as,
Heureux celui qui craint le Seigneur.

(2) before a Genitive referring to a noun already mentioned: as,
La capitale de la France est grande, celle de l'Angleterre est encore plus grande.

§ 60. **celui-ci, celle-ci,** etc., are used with reference to objects near to the speaker: as,
Ce pays-là est plus fertile que celui-ci.

celui-là, celle-là, etc., are used with reference to something remote: as,
Cette ville-ci est plus populeuse que celle-là.

§ 61. In referring to different antecedents
celui-ci, celle-ci, etc., are used to denote the **latter;**
celui-là, celle-là, etc., the **former:** as,

Un magistrat intègre et un brave officier sont également estimables; celui-là fait la guerre aux ennemis domestiques, celui-ci nous protège contre les ennemis extérieurs.

D. RELATIVE PRONOUNS. (PRONOMS RELATIFS.)

§ 62. These are **qui, lequel, quoi, dont,** which are declined thus:

SINGULAR & PLURAL.

1) Nom. or Subj. **qui,** *who, which, that.*
   Acc. or Dir. Obj. **que** (**qui** after prepositions), *whom, which, that.*
   Genitive **de qui, dont,** *whose, of whom, of which.*
   Dative **à qui,** *to whom, to which.*

Qu' instead of **que** before a vowel or silent h: as,
qu'il instead of **que il; qu'on** instead of **que on.**

§ 63. (2) SING.   PLUR.
N. & A.   lequel,   laquelle;   lesquels,   lesquelles, who
                                                 whom, which.
Gen.   duquel,   de laquelle;   desquels,   desquelles, of
                                                 whom, of which
Dat.   auquel,   à laquelle;   auxquels,   auxquelles, to
                                                 whom, to which

Obs. Qui is derived from the corresponding Latin Relat. Pronoun qui; lequel from le and quel, *Lat.* qualis; que from quem; dont, originally an Adverb, **from** de unde.

§ 64. (3) Relative Pronoun used absolutely:
Nom. **ce qui** (id quod) *what, that which.*
Acc. **ce que**
Gen. **ce dont**
Dat. (**ce**) **à quoi.**   (See also §§ 209—218.)

E. INTERROGATIVE PRONOUNS (PRONOMS INTERROGATIFS).

§ 65. These are employed either (a) adjectively: as,
Quel homme? *which, what, man?*

or (b) substantively: as,
Qui va là? *Who goes there?*   Lequel de vous? *which of you?*

(A) INTERROGATIVE PRONOUNS USED ADJECTIVELY.
              SING.   PLUR.
N. & A. **quel,   quelle?**   **quels,   quelles?** *which? what?*
Gen.   de quel, de quelle?   de quels, de quelles?
Dat.   à quel, à quelle?   à quels, à quelles?

§ 66. (B) INTERROGATIVE PRONOUNS USED SUBSTANTIVELY
(1) *Nom. & Acc.*   qui? *who? whom?* | que? quoi? *what?*
    Gen.   de qui? | de quoi?
    Dat.   à qui? | à quoi?

              SING.   PLUR.
(2) **lequel? laquelle?**   **lesquels? lesquelles?** *which?*
declined like the Relative lequel § 63.   (See also §§ 219—221.)

Observe that **qui**, *Interrog.* or *Absolute*, is used both as *Subject* and *Dir. Object*; whilst **qui**, *Relative* Pron., is used as Subject only.

Qui? refers to **Persons** only.—**Que?** and **Quoi?** refer to **things**.
Quoi? and not **Que?** must be used after Prepositions: as,

De quoi vous plaignez-vous? Of what *do you complain?*
A quoi songez-vous? What *are you thinking* of?
but Que faites-vous? What *are you doing?*

Lequel? refers to both persons and things.

§ 67.   PERIPHRASTIC INTERROGATION.
Nom. qui est-ce qui? *who?*   qu'est-ce qui? *what?*
Acc. qui est-ce que?   qu'est-ce que?
Gen. de qui est-ce que?   de quoi est-ce que?
Dat. à qui est-ce que?   à quoi est-ce que?

F. **INDEFINITE PRONOUNS.**   (PRONOMS INDÉFINIS.)
§ 68.   These are of three kinds,
(a) those used as **Adjectives**, i.e., qualifying a Noun: as,
chaque élève, *every pupil.*
(b) those used as **Pronouns Proper**, i.e., instead of a Noun: as,
chacun pour soi, *every one for himself.*
(c) those used both as **Adjectives** and as **Pronouns**: as,
un tel homme, *such a man.*
un tel, *such a one.*

§ 69. (A) INDEFINITE PRONOUNS USED ADJECTIVELY.
certain, -e, certains, -nes (Low Lat. certanus), *certain, some.*
quelque, -s (Lat. qualis *and* que), *some, any, a few.*
quelconque (Lat. qualiscunque), **whatever**, *whichever.*
chaque (Lat. quisque), **each**, *every.*
différents, -tes (Lat. differentem), *different.*
divers, diverses (Lat. diversus), *different* (*divers*).
maint, -e; maints, -es, (Germ. manch), *many.*

§ 70. (B) INDEFINITE PRONOUNS USED SUBSTANTIVELY.

autrui, (Lat. alterius), *others, other people.*
chacun, -e, (quisque unus) *each one, every one.*
on, l'on, (hominem) *one, they, people.*
personne, (persona) *any one.*
personne . . . ne, *no one, no body, not any body.*
quelqu'un, -e, (*composed of* quelque *and* un) *some one, some body.*
quelques -uns, -unes, *some people.*
qui . . . . . que, quiconque, (Lat. quicunque) *whoever, whomsoever.*
rien, (L. rem) *anything.*
rien . . . ne, *nothing, not anything.*

§ 71. (C) INDEFINITE PRONOUNS USED BOTH ADJECTIVELY AND SUBSTANTIVELY.

autre, -s, (Lat. alter) *other, others.*
l'un l'autre, les uns les autres, *one another, each other.*
l'un et l'autre, *both;* **l'un ou l'autre,** *either;*
ni l'un ni l'autre, *neither.*
aucun, -e, . . . ne (Lat. aliquis . . unus) *no one, no.*
nul (nulle) . . . ne, nuls (nulles) . . . ne, (nullus) *no one, no.*
tout, -e; tous, toutes (totus), *every, each, whole, all, everything.*
plusieurs, m. & f. (Low Lat. pluriores), *several.*

(See also §§ 225—237.)

The Verbs.

AUXILIARY VERBS.

§ 72. AVOIR, *to have.*

	INFINITIVE.		PARTICIPLE.
Pres.	avoir, *to have,*	*Pres.*	ayant, *having,*
Past.	avoir eu, *to have had.*	*Past.*	eu, *had.*

	INDICATIVE.		SUBJUNCTIVE.
PRESENT.	j' ai, *I have,* etc. tu as il a nous avons vous avez ils ont	**PRESENT.**	*[(should) have,* etc. que j' aie, *that I may* que tu aies qu'il ait que nous ayons que vous ayez qu'ils aient
IMPERFECT.	j' avais, *I had,* etc. tu avais il avait nous avions vous aviez ils avaient		
PRETERITE.	j' eus, *I had,* etc. tu eus il eut nous eûmes vous eûtes ils eurent	**IMPERFECT.**	*[(should) have,* etc. que j' eusse, *that I might* que tu eusses qu'il eût que nous eussions que vous eussiez qu'ils eussent

VERBS.

	INDICATIVE.		SUBJUNCTIVE.
P. INDEFINITE.	j' ai eu, *I have had*, etc. tu as eu il a eu nous avons eu vous avez eu ils ont eu	**PERFECT.**	*that I may have had*, etc. que j' aie eu que tu aies eu qu' il ait eu que nous ayons eu que vous ayez eu qu' ils aient eu
PLUPERFECT.	j' avais eu, *I had had*, etc. tu avais eu il avait eu nous avions eu vous aviez eu ils avaient eu		
P. ANTERIOR.	j' eus eu, *I had had*, etc. tu eus eu il eut eu nous eûmes eu vous eûtes eu ils eurent eu	**PLUPERFECT.**	*that I might have had*, etc. que j' eusse eu que tu eusses eu qu' il eût eu que nous eussions eu que vous eussiez eu qu' ils eussent eu
FUTURE PRESENT.	j' aurai, *I shall have*, etc. tu auras il aura nous aurons vous aurez ils auront	**PRESENT.**	CONDITIONAL. j' aurais, *I should have*, etc. tu aurais il aurait nous aurions vous auriez ils auraient
FUTURE PAST.	j' aurai eu, *I shall have [had*, etc. tu auras eu il aura eu nous aurons eu vous aurez eu ils auront eu	**PAST.**	*I should have had*, etc j' aurais eu tu aurais eu il aurait eu nous aurions eu vous auriez eu ils auraient eu

IMPERATIVE.

aie, *have (thou)*
qu'il ait, *let him have*

ayons, *let us have*
ayez, *have (ye)*
qu'ils aient, *let them have.*

§ 73. ÊTRE, *to be*.

	INFINITIVE.		PARTICIPLE.
Pres.	être, *to be*	*Pres.*	étant, *being*
Past.	avoir été, *to have been*	*Past.*	été, *been*

	INDICATIVE.		SUBJUNCTIVE.
PRESENT.	*I am,* etc. je suis, tu es il est nous sommes vous êtes ils sont	**PRESENT.**	*that I may (should) be,* etc. que je sois que tu sois qu' il soit que nous soyons que vous soyez qu' ils soient
IMPERFECT.	*I was,* etc. j' étais, tu étais il était nous étions vous étiez ils étaient		
PRETERITE.	*I was,* etc. je fus, tu fus il fut nous fûmes vous fûtes ils furent	**IMPERFECT.**	*that I might (should) be,* etc. que je fusse que tu fusses qu' il fût que nous fussions que vous fussiez qu' ils fussent
P. INDEFINITE.	*I have been,* etc. j' ai été tu as été il a été nous avons été vous avez été ils ont été	**PERFECT.**	*that I may have been,* etc. que j' aie été que tu aies été qu' il ait été que nous ayons été que vous ayez été qu' ils aient été
PLUPERFECT.	*I had been,* etc. j' avais été tu avais été il avait été nous avions été vons aviez été ils avaient été		

VERBS.

	INDICATIVE.		SUBJUNCTIVE.
P. ANTERIOR.	*I had been,* etc. j' eus été tu eus été il eut été nous eûmes été vous eûtes été ils eurent été	**PLUPERFECT.**	*that I might have been,* etc. que j' eusse été que tu eusses été qu' il eût été que nous eussions été que vous eussiez été qu' ils eussent été
FUTURE PRESENT.	je serai, *I shall be,* etc. tu seras il sera nous serons vous serez ils seront	**PRESENT.**	CONDITIONAL. je serais, *I should be,* etc. tu serais il serait nous serions vous seriez ils seraient
FUTURE PAST.	*I shall have been,* etc. j' aurai été tu auras été il aura été nous aurons été vous aurez été ils auront été	**PAST.**	*I should have been,* etc. j' aurais été tu aurais été it aurait été nous aurions été vous auriez été ils auraient été

IMPERATIVE.

sois, *be* (thou)   soyons, *let us be*
qu'il soit, *let him be*   soyez, *be* (ye)
                                       qu'ils soient, *let them be.*

Auxiliary Verbs conjugated Interrogatively and Negatively.

§ 74. 1. **Interrogatively.** The Personal Pronoun is placed after the verbs and connected with it by a hyphen. When the Third Pers. Sing. terminate, in a vowel, a euphonic **-t- is** inserted:

have I? etc.	*had I?* etc.	*am I?* etc.	*was I?* etc.
ai-je?	avais-je?	suis-je?	étais-je?
as-tu?	eus-je?	es-tu?	fus-je?
a-t*-il (elle ;-on)?	ai-je eu?	est-il (elle ;-on)?	ai-je été?
avons-nous?	avais-je eu?	sommes-nous?	avais-je été?
avez-vous?	eus-je eu?	êtes-vous?	eus-je été?
ont-ils?	aurai-je?	sont-ils?	serai-je?

VERBS. 33

Obs. If the subject is a Noun, it is left before the Verb, and repeated after it, in the form of a corresponding **Conjunctive Pers. Pronoun**:

Cet homme a-t-il un livre?	Ces hommes ont-ils de l'argent?
Cette femme a-t-elle un livre?	Ces femmes ont-elles de l'argent?

(For further particulars, see § 121.)

Periphrastic interrogation. This is formed by placing **est-ce que** (lit. *is it that?*) before the affirmative form: as,

est-ce que j'ai? *have I?*	est-ce que Jean est ici?
est-ce que tu as? *hast thou?*	*Is John here?*
est-ce qu'il (elle) a? *has he (she)?* etc.	

§ 75. 2. **Negatively.** In Simple **tenses** the verb is placed between the negations **ne .. pas, ne ... point, ne .. jamais** etc.; in Compound tenses the auxiliary only is placed between the negations, and the Past Part. at the end (**n'** *instead of* **ne** *before a vowel*): as,

je	n'ai	pas, *I have not,* etc.	je	ne suis	pas, *I am not,* etc.
tu	n'as	pas	tu	n'es	pas
il	n'a	pas	il	n'est	pas
nous	n'avons	pas	nous	ne sommes	pas
vous	n'avez	pas	vous	n'êtes	pas
ils	n'ont	pas	ils	ne sont	pas

Je n'ai pas eu, *I have not had,* etc.   Je n'ai pas été, *I have not been,* etc.
Je n'avais point, *I had not at all;*   je n'ai jamais eu, *I have never had;*
     Je n'aurai rien, *I shall not have anything,* etc.

§ 76. 3. **Negatively and Interrogatively.** In Simple tenses the Verb Interrogative and the Pronoun are placed between the negations; in Compound tenses, the Past Part. at the end: as,

n'ai-je pas? *have I not?*	ne suis-je pas? *Am I not?* etc.
n'as-tu pas? *hast thou not?*	n'es-tu pas?
n'a-t-il pas? *has he not?* etc	n'est-il pas?

n'ai-je pas eu? *have I not had?* n'aurai-je point eu? *Shall I not have had?*
     n'as-tu pas été? *hast thou not been?*

Periphrastic interrogation used negatively:
     est-ce que je n'ai pas?   *have I not?*
     est-ce que tu ne seras pas?   *wilt thou not be?* etc.

Regular Verbs. Formation of Tenses.

§ 77. There are four Regular Conjugations, distinguished by their Infinitive Terminations:

1. **-er** (aimer, *to love*). 2. **-ir** (finir, *to finish*). 3. **-oir** (recevoir, *to receive*). 4. **-re** (vendre, *to sell*).

Obs. Strictly speaking there are only three regular conjugations, the Verbs in **-oir** being all irregular, since a part of their stem is dropped in several Tenses and Persons. To avoid confusion, however, the old classification is retained, according to which the seven Verbs in **-evoir** represent the Regular Third Conjugation.

§ 78. In order to conjugate a Verb it is necessary to know its Principal Parts from which the *Derived Parts* are formed thus

	I. aim-er	II. fin-ir	III. recev-(oi)r	IV. vend-r(e)
(a) from the Infinitive				
1) the *Future Pres.* by adding the inflections ai, as, a; ons, ez, ont¹).	1. aimer-ai, -ons 2. — -as, -ez 3. — -a,²) -ont	finir-ai, -ons — -as, -ez — -a, -ont	recevr-ai, -ons — -as, -ez — -a, -ont	vendr-ai, -ons — -as, -ez — -a, -ont
2) the *Conditional Pres.* by adding the inflections ais, ais, ait; ions, iez, aient.	1. aimer-ais, -ions 2. — -ais, -iez 3. — -ait, -aient	finir-ais, -ions — -ais, -iez — -ait, -aient	recevr-ais, -ions — -ais, -iez — -ait, -aient	vendr-ais, -ions — -ais, -iez — -ait, -aient
(b) from the Pres. Part.	aim-ant	fin-iss-ant	recev-ant	vend-ant
1) the *Pres. Indic. Plur.* by changing -ant into ons, ez, ent.	1. aim-ons 2. — -ez 3. — -ent	fin-iss -ons — -iss -ez — -iss -ent	recev-ons — -ez — reçoiv-ent	vend-ons — -ez — -ent
2) the *Imperfect Indic.* by changing -ant into ais, ais, ait; ions, iez, aient.	1. aim-ais, -ions 2. — -ais, -iez 3. — -ait, -aient	fin-iss -ais, -iss -ions — -iss -ais, -iss -iez — -iss -ait, -iss -aient	recev-ais, -ions — -ais, -iez — -ait, -aient	vend-ais, -ions — -ais, -iez — -ait, -aient
3) the *Pres. Subjunctive* by changing -ant into e, es, e; ions, iez, ent.	1. aim-e, -ions 2. — -es, -iez 3. — -e,²) -ent	fin-iss -e, -iss -ions — -iss -es, -iss -iez — -iss -e, -iss -ent	reçoiv-e*, recev-ions — -es, -iez — -e, reçoiv-ent	vend-e, -ions — -es, -iez — -e, -ent

see obs. to (d).

VERBS. 35

1) all *Compound Tenses* with avoir or être	j'ai j'avais j'eus j'aurai j'aurais } aimé.	fini.	reçu.	vendu.
2) the *Passive Voice* with être	je suis j'étais je fus je serai je serais } aimé *or* aimée.	fini *or* finie.	reçu *or* reçue.	vendu *or* vendue.
(d) from the Pres. Indicative.	1. aim-e, -ons 2. -es, -ez 3. -e²), -ent	fin-is, -issons -is, -issez -it, -issent	reç-ois, recev-ons -ois, -ez -ois, reçoi-vent	vénd-s, -ons -s, -ez -²), -ent
1) the *Imperative* by dropping the Pers. Pron.	1. aim-ons 2. aim-e*, -ez *s *dropped in the 1st Conj.*	fin-is, fin-iss-ons -iss-ez	reç-ois, recev-ons -ez	vend-s, vend-ons -ez
also the *Pres. Subj. Sing. & the 3d pers. pl. of the 3d Conj. & of nearly all Irr. Verbs;* by cutting off -ent of the 3d p.pl.			{ 1. reçoiv-e, 2. -es, 3. -e, reçoiv-ent }	
(e) fr. the Preterite (Défini) 2d pers. Sing.	1. aim-ai, -âmes 2. -as, -âtes 3. -a²), -èrent	fin-is, -îmes -is, -îtes -it, -irent	reç-us, -ûmes -us, -ûtes -ut, -urent	vend-is, -îmes -is, -îtes -it, -irent
the *Imperfect Subjunctive* by changing the final s into -sse, -sses, -t -ssions, -ssiez -ssent.	1. aim-asse, -assions 2. -asses, -assiez 3. -ât, -assent	fin-isse, -issions -isses, -issiez -ît, -issent	reç-usse, -ussions -usses, -ussiez -ût, -ussent	vend-isse, -issions -isses, -issiez -ît, -issent

1) These tense-inflections of the Future and Conditional are derived from the *Pres.* and *Imperf.* of avoir (ai and av-ais) respectively. (See Introd. § 10, last section).

2) The person-inflection -t is always dropped after the final stem-consonants d, t, c, after e mute and a (*Imperf. Subj.* excepted).

Obs. Exceptions to these Rules are collected and explained § 91. The personal inflections are explained in the Introduction § 21.

3*

A. ACTIVE VOICE.

§ 80. First Conjugation: aim-er, to love.

	INFINITIVE.		PARTICIPLE.
Pres.	aim-er, to love	Pres.	aim-ant,¹) loving
Past.	avoir aim-é, to have loved	Past.	aim-é, f. -ée,²) loved

	INDICATIVE.		SUBJUNCTIVE.
PRESENT.	*I love, I am loving, I do love,* j' aime³) [etc. tu aimes il aime nous aimons vous aimez ils aiment	**PRESENT.**	*that I may (should) love, etc.* que j' aime que tu aimes qu' il aime que nous aimions que vous aimiez qu' ils aiment
IMPERFECT.	*I loved, I was loving, I did* j' aimais⁴) [*love, etc.* tu aimais il aimait nous aimions vous aimiez ils aimaient		
PRETERITE.	j' aimai,⁵) *I loved, etc.* tu aimas il aima nous aimâmes vous aimâtes ils aimèrent	**IMPERFECT.**	*that I might (should) love, etc.* que j' aimasse⁶) que tu aimasses qu' il aimât que nous aimassions que vous aimassiez qu' ils aimassent
INDEFINITE.	j' ai aimé, *I have loved, etc.* tu as aimé, etc.	**PERFECT.**	*that I may have loved, etc.* que j' aie aimé, que tu aies aimé, etc.

VERBS.

	INDICATIVE.		SUBJUNCTIVE.
PLUPERFECT.	j' avais aimé, *I had loved*, etc. tu avais aimé, etc.		
P. ANTERIOR.	j' eus aimé, *I had loved*, etc. tu eus aimé, etc.	PLUPERFECT.	*that I might have loved*, etc. que j' eusse aimé que tu eusses aimé, etc.
FUTURE PRESENT.	j' aimerai, *I shall love*, etc. tu aimeras il aimera nous aimerons vous aimerez ils aimeront	PRESENT.	**CONDITIONAL.** j' aimerais, *I should love*, [etc. tu aimerais il aimerait nous aimerions vous aimeriez ils aimeraient
FUTURE PAST.	[*loved*, etc. j' aurai aimé, *I shall have* tu auras aimé, etc.	PAST.	*I should have loved*, etc. j' aurais aimé tu aurais aimé, etc.

IMPERATIVE.

aime, *(love thou)*   aimons, *let us love*
                                                                aimez, *love (ye)*
(qu'il aime, *let him love*)   (qu'ils aiment, *let them love*).

1. From the Lat. Part. Pres. Acc. **amantem** (not from the Nom.; see Introd. § 19).
2. From the Lat. Part. Perf. Pass. **amatus**. (The Lat. ending **-atus** becomes é in Fr., comp. clericatus = **clergé**.)
3. From the Lat. Pres. Indicat.   ⎫
4. From the Lat. Imperf. **-a(b)am, a(b)as**.   ⎬ see Introd. § 21.
5. From the Lat. Perf. **-a(v)i**, by the dropping of v. ⎪
6. From the Lat. **contracted** Pluperf. Subj. **-assem**. ⎭

§ 81. Second Conjugation: **finir**, to finish.

	INFINITIVE.		PARTICIPLE.
Pres.	**fin-ir,** *to finish*	*Pres.*	fin-iss-ant, *finishing*
Past.	avoir fin-i, *to have finished*	*Part.*	fin-i, f. -ie, *finished*

	INDICATIVE.		SUBJUNCTIVE.
PRESENT.	*I finish, I am finishing, I do [finish, etc.* je finis tu finis il finit nous finissons vous finissez ils finissent	**PRESENT.**	*that I may (should) finish,* etc. que je finisse que tu finisses qu' il finisse que nous finissions que vous finissiez qu' ils finissent
IMPERFECT.	*I finished, I was finishing, I* je finissais [*did finish, etc.* tu finissais il finissait nous finissions vous finissiez ils finissaient		
PRETERITE.	je finis, *I finished, etc.* tu finis il finit nous finîmes vous finîtes ils finirent	**IMPERFECT.**	*that I might (should) finish,* etc. que je finisse que tu finisses qu' il finît que nous finissions que vous finissiez qu' ils finissent
INDEFINITE.	j' ai fini, *I have finished, etc.* tu as fini, *etc.*	**PERFECT.**	*that I may have finished,* etc. que j' aie fini que tu aies fini, *etc.*
PLUPERFECT.	*I had finished, etc.* j' avais fini tu avais fini, *etc.*		

VERBS.

	INDICATIVE.		SUBJUNCTIVE.
P. ANTERIOR.	j' eus fini, *I had finished*, etc. tu eus fini, etc.	PLUPERFECT.	*that I might have finished* etc. que j' eusse fini que tu eusses fini, etc.
FUTURE PRESENT.	je finirai, *I shall finish*, etc. tu finiras il finira nous finirons vous finirez ils finiront	PRESENT.	CONDITIONAL. je finirais, *I should finish,* tu finirais [etc. il finirait nous finirions vous finiriez ils finiraient
FUT. PAST.	*I shall have finished.* etc. j' aurai fini tu auras fini, etc.	PAST.	*I should have finished,* etc j' aurais fini tu aurais fini, etc.

IMPERATIVE.

finis, *finish (thou)* finissons, *let us finish*
(qu'il finisse, *let him finish*) finissez, *finish (ye)*
　　　　　　　　　　　　　　(qu'ils finissent, *let them finish.*)

Obs. The regular form of the Second Conjugation is derived from Lat. *Inchoative (Inceptive)* Verbs, as **flor-esc-o,** the character **esc** of which became in French **iss,** — the character of the regular Second Conjugation.

The ss of -iss- is retained before **vowel-inflections only;** in all other cases it is dropped :

　fin-iss-ant, fin-iss-ons, fin-iss-ais, que je fini-ss-e, etc.
but fini-r, je fini-s, il fini-t, je fini-rai, etc.

A great many Verbs which are **not** derived from Lat. inchoatives or from Latin at all, take the Character **-iss.** For the few which do not take it see §§ 93 and 94.

§ 82. Third Conjugation: recevoir, *to receive.* (see Obs.)

	INFINITIVE.		PARTICIPLE.
Pres.	rec(ev)-oir, *to receive*	Pres.	rec(ev)-ant, *receiving*
Past.	avoir reç-u, *to have received*	Past.	reç-u, f. -ue, *received*

	INDICATIVE.		SUBJUNCTIVE.
PRESENT.	*I receive, I am receiving, I do* [*receive*, etc. je reçois tu reçois il reçoit nous recevons vous recevez ils reçoivent	**PRESENT.**	*that I may (should) receive,* etc. que je reçoive que tu reçoives qu' il reçoive que nous recevions que vous receviez qu' ils reçoivent
IMPERFECT.	*I received, I was receiving, I did* [*receive*, etc. je recevais tu recevais il recevait nous recevions vous receviez ils recevaient		
PRETERITE.	je reçus, *I received,* etc. tu reçus il reçut nous reçûmes vous reçûtes ils reçurent	**IMPERFECT.**	*that I might (should) receive,* que je reçusse [etc. que tu reçusses qu' il reçût que nous reçussions que vous reçussiez qu' ils reçussent
INDEF-INITE.	j' ai reçu, *I have received,* etc. tu as reçu, etc.	**PERFECT.**	*that I may have received,* etc. que j' aie reçu que tu aies reçu, etc.
PLUPER-FECT.	*I have received,* etc. j' avais reçu tu avais reçu, etc.		
ANTE-RIOR.	*I had received,* etc. j' eus reçu tu eus reçu, etc.	**PLUPER-FECT.**	*that I might have received,* etc. que j' eusse reçu que tu eusses reçu, etc.

VERBS.

	INDICATIVE.		CONDITIONAL.
FUTURE PRES^t	je recevrai, *I shall receive*, tu recevras [etc. il recevra nous recevrons vous recevrez ils recevront	**PRESENT.**	je recevrais, *I should receive*, tu recevrais [etc il recevrait nous recevrions vous recevriez ils recevraient
FUTURE PAST.	*I shall have received*, etc. j' aurai reçu tu auras reçu, etc.	**PAST.**	*I should have received*, etc. j' aurais reçu tu aurais reçu, etc.

IMPERATIVE.

reçois,	*receive (thou)*	recevons,	*let us receive*
		recevez,	*receive (ye)*
(qu'il reçoive,	*let him receive*)	(qu'ils reçoivent,	*let them receive*)

Obs. 1. Three stems must be distinguished in Verbs of this Conjugation:

(1)* **recev-** for the *Pres. Part. and its derived Tenses:* —

      recev-ant, recev-ons, recev-ais, etc.;

(*but* **recevr-** for the *Fut. and Condit.:* — recevr-ai, recevr-ais, etc.)

(2)***reçoi(v)-** for the Sing. and 3^d. p. plur. of the *Pres. Indic.* and *Subj.* and of the *Imperative:*

      je reçoi-s, il reçoi-t, que je reçoiv-e, reçoi-s, etc.

(3)**reç-** for the *Past. Part. Preterite* and *Imperf. Subj.:* —

      reç-u, je reç-us, je reç-usse, etc.

*The real difference between these two stems is that **recev-** stands before sonorous inflections only — **ant, ons, ais,** etc.; whilst the strengthened stem **reçoi(v)-** stands before mute inflections e, es, ent; s, t; (v dropped before consonants: reçoi-(v)s, -(v)t), on the same principle as
ten-ir = tien-s, tienn-ent; men-er = mèn-e, mèn-ent; appel-er = appell-e, etc.

Verbs ending in **-evoir** only are conjugated like **recevoir**: as, devoir, *to owe, to be obliged;* apercevoir, *to perceive;* concevoir, *to conceive;* décevoir, *to deceive;* percevoir, *to collect,* (taxes etc.)

Obs. 2. devoir, takes a circumflex in the Past. Part. **dû,** *masc.* but *fem.* **due,** and *plur.* **dus** without circumflex.

Obs. 3. In Verbs ending in **-evoir** the **c** takes a *cedilla* before **o** and **u**.

§ 83. *Fourth Conjugation:* **vendre,** *to sell.*

	INFINITIVE.		PARTICIPLE.
Pres.	vend-re, *to sell*	*Pres.*	vend-ant, *selling*
Past.	avoir vend-u, *to have sold*	*Part.*	vend-u, f. -ue, *sold*

	INDICATIVE.		SUBJUNCTIVE.
PRESENT.	*I sell, I am selling, I do sell,* je vends [etc. tu vends il vend ¹) nous vendons vous vendez ils vendent	**PRESENT.**	*that I may (should) sell,* etc. que je vende que tu vendes qu' il vende que nous vendions que vous vendiez qu' ils vendent
IMPERFECT.	*I sold, I was selling, I did sell,* je vendais [etc. tu vendais il vendait nous vendions vous vendiez ils vendaient		
PRETERITE.	je vendis, *I sold,* etc. tu vendis il vendit nous vendîmes vous vendîtes ils vendirent	**IMPERFECT.**	*that I might (should) sell,* etc. que je vendisse que tu vendisses qu' il vendît que nous vendissions que vous vendissiez qu' ils vendissent
INDEFINITE.	j' ai vendu, *I have sold,* etc. tu as vendu, etc.	**PERFECT.**	*that I may have sold,* etc. que j' aie vendu que tu aies vendu, etc.
PLUPER- FECT.	j' avais vendu, *I had sold,* etc. tu avais vendu, etc.		

VERBS.

	INDICATIVE.		SUBJUNCTIVE.
ANTERIOR.	j' eus vendu, *I had sold*, etc. tu eus vendu, etc.	PLUPER- FECT.	*that I might have sold*, etc. que j' eusse vendu que tu eusses vendu, etc.
FUTURE PRESENT.	je vendrai, *I shall sell*, etc. tu vendras il vendra nous vendrons vous vendrez ils vendront	PRESENT.	CONDITIONAL. je vendrais, *I should sell*, tu vendrais [etc. ils vendrait nous vendrions vous vendriez ils vendraient
FUTURE PAST.	j' aurai vendu, *I shall have* tu auras vendu, etc. [*sold*, etc.	PAST.	*I should have sold*, etc. j' aurais vendu, tu aurais vendu, etc.

IMPERATIVE.

                    vends, *sell (thou)*   vendons, *let us sell*
            (qu'il vende, *let him sell*)   vendez, *sell (ye)*
                                           (qu'ils vendent, *let them sell*.)

---

1) The person-inflection -t is always dropped after dentals (d, t) and after c:

        perd-re; il perd-,   *but* romp-re,   il romp-t
        vainc-re, il vainc-,   plai-re,   il plai-t
        mett-re, il met-,   construi-re, il construi-t, etc.

§ 84. *a.* The rules for conjugating Verbs *interrogatively* and *negatively* are given in §§ 74—76:

Obs. For the sake of euphony the 1st pers. sing. of the Pres. Indic. takes an acute accent on the final e: j'aime, *interrogatively* aimé-je?

I do not love, etc.			*Do I love?*	*Do I not love?* etc.			
Je	n'aime	pas	aimé-je?	N'aimé-je*	pas?	*I have not loved,* etc.	
tu	n'aimes	pas	aimes-tu?	n'aimes-tu	pas?	Je n'ai pas aimé, etc.	
il	n'aime	pas	aime-t-il?	n'aime-t-il	pas?	*Have I loved?*	
nous	n'aimons	pas	aimons-nous?	n'aimons-nous	pas?	ai-je aimé? etc.	
vous	n'aimez	pas	aimez-vous?	n'aimez-vous	pas?	*Have I not loved?* etc.	
ils	n'aiment	pas	aiment-ils?	n'aiment-ils	pas?	N'ai-je pas aimé? etc.	

* The interrogative construction with **est-ce que . . .?** is preferred with certain verbs for the sake of euphony:
  est-ce que je corrige? *instead of* corrigé-je?

β. REMARKS ON SOME PECULIARITIES OF THE FIRST AND SECOND CONJUGATIONS.

1) In Verbs ending in **-ger**: as, **manger**, *to eat,* an e mute is inserted between the stem and the inflection, whenever the latter begins with a or o; as,

mang-er	je mang-e, n. mange-ons	je mange-ais, n. mang -ions
mang-e-ant	tu - -es, v. mang-ez	tu - -e-ais, v. - -iez
mang-é	il - -e, ils - -ent	il - -e-ait, ils - -e-aient, etc.

2) In Verbs ending in **-cer**, as: **tracer**, *to trace,* the c takes a *cedilla* whenever the inflection begins with **a** or **o**; as,

trac-er	je trac-e, n. traç-ons	je traç-ais, n. trac-ions
traç-ant	tu - -es, v. trac-ez	tu - -ais, v. - -iez
trac-é	il - -e, ils - -ent	il - -ait, ils traç-aient, etc.

Obs. to 1 and 2. The Final stem consonants **g** and **c** thus retain their soft pronunciation throughout the whole conjugation.

3) In Verbs ending in **-eler** and **-eter**, as **appeler**, *to call,* **jeter**, *to throw,* the t or l is doubled before an e mute: as,

appel-er	j' appell-e, n. appel-ons	appell-erai -erons	appell-erais, etc.
appel-ant	tu - -es, v. - -ez	- -eras -erez	
appel-é	il - -e, ils appell-ent	- -era -eront	

jet-er	je jett-e, n. jet-ons	jett-erai -erons	jett-erais, etc.
jet-ant	tu - -es, v. - -ez	- -eras -erez	
jet-é	il - -e, ils jett-ent	- -era -eront	

Exceptions: bourreler, celer, geler, harceler, peler; acheter, colleter, étiqueter, and their compounds, instead of doubling the consonant, take an accent grave over the e before l or t, as: il gèle, j'achète, etc.

4) Verbs with an e mute or é in the Penultima, as: mener, *to lead*, céder, *to yield*, take a grave accent whenever the vowel of the following syllable is an e mute (in the Fut. and Condit., however, é is retained): as,

men-er	je **mèn-e,**	n. men-ons	mèn-erai	-erons	**mèn-erais,** etc.
men-ant	tu **mèn-es,**	v. men-ez	mèn-eras	-erez	
men-é	il **mèn-e,**	ils mèn-ent	mèn-era	-eront	

céd-er	je **cèd-e,**	n. céd-ons		
céd-ant	tu **cèd-es,**	v. céd-ez	but *Fut. & Condit.*	je céd-erai,
céd-é	il **cèd-e,**	ils cèd-ent	unchanged	je céd-erais, etc.
protég-er	je **protèg-e,**	n. protég-eons		je protég-erai,
protég-eant	tu **protèg-es,**	v. protég-ez		je protég-erais,
protég-é	il **protèg-e,**	ils **protèg-ent**		etc.

5) Verbs ending in -ayer, -oyer, -uyer, change y into i before an e mute: as,

essayer, *to try,*	j' essaie,	nous essayons,	j' essaierai, etc.
ployer, *to fold,*	je ploie,	nous ployons,	je ploierai, etc.
essuyer, *to wipe,*	j' essuie,	nous essuyons,	j' essuierai, etc.

Obs. 1. Those in -ayer (also grasseyer), may be conjugated without changing y, as: je paye etc.

Obs. 2. Verbs in -ier are spelt regularly: the final i- of the *stem* coming together with the initial -i of the *inflection* in the 1st and 2nd p. pl. of *Impf. Indic.* and Pres. Subj.:

pri-er; *Indic.* n. pri-ons, *Pres. Subjunct.* { n. pri-ions,
v. pri-ez, *and Impf. Indic.* { v. pri-iez.

---

6) Haïr (Old Germ. hatjan) *to hate,* retains the diæresis throughout except in the Sing. of the Prest. Indic. and Imperat.: **as,**

je hais, tu hais, il hait, *but*, nous haïssons, etc.

Obs. Haïr is the only verb which does not take an accent circumflex in the 3 P. Sing. Imperf. Subj.: qu'il haït.

7) **Bénir** (Lat. benedicere) *to bless,* has two forms for the Past Part.:
béni, *fem.* bénie, *blessed;* and bénit, *fem.* bénite, *consecrated:* as,
Un peuple béni de Dieu; eau bénite, *holy water.*

8) Fleurir (Lat. floresco) in its literal sense *to blossom,* is always regular; but in the figurative sense *to be prosperous, to flourish,* it forms the Pres. Part. and Imperf. Indicat. thus: florissant, je florissais, etc.

§ 85. *B.* PASSIVE VOICE.

INFINITIVE.

Pres. **être aimé,** *to be loved.* *Past.* **avoir été aimé,** *to have been loved.*

PARTICIPLE.

Pres. **étant aimé,** *being loved.* *Past.* **ayant été aimé,** *having been loved.*

INDICATIVE.

PRESENT.				P. INDEFINITE.			
je	suis	aimé	(aimée) *I am*	j'	ai	été aimé,	*I have been*
tu	es	aimé	„ *[loved,*	tu	as	été aimé	*[loved,*
il, on,	est	aimé		il, on,	a	été aimé	
elle	est	aimée		elle	a	été aimée	
nous	sommes	aimés	(aimées)	nous	avons	été aimés	
vous	êtes	aimés	„	vous	avez	été aimés	
ils	sont	aimés		ils	ont	été aimés	
elles	sont	aimées.		elles	ont	été aimées.	

IMPERFECT. **PLUPERFECT.**

j' étais aimé, etc., *I was loved,* j' avais été aimé, etc., *I had been*
nous étions aimés, etc. nous avions été aimés, etc. *[loved,*

PRETERITE. **ANTERIOR.**

je fus aimé, etc., *I was loved,* j' eus été aimé, etc., *I had been*
nous fûmes aimés, etc. nous eûmes été aimés, etc. *[loved,*

FUT. PRES. **FUTURE PAST.**

je serai aimé, etc., *I shall be loved,* j' aurai été aimé, etc., *I shall have*
nous serons aimés, etc. nous aurons été aimés, etc. *[been loved,*

CONDITIONAL PRES. **CONDITIONAL PAST.**

je serais aimé, etc., *I should be* j' aurais été aimé, etc., *I should have*
nous serions aimés, etc. *[loved,* nous **aurions** été aimés, etc. *[been loved.*

IMPERATIVE.

sois aimé, *be (thou) loved.*
soyons aimés, *let us be loved*
soyez aimés, *be (ye) loved.*

SUBJUNCTIVE.

PRESENT. **PERFECT.**

(que) je sois aimé, etc., *I may be* (que) j' **aie** été aimé, etc., *I may have*
(que) n. soyons aimés, etc. *[loved,* (que) n. ayons été aimés, etc. *[been loved,*

IMPERFECT. **PLUPERFECT.**

(que) je **fusse** aimé, *I might (should)* (que) j' eusse été aimé, *I might*
 be loved, *(should) have been loved,*
(que) n. fussions aimés, etc. (que) n. eussions été aimés, etc.

C. INTRANSITIVE VERBS (VERBES NEUTRES).

§ 86. **Intransitive** Verbs are generally conjugated with **avoir**, except the following, which are conjugated with **être**:

aller	*to go*	éclore *to be hatched, to blow*	retourner	*to return*
arriver	*to arrive*	entrer *to enter*	sortir	*to go out*
décéder	} *to die*	naître *to be born*	tomber	*to fall*
mourir		partir *to depart*	venir	*to come*

Obs. 1. Two compounds of venir: **contrevenir à**, *to contravene;* **subvenir à**, *to relieve;* **prévenir**, *to inform, anticipate*, are conjugated with **avoir**.

Obs. 2. Whenever an Intransitive Verb is used transitively, it must be conjugated with **avoir**, as,

Il a **sorti** le cheval de l'écurie; *He has brought the horse out of the stable.*

§ 87. Some Intransitive Verbs may be conjugated with **avoir** and **être**:

(1) with **avoir** to denote the *action:* | (2) with **être** to denote the *result* of the action, the actual *state* or *condition*.

La rivière **a** baissé aujourd'hui. | La rivière **est** bien baissée.
*The river **has** fallen to-day.* | *The river **is** very low.*

Thus—

accourir	*to hasten*	déchoir	*to decay*	embellir *to embellish*
apparaître	*to appear*	déborder	*to overflow*	empirer *to grow worse*
disparaître	*to disappear*	monter	*to ascend*	grandir *to grow*
baisser	*to sink*	descendre	*to descend*	passer *to pass*
changer	*to change*	échouer	*to* {*strand* / *fail*}	rajeunir *to grow young again*
croître	{*to grow* / *to increase*}			vieillir *to grow old*

With the following **Verbs, avoir** or **être** may be used according to meaning:

	with **avoir**:	with **être**:
convenir	(à quelqu'un) *to suit*	(de quelque chose) *to agree, confess*
demeurer rester	} *to reside*	} *to remain, to be left*
échapper	{*to escape unnoticed* / *to escape the notice of*}	*to escape inadvertently*
partir	*to go off* (fire-arms, etc.)	*to set off, leave*
repartir	*to reply, retort*	*to set off* (*leave*) *again*

§ 88. D. REFLECTIVE VERBS (VERBES RÉFLÉCHIS.)

All Reflective Verbs are conjugated with **être**, *to be*, in the Compound Tenses.

INFINITIF.

Présent: **se laver**, *to wash one's self*. | *Passé*: **s'être lavé**, *to have washed one's self*.

PARTICIPE.

Présent: **se lavant**, *washing one's self*. | *Passé*: **s'étant lavé**, *having washed one's self*.

INDICATIF.

A. *Affirmatif.* PRÉSENT.   **B.** *Négatif.*

Je	me	lave,	*I wash myself*		Je	ne me	lave	pas
tu	te	laves,	*thou washest thyself*		tu	ne te	laves	pas
il	se	lave,	*he washes himself*		il	ne se	lave	pas
on	se	lave,	*one washes one's self*		on	ne se	lave	pas
elle	se	lave,	*she washes herself*		elle	ne se	**lave**	pas
nous	nous	lavons,	*we wash ourselves*		nous	ne **nous**	lavons	pas
vous	**vous**	lavez,	*you wash yourselves*		vous	ne **vous**	lavez	pas
ils	**se**	lavent,	*they wash themselves*		ils	ne se	lavent	pas
elles	**se**	lavent,	*they wash themselves*		elles	ne se	**lavent**	pas

C. *Interrogatif.*   **D.** *Négatif & Interrogatif.*

Me	lavé-je ?*	*Do I wash myself?*	Ne me	lavé-je	pas ?* *Don't I wash*
te	laves-tu ?		ne te	laves-tu	**pas** ? [*myself?* etc.
se	**lave-t-il** (-t-elle, -t-on **?**)		ne se	lave-t-il (-t-elle, -t-on) pas ?
nous	lavons-nous ?		ne nous	lavons-nous pas ?
vous	lavez-vous ?		ne vous	lavez-vous pas ?
se	lavent-ils (-elles) ?		ne se	lavent-ils pas ?

IMPARFAIT.   FUTUR PRÉSENT.

Je me lavais, *I was washing myself.*   Je me laverai, *I shall wash myself.*

PRÉTÉRIT (DÉFINI).   CONDITIONNEL PRÉSENT.

Je me lavai, *I washed myself.*   Je me laverais, *I should wash myself.*

A. *Affirmatif.* IMPÉRATIF.   **B.** *Négatif.*

lave-toi,	*wash thyself*	Ne te lave pas,	*Do not wash thyself*
lavons-nous,	*let us wash ourselves*	ne nous lavons pas,	*let us not wash ourselves*
lavez-vous,	*wash yourselves*	ne vous lavez pas,	*do not wash yourselves*

*or **Est-ce que** je me lave ? etc.   Est-ce que je ne me lave pas ? etc.

VERBS.   49

PASSÉ INDÉFINI.

A. *I have washed (been washing) myself,* etc.

Je	me	suis	lavé (ou lavée)
tu	t'	es	lavé ,,
il	s'	est	lavé ,,
elle	s'	est	lavée
on	s'	est	lavé ,,
nous	nous	sommes	lavés (ou lavées)
vous	vous	êtes	lavés ,,
ils	se	sont	lavés
elles	se	sont	lavées

B. *I have not washed myself,* etc.

Je	ne me	suis	pas lavé (-ée)
tu	ne t'	es	pas lavé ,,
il	ne s'	est	pas lavé
elle	ne s'	est	pas lavée
on	ne s'	est	pas lavé ,,
nous	ne nous	sommes	pas lavés (-ées)
vous	ne vous	êtes	pas lavés ,,
ils	ne se	sont	pas lavés
elles	ne se	sont	pas **lavées**

C. *Have I washed myself?* etc.

Me	suis-je	lavé (ou lavée) ?*
t'	es-tu	lavé ,, ?
s'	est-il (-elle)	lavé ,, ?
nous	sommes-nous	lavés (ou lavées) ?
vous	êtes-vous	lavés ,, ?
se	sont-ils	lavés ?
se	sont-elles	lavées ?

*or Est-ce que je me suis lavé ? etc.

D. *Have I not washed myself?*

Ne me	suis-je	pas lavé (-ée)?*
ne t'	es-tu	pas lavé ,, ?
ne s'	est-il (-elle)	pas lavé ,, ?
ne nous	sommes-nous	pas lavés (-ées)?
ne **vous**	êtes-vous	pas lavés ,, ?
ne se	sont-ils	pas lavés ?
ne se	sont-elles	pas lavées ?

Est-ce que je ne me suis pas lavé ? etc.

PLUSQUEPARFAIT.

Je m'étais lavé, *I had washed myself.*

ANTÉRIEUR.

Je **me** fus lavé, *I had washed myself.*

FUTUR PASSÉ.

Je me serai lavé, *I shall have* **washed** *myself.*

CONDITIONNEL PASSÉ.

Je me serais lavé, *I should have washed myself.*

The Subjunctive **is** conjugated in the same manner :
Que je me lave (lavasse), etc.

Reciprocal Verbs are conjugated like Reflective Verbs : thus, Ils se trompent, can signify *They deceive each other* or *themselves.*

The ambiguity **is** avoided by adding l'un l'autre, les uns les autres, *one another* (§ 71 & 228).

Eugène, French Grammar.

§ 89. E. IMPERSONAL VERBS (VERBES IMPERSONNELS).

The following are the principal Impersonal Verbs:

il neige	(Lat. ningit)	*it snows*	il gèle	(gelare)	*it freezes*
il tonne	(tonat)	*it thunders*	il dégèle		*it thaws*
il grêle	(grandinat)	*it hails*	il bruine		*it drizzles*
il pleut	(pluit)	*it rains*	il vente		*it is windy*

Obs. All these belong to the first Conjugation, except **il pleut** (pleuvoir).

il **fait** chaud,	*it **is** warm*		il **fait** du vent,	*it is windy*
,, froid,	,, *cold*		,, du brouillard,	,, *foggy*
,, beau,	,, *fine weather*		,, de la poussière,	,, *dusty*
,, frais,	,, *cool*		,, nuit,	,, *dark*
,, doux,	,, *mild*		,, jour,	,, *daylight*
,, bon,	,, *comfortable, cozy*		,, du soleil,	,, *sunny*
			,, clair de lune,	*the moon shines,* etc.

---

§ 90. The **following (with the exception of** il faut, il s'ensuit, il sied,) are Impersonal **in a certain** meaning only:

il **y a,** il **est,**	*there is, there are*		il **semble**	*it seems*
il **s'agit de,**	*the question is*		il **paraît**	*it appears*
il **importe**	*it behoves, it is important*		il **plaît**	*it pleases*
il convient	*it is convenient*		il dépend	*it depends*
il sied	*it is becoming*		il s'ensuit	*it follows*
il vaut mieux	*it is better*		il y va	*there is ... at stake*
il me tarde	*I long*		il suffit	*it suffices*
il **faut** (il me faut etc.,)	*it is necessary (I must, etc.)*		il se peut	*it may be,* etc. etc.

F. STRONG AND ANOMALOUS VERBS.

§ 91. Principal Exceptions to the Rules on the Formation of Tenses, § 77—79,:

NB. The letters (a) (b) etc. refer to those in § 77—79.

(a) **Future & Condit. 1.** *formed from a different root:* aller: j'irai, -s,

    2. *syllables contracted or strengthened:*

envoyer = **enverrai**	acquérir = acquerrai	asseoir = assiérai
courir = **courrai**	venir = vien-d-rai	voir = verrai, etc.

  3. *the final stem consonant* l *or* v *changed into* **u** (Introd. § 20).

    valoir = vau-d-rai   vouloir = vou-d-rai
    falloir = il fau-d-ra   savoir = saurai

(b) **Pres. Part. 1.** *Pres. Indic. pl. & Imperf.* formed from the *Inf. stem:*
   savoir (sachant) nous savons, je savais,

  2. 2ᵈ *& 3ᵈ p. of Pres. Indic. pl. anomalous:* as

  faire,   fais -ant,   **vous** faites, ils font.
  dire,   dis **-ant,**   **vous** dites,
  prendre, pren -ant,   ils prennent.
  mourir, **mour** -ant,   ils meurent, etc.

(c) **Past Part.** and (e) **Preterite:** *Exceptions to the Normal terminations:*

Normal (II): *Pret.* **-is**; *Past Part.* **-i.**			(IV): *Pret.* **-is**; *Past Part.* **-u.**		
cour-ir = cour-us,	cour-u.		condui-re = condui-s-is,	condui-t.
ten-ir = **tin-s**,	ten-u.		résoud-re = résol-us,	**résou-s.**
mour-ir = mour-us,	mort.		connaît-re = conn-us,	
ouvr-ir =	ouvert.		naît-re = naquis,	né.
			viv-re = vécus,	vécu.
Normal (III): *Pret.* **-us**; *Past Part.* **-u.**			mett-re = **mis,**	mis.
asseoir = ass-is,	ass-is.		prend-re = **pris,**	pris.

(d) **Pres. Indic. 1.** *formed from a different root:*
   je vais, tu vas, il va; —, —, ils vont.

 2. *following a different conjugation:*
   ouvr-ir = j'ouvr-e, -es, -e; ten-ir = je tien-s, -s, -t.

 3. *strengthening of the stem:*
   ven-ir = je viens;   mour-ir = je meur-s.
   asse-oir = j' assied-s; acquér-ir = j' acquier-s; etc.

 4. *dropping of the final stem consonant:*
dor-m-ir = je dor-s, -s, -t; plain-d-re = je plain-s; connaî-t-re = je connai-s;
vi-v-re = vi-s, -s, -t; pou-v-oir = je pui-s; sa-v-oir = je sai-s; etc.

 5. **x** *instead of* **s** *added in the 1ˢᵗ & 2ᵈ p. sing.:* peux, veux, vaux.

 6. *Pres. Subj.* **formed** *irregularly:*

aller = j' aille.	**savoir** = je sache.	*Imperative:* sache, etc.
pouvoir = je puisse.	**vouloir** = je veuille.	„ veuille, etc.
valoir = je vaille.	**faire** = je fasse.	

4*

§ 92. FIRST

INFINITIVE.	PRES. PART.	PRESENT INDICAT.	PRETER.	PAST PART.	FUTURE.
aller, *to go*	allant	je vais, nous allons tu vas, vous allez il va, ils vont	j'allai	**allé**	j'irai
				INDEFINITE.	
s'en aller *to go away*	s'en allant	je m'en vais tu t'en vas il s'en va nous nous en allons vous vous en allez ils s'en vont	je m'en suis allé tu t'en es allé il s'en est allé nous nous en sommes allés vous vous en êtes allés ils s'en sont allés		

Negatively.

I am not going away, etc.

je ne m' en vais pas
tu ne t' en vas „
il ne s' en va „
nous ne nous en allons „
vous ne vous en allez „
ils ne s' en vont „

I have not gone away, etc.

je ne m' en suis pas allé
tu ne t' en es „ „
il ne s' en est „ „
nous ne nous en sommes „ allés
vous ne vous en êtes „ „
ils ne s' en sont „ „

Interrogatively.

Am I going away, etc.

m' en vais-je?
t' en vas-tu?
s' en va-t-il?
nous en allons-nous?
vous en allez-vous?
s' en vont-ils?

Have I gone away? etc.

m' en suis-je allé?
t' en es-tu „
s' en est-il „
nous en sommes-nous allés?
vous en êtes-vous „
s' en sont-ils „

Negatively and Interrogatively.

Am I not going away? etc.

ne m' en vais-je pas?
ne t' en vas-tu „
ne s' en va-t-il „
ne nous en allons-nous „
ne vous en allez-vous „
ne s' en vont-ils „

Have not I gone away? etc.

ne m' en suis-je pas allé?
ne t' en es-tu „ „
ne s' en est-il „ „
ne nous en sommes-nous „ allés?
ne vous en êtes-vous „ „
ne s' en sont-ils „ „

After these all other **simple** and Compound Tenses **of s'en** aller may be conjugated.

envoyer, (comp^d. of inde & viare) *to send* | Irregular in the FUTURE **and** CONDITIONAL **only:** j'enverrai.

CONJUGATION.

IMPERATIVE.	PRESENT SUBJUNCTIVE.	
va allons allez	que j'aille, que nous allions que tu -es, que vous -iez qu' il -e, qu' ils aillent	The Conjug. of this Anomalous Verb forms the Sing. and the 3^d Pers. Pl. of the Pres. Indic., and also the 3^d Pers. Sing. of the Imper. from the Lat. Verb vadere; the Fut. and Condit. from ire.
va-t'en allons-nous-en allez-vous-en	que je m' en aille que tu t' en -es qu' il s' en -e que nous nous en allions que vous vous en alliez qu' ils s' en aillent	Obs. 1. The IMPERAT. va takes a euphonic s before en and y; as, vas-en, vas-y. Obs. 2. The most probable etymology of aller is from the Lat. adnare.
ne t'en va pas ne nous en allons pas ne vous en allez pas	que je ne m'en aille pas, etc.	

Idiomatic Conjugation of aller, *to go.*

IMMEDIATE FUTURE PRES.	IMMEDIATE FUTURE PERF.
I am going to.., or I am about to...	*I was going to.., or I was about to...*
je vais finir	j' allais finir
tu vas sortir	tu allais sortir
il va partir	il allait partir
nous allons nous réjouir	nous allions nous réjouir
vous allez vous amuser	vous alliez vous amuser
ils vont se baigner	ils allaient se baigner.

Like **envoyer** is conjugated:— **renvoyer**, *to send back, to discharge, to postpone.*

SECOND

§ 93. I. Verbs which in the PRESENT INDICATIVE Sing. take the contracted endings -s, -s, -t:

A. The following drop their Stem Consonant (m, t, v) in the Singular of the Present Indicative:—

dorm-ir (dormire) *to sleep*	**dorm-ant**	je dor-s, n. dorm-ons tu - -s, v. - -ez il - -t, ils - -ent	je dorm-is	dorm-i
mentir (mentiri) *to lie*	mentant	je men-s, n. ment-ons	je mentis	menti
partir (partiri) *to depart*	partant	je **par-s,** n. part-ons	je partis	parti
sentir (sentire) *to feel, smell*	sentant	je **sen-s,** n. sent-ons	je sentis	senti
servir (servire) *to serve*	servant	je ser-s, n. serv-ons	je servis	servi
sortir (sortiri) *to go out*	sortant	je **sor-s,** n. sort-ons	je sortis	sorti
se repentir (pœnitere) *to repent*	se repent-ant	je me repen-s nous nous repent-ons	je me repentis	repenti
bouill-ir (bullire) *to boil*	bouill-ant	je **bou-s,** n. bouill-ons, tu - -s, v. - -ez, il - -t, ils - -ent,	je bouill-is,	bouill-i

B. The following do not alter their stem:—

cour-ir (currere) *to run*	cour-ant	je cour-s, n. cour-ons tu - -s, v. - -ez il - -t, ils - -ent	je cour-us	cour-u	je cour (contra-ed fro courir
fu-ir (fugere) *to flee*	fuy-ant	je fui-s, n. **fuy-ons** tu - -s, v. - -ez il - -t, ils fui-ent	je fuis	fui
vêt-ir (vestire) *to clothe*	vêt-ant	je vêt-s, n. vêt-ons tu - -s, v. - -ez il - -, ils - -ent	je vêt-is	vêt-u

CONJUGATION.

REMARKS AND COMPOUND VERBS.

All strong verbs of the Second Conjugation form their Pres. Part. and the tenses derived from it) without the character -iss- *of the regular conjugation. Compare (§ 81. Obs.)—*

fin-ir, fin-iss-ant,	*with*	ment-ir, ment-ant,
nous fin-iss-ons, etc.		nous ment-ons, etc.
je fin-iss-ais, etc.		je ment-ais, etc.

endormir, *to lull.*
s'endormir, *to fall asleep,* se rendormir, *to fall asleep again.*

démentir, *to give the lie, to contradict.*

repartir, *to set off again, to reply.* — Répartir, *to distribute, to portion out,* is conjugated regularly.

consentir, *to consent;* pressentir, *to have a presentiment;* ressentir, *to feel, to resent.*

desservir, *to clear the table, to disoblige.* — asservir, *to enslave,* is conjugated regularly.

ressortir, *to go out again.* — Ressortir de, *to be in the jurisdiction of,* is regular.

The final -ill- of the stem is dropped in the Sing. of the Present Indicative.

bouillir, is a neuter verb. *To boil,* transitive, is rendered by faire bouillir.

accourir à, *to run, to hasten to,*   parcourir, *to run over, through.*
concourir, *to concur, to compete,*   recourir, *to have recourse.*
discourir, *to discourse,*   secourir, *to help, to relieve.*
encourir, *to incur.*

s'enfuir, *to run away.*

dévêtir, *to divest.*
revêtir, *to invest.*

C. *The following alter the vowel of their stem:—*

ven-ir (ven-ire) *to come,*	ven-ant	je vien-s, n. ven-ons tu - -s, v. - -ez il - -t, ils vienn-ent	je vin-s	venu-u	je viendrai
ten-ir (ten-ere) *to hold,*	ten-ant	je tien-s, n. ten-ons tu - -s, v. - -ez il - -t, ils tienn-ent	je tin-s	ten-u	je tiendrai
acquér-ir (acquirere) *to acquire,*	acquér-ant	j'acquier-s, n. acquér-ons tu - -s, v. - -ez il - -s, ils acquièr-ent	j'acqu-is	acqu-is	j'acquerrai (contracted)
mour-ir (mori) *to die,*	mour-ant	je meur-s, n. mour-ons tu - -s, v. - -ez il - -t, ils meur-ent	je mour-us	mort	je mourrai (contracted)

Obs. 1. The stem is strengthened by the insertion **of i.** (Compare **bien** with the Lat. **bene**; **rien** with the Lat. **rem**.)

Obs. 2. A euphonic **d** is inserted in the Fut. and Condit. between n and r. (Compare gendre, Lat. gener; tendre, Lat. tener; Greek ἀνήρ, Genit. ἀνδρός. see also § 99.)

§ 94. II. Verbs which follow the FIRST Conjugation—

A. *in the Present Tense* (*Perf. Participle* -ert):

ouvr-ir *to* (aperire) *open,*	ouvr-ant	j'ouvr-e, n. ouvr-ons tu - -es, v. - -ez il - -e, ils - -ent	j'ouvr-is	ouvert
couvrir (cooperire) *to cover,*	couvr-ant	je couvre, etc.	je couvr-is	couvert
offrir (offerre) *to offer,*	offr-ant	j'offre, etc.	j'offr-is	offert
souffrir (sufferre) *to suffer,*	souffr-ant	je souffre, etc.	je souffr-is	souffert

B. *in the Present,* Future *and* Conditional:

cueill-ir (colligere) *to collect, gather*	cueill-ant	je cueill-e, n. cueill-ons tu - -es, v. - -ez il - -e, ils - -ent	je cueill-is	cueilli	je cueillerai
saill-ir (sal-ire) *to project, to jut out*	saill-ant	il saill-e,		il saill-it	sailli	il saillera

REMARKS AND COMPOUND VERBS.

nvenir (de)	*to agree*	intervenir	*to interfere*	revenir	*to come back*
— (à)	*to suit*	parvenir	*to attain, to reach*	se souvenir	*to remember*
evenir	*to become*	prévenir	*to warn*	subvenir	*to relieve*
isconvenir	*to disagree*	provenir	*to proceed from*	survenir	*to happen*
abstenir	*to abstain*	détenir	*to detain*	obtenir	*to obtain*
ppartenir	*to belong*	entretenir	*to keep up*	retenir	*to retain*
ntenir	*to contain*	maintenir	*to maintain*	soutenir	*to sustain, to assert*

nquérir	*to conquer*	quérir *to fetch*, used in the Infinit. only, after **aller**,
enquérir	*to inquire*	envoyer, venir.
quérir	*to require*	

Obs. 3. The stem consonant **n** is doubled before e mute.

Obs. 4. The Preterite and Perf. Part. **acquis** is a contraction of the Lat. cquisivi, acquisitum.

couvrir *to reopen*. **Obs.** For the Past Participles ouvert, couvert, etc., comp. the Lat. apertum, coopertum, etc.

découvrir, *to discover*, recouvrir, *to cover again*.

accueillir, *to receive, to welcome*, recueillir *to gather, to reap*.

saillir, *to gush*, is regular.
assaillir, *to attack*, } are conjugated like saillir, except in the Fut. and Conditional
tressaillir, *to start*, } which they form regularly, as: j'assaillirai, je tressaillirai.

THIRD

§ 95. **I. Verbs the stems of which end in 'v'**, *(which is dropped in the Singular of the Pres. Indicat.; in the Preterite Definite, the Imperfect Subj., and the Perf. Participle; — hence the contraction.)*

pouv-oir (Low. L. potere) *to be able*	pouvant	je peu-x (puis) n. pouv-ons tu - -x, v. - -ez il - -t, ils peuv-ent	je pus	pu	je pourrai
mouv-oir (movere) *to move*	mouvant	je meu-s, n. mouv-ons tu - -s, v. - -ez il - -t, ils meuv-ent	je mus	mû (mue)	je mouvrai
pleuv-oir (pluere) *to rain*	pleuvant	il pleut,	il plut	plu	il pleuvra
sav-oir (sapere) *to know*	sach-ant	je sai-s, n. sav-ons tu - -s, v. - -ez il - -t, ils - -ent	je sus	su	je saurai

§ 96. **II. Verbs the stems of which end in 'l'**, *which is changed into* u, *or dropped in the Sing. Pres. Indicat., in the Future and Conditional.* See § 91. g. and Introd. § 20.

fall-oir (fallere) *to be necessary*	*wanting*	il fau-t	il fallut	fallu	il faudra
val-oir (valere) *to be worth*	valant	je vau-x, nous val-ons tu - -x, vous - -ez il - -t, ils - -ent	je valus	valu	je vaudrai
voul-oir (Low. L. volere) *to wish*	voulant	je veu-x, nous voul-ons tu - -x, vous - -ez il - -t, ils veul-ent	je voulus	voulu	je voudrai

CONJUGATION.

NB. To this **class** belong all Verbs **in -evoir,** the full Conjugation of which is given § 82.

PRESENT **SUBJ.**
que je **puisse,** etc. | 1st. Person Sing. Present Indic. je **peux,** *or* je **puis;** but interrogatively **puis-je,** only.

    émouvoir, **PERF. PART.:—** ému, *to affect, to touch,*
    promouvoir, -   promu, *to promote.*

que je **sach-e,** n. **sach-ions** | IMPERATIVE:— **sache, sachons, sachez.**
 tu - **-es,** v. - **-iez** | IMPERF. INDIC.:— je **savais,** etc.
 il - **-e,** ils - **-ent** |

qu'il **faille,** |

que je **vaille,** es, e, | équivaloir, *to be equivalent,* revaloir, *to requite.*
que nous **valions,** -iez, | Prévaloir, *to prevail,* forms its Pres. Subj. regularly: as,
qu' ils **vaillent,** | que je **prévale.**

que je **veuille,** es, e, | The IMPER. proper: **veux, voulons, voulez,** is but rarely used.
que nous **voulions,** -iez, | The OPTATIVE form **veuille, veuillons, veuillez,** is equi-
qu' ils **veuillent,** | valent to the Engl. *be so good as to* …

§ 97. III. Verbs which cannot be classified.

asse-oir (assidere) *to set down*	'assey-ant	j' assied-s, n. assey-ons tu - -s, v. - -ez il - -, ils assey-ent	j'assis	assis	j'assié⟨rai⟩
voir (videre) *to see*	voy-ant	je voi-s, nous voy-ons tu - -s, vous - -ez il - -t, ils voi-ent	je vis	vu	je ver⟨rai⟩
pourv-oir (providere) *to provide*	pourvoy-ant	je pourvois, n. pourvoyons	je pourvus	pourvu	je pour⟨voirai⟩
déch-oir (cadere) *to decay*	wanting	je déchoi-s, n. déchoy-ons tu - -s, v. - -ez il - -t, ils déchoi-ent	je déchus	déchu	je déch⟨rai⟩
surse-oir (supersedere) *to suspend,* *to defer*	sursoy-ant	je sursoi-s, n. sursoy-ons tu - -s, v. - -ez il - -t, ils sursoi-ent	je sursis	sursis	je surs⟨irai⟩

FOURTH

§ 98. I. Verbs the stems of which end in a VOWEL.

All these are regular in the Singular of the Pres. Indicat. T⟨hey⟩ insert a Consonant, (in most cases the Original stem consonants s *or* ⟨t⟩ *between the stem and the* **inflection** *which begins with a Vowel.*

A. Preterite -s-is, Perf. Part. i-t.

condui-re (conducere) *to conduct*	condui-s-ant	je condui-s, n. condui-s-ons tu - -s, il - -t,	je condui-s-is	condu⟨it⟩
construire (construere) *to construct*	construisant	je construis, n. construisons	je construisis	constr⟨uit⟩
cuire (coquere) *to cook*	cuisant	je cuis, nous cuisons	je cuisis	cuit

The t of the Perf. Part. is dropped in the following two ver⟨bs⟩

nuire (nocere) *to hurt*	nuisant	je nuis, nous nuisons	je nuisis	nui
luire (lucere) *to shine*	luisant	je luis, nous luisons	wanting	lui
écri-re (scribere) *to write*	écri-v-ant	j'écri-s, nous écri-v-ons	j'écri-v-is	écri-t

VERBS.

Asseoir is most commonly used as a Reflective Verb: **s'asseoir,** *to sit down;* as,
m' assieds, etc.
m' assis, etc.
me suis assis, etc.

Obs. Another form of asseoir, much less frequently used, is:

PRESENT INDICATIVE.	PRESENT PART.	FUTURE.
j'assois, s, t, n. assoyons -ez, ils **assoient,**	**assoyant,**	j'assoirai, etc. j'asseyerai,

Like s'asseoir, is conjugated: **se rasseoir,** *to sit down again.*

ntrevoir, *to catch a glimpse of.*—Prévoir, *to foresee,* forms its Future **regularly,** like pourvoir :—je prévoirai,

evoir, *to see* **again.**

CONJUGATION.
REMARKS AND COMPOUND VERBS.

Obs. For the Past Partic. in **-it,** as: **conduit, construit, dit, fait,** etc. ompare the Latin conductum, constructum, dictum, factum, etc. As a rule the at. **ct** preceded by a vowel becomes **-it** in French: as, noctem = nuit; lactem = it; fructum = fruit, etc. but ct preceded by a consonant becomes simply **t,** as, unctum = point, see also § 99, planctum = plaint.

conduire,	**to** *reconduct*	introduire, **to** *introduce*	réduire, **to** *reduce*
éduire,	**to** *deduct*	produire, **to** *produce*	séduire, **to** *seduce*
nduire,	**to** *plaster*	reproduire, *to reproduce*	traduire, **to** *translate*
duire,	**to** *lead into*		

Obs. The simple Verb duire (ducere) is not in use.

étruire, **to** *destroy,* reconstruire, *to rebuild.*
struire, **to** *instruct,*

cuire, **to** *cook* *again,*

luire, **to** *glitter.*
scrire, **to** *inscribe.*   souscrire, *to subscribe.*   décrire, *to describe.*
escrire, **to** *prescribe.*   transcrire, **to** *transcribe.*   proscrire, *to proscribe.*

VERBS.

B. Preter. Definite: -s (Contracted).

Infinitive	Pres. Part.	Present		Preterite	Perf. Part.
di-re (dicere) to *say, to tell*	di-s-ant	je dis, tu dis, il dit,	nous dis-ons vous dit-es ils dis-ent	je **dis**	dit
maudi-re (maledicere) to *curse*	maudi-ss-ant	je **maudis**,	n. maudiss-ons	je maudis	maudit
fai-re (facere) to *make, to do*	fai-s-ant	je fais, tu fais, il fait,	nous fais-ons vous fait-es ils font	je **fis**	fait
confire (conficere) to *preserve, pickle*	confisant	je confis,	**nous** confisons	je confis	confit
suffire (sufficere) to *suffice*	suffisant	je **suffis**,	nous suffisons	je suffis	suffi

No consonant is inserted the between stem and the Inflection in

| ri-re (ridere) to *laugh* | ri-ant | je ris, | nous ri-ons | je ris | ri |

The i of the stem is changed into y before a vowel in

| trai-re (trahere) to *milk* | tray-ant | je trais, nous trayons | | *wanting* | trai-t |

C. *The vowel of the stem is changed into* u: *Preterite* -us; *Perf. Part.* -u.

plai-re (placere) to *please*	plai-s-ant	je plais, nous plais-ons		je plus	plu
tai-re (tacere) to *keep secret*	tai-s-ant	je tais,	nous taisons	je tus	tû (fem. tue)
li-re (legere) to *read*	li-s-ant	je lis,	nous lisons	je lus	lu
boi-re (bibere) to *drink*	bu-v-ant	je bois,	nous buv-ons vous - -ez ils boivent	je bus	bu

The i of the stem is changed into y before a vowel in

| croi-re (credere) to *believe* | croy-ant | je crois, nous croyons | | je crus | cru |

No consonant is inserted between the stem and the Inflection in

| conclu-re (concludere) to *conclude* | conclu-ant | je conclus, nous concluons | | je conclus | conclu |

VERBS.

ntredire, *to contradict*
dire, *to gainsay*
terdire, *to forbid*
dire, *to speak ill*
édire, *to predict*

Obs. All compounds, with the exception of **redire,** *to say again, to object,* form the 2^d. pers. plur. Pres. Indicat. and Imperative **regularly;** as,
vous **contredisez** etc.

T. je **ferai,** etc.
es. Subj. je **fass**-e, -es, -e;
n. **fass**-ions, -iez, -ent.

contrefaire, *to counterfeit, to feign.*
défaire, *to undo, to defeat.*
refaire, *to do again, to restore.*

satisfaire, *to* [*satisfy,*
surfaire, *to* [*overcharge,*

REMARKS AND COMPOUND VERBS.

urire, ***to smile.***

straire, *to distract.*
traire, *to extract.*
ustraire, *to subtract.*

mplaire, **to** *please,* **to** *gratify;* déplaire, **to** *displease.*

taire, *to be silent.*

lire, *to read* ***again,*** élire, **to** ***elect.***

croire, **only** used in the expression **faire accroire,** *to make believe, to impose upon.*

§ 99. II. Verbs the stems of which end in a CONSONANT

The original stem Consonant of these **Verbs** *is shown in the* **Present Participle** *(as will be readily seen from comparison with Latin). The* Dentals **d** *and* **t** *in the* **Infinitive, Future** *and* **Conditional,** *are inserted, for the sake of euphony, between the final Consonant of the* stem *and the initial* **r** *of the* **inflection.** *(Compare also* **Venir, tenir** *in the* **Future** *and* **Conditional.)**

A. Infinitive: **in-d -re;** *Pres. Part.* **-gn -ant;** *Sing. Pres. Indic.* **-ns;**
Preterite **-gn -is;** *Past Participle* **-nt:**

plain-d-re	plai-gn-ant	je plain-s, n. plai-gn-ons	je plai-gn-is plain-
(plangere)		tu - -s, v. - -gn-ez	
to pity		il - -t, ils - -gn-ent	

Conjugate in the same manner, all Verbs in **-aindre, -eindre, -oindre:**

craindre (tremere) *to fear*	éteindre (extinguere) *to extinguish*
contraindre (constringere) *to constrain*	feindre (fingere) *to feign*
astreindre (astringere) *to compel*	peindre (pingere) *to paint*
atteindre (attingere) *to reach*	teindre (tingere) *to dye*
ceindre (cingere) *to gird*	joindre (jungere) *to join*
enfreindre (infringere) *to infringe*	oindre and poindre, see Defect. Verbs § 1

B. Infin. **-ou-d-re;** *Pres. Part.* **-s-ant;** *or* **-l (lv)-ant:**

cou-d-re	cou-s-ant	je coud-s, nous cousons	je cousis	cousu
(consuere)		tu - -s,		
to sew		il - -,		
mou-d-re	**mou-l-ant**	je moud-s, nous moulons	je moulus	moult
(molere)		tu - -s,		
to grind		il - -, .		
absou-d-re	absol-v-ant	j' absou-s, nous absolvons	*wanting*	absou
(absolvere)		tu - -s,		
to absolve		il - -t,		
résou-d-re	résol-v-ant	je résou-s, nous résolvons	je résolus	résous
(resolvere)		tu - -s,		résolu
to resolve		il - -t.		

VERBS.

Obs. For the Perf. Partic. plaint, ceint, joint, etc compare the Latin Supines planctum, cinctum, junctum, etc. see § 93 Obs.

peindre, *to describe*, *to depict*; repeindre *to paint again.*
reindre, *to grasp*; restreindre, *to restrict;*

joindre, *to disjoin.*   rejoindre, *to rejoin.*
joindre, *to enjoin.*

coudre, *to unsew, to rip.*
coudre, *to sew again.*

noudre, *to whet,* | remoudre, *to grind again.*
moudre, *to whet again,* |

solu, the other form of the Perf. Part. is only used adjectively.

ssoudre, *to dissolve,* Perf. Part. **dissous.** — Dissolu is only used adjectively.

VERBS.

C. Infinit.:— -ît -re; *Pres. Part.* -îss-ant; *Preterite* **-us;** *Perf. Part.* -u.

connaî-t-re (cognoscere) *to know*	connai-ss-ant	je connai-s, n. connaiss-ons tu - -s, v. - -ez il - -t, ils - -ent	je conn-us	conn-u
paraî-t-re (Low Lat. parescere) *to appear*	paraissant	je parais, nous paraissons	je parus	paru
paî-t-re (pascere) *to graze*	paissant	je pais, nous paissons	*wanting*	*wantin*
croî-t-re (crescere) *to grow*	croissant	je croîs, nous croissons	je crûs	crû

The *Preterite* and *Perf. Part.* are quite **irregular in—**

naît-re (nascor) *to be born*	naissant	je nais, nous naissons	je naquis	né

D. *A few Verbs, offering peculiar Anomalies, cannot strictly be classified:*

The **final** stem Consonant (**v** or **t**) *is dropped in the* Sing. Present Indic. *in—*

viv-re (vivere) *to live*	vivant	je vi-s, nous vivons	je vécus	vécu
suiv-re (sequi) *to follow*	suivant	je sui-s, nous suivons	je suivis	suivi
mett-re (mittere) *to put*	mettant	je met-s, nous mettons tu - -s, il - -,	je mis	mis

The *final stem* Consonant *is dropped before a* Vowel, *in—*

prend-re (prehendere) *to take*	**pren-ant**	je prend-s, n. pren-ons tu - -s, v. - -ez il - -, ils prenn-ent	je pris	pris

The *stem* **Consonant c** *is changed into* **qu** *before a* Vowel (Perf. Part. excepted)

vainc-re (vincere) *to conquer*	vainqu-ant,	je vainc-s, n. vainqu-ons tu - -s, v. - -ez il - -, ils - -ent	je vainquis	vaincu

Obs. battre, *to beat,* **drops one t,** like mettre, in the Sing. Pres. Indic. but **is regular** in all other parts.

VERBS. 67

Obs. The original Stem Conson^t. is -ss, from Lat. sc. In the process of formation of the language, the dental t was inserted between the consonants s and r; old *Fr.* cognoistre; the g however was subsequently assimilated to n, and s replaced by a circumflex. Hence all verbs of this class take a circumflex on the i before a t.

méconnaître, *to slight, not to recognize.*
reconnaître, *to recognize, to acknowledge.*

apparaître, *to appear,*	disparaître, *to disappear.*
comparaître, *to appear, (before the judge)*	reparaître, *to reappear.*

repaître, *to feed.* PRETERITE: **repus;** PAST PART.: **repu.**

accroître, (PP. accru) *to increase,*	recroître, *to grow again.*
décroître, (PP. décru) *to decrease,*	

renaître, *to be born again, to reappear.*

revivre (intrans.), *to come to life again.* To revive (trans.) *is rendered by* faire revivre.

poursuivre, *to pursue, to prosecute*		
admettre, *to admit*	promettre, *to promise*	soumettre, *to submit.*
commettre, *to commit*	compromettre, *to compromise*	transmettre, *to transmit.*
permettre, *to permit*	remettre, *to put again, to put off*	

Obs. The n is doubled before e mute.

apprendre, *to learn*	méprendre, *to mistake.*
comprendre, *to understand*	reprendre, *to take, to reprove.*
entreprendre, *to undertake*	surprendre, *to surprise.*

convaincre, *to convince.*

5*

§ 100.   G. DEFECTIVE VERBS.

Defective Verbs are those which want several Tenses and Persons.

NB. A blank indicates that a Mood, Tense or Person is wanting.

§ 101. 2ᵈ Conj.

	Pres. Part.	Pres. Indic.	Imperfect.		
gésir (jacere) *to lie*	gisant	n. gis-ons · v. · -ez il gît, ils · -ent	je gisais, etc.	The s in the *Pres. Part., Pres. Indic.,* and *Imperf.* is pronounced = ss. Ci-gît = *Here lies,* etc.	
férir (ferire) *to strike*		occurs only in the expression 'sans coup férir' = *without striking a blow.*			
			Preterite.	Past Part.	Fut. & Condit.
faillir (fallere) *to fail, to err*		il faut,	je faillis, etc.	failli, used in all Comp. Tenses	
ouïr (audire) *to hear*				ouï	
saillir	saillant	(see Ir. Verbs § 94b)			

§ 102. 3ᵈ Conj.

	Pres. Part.	Pres. Indic.	Imperfect.	Past Part.	Fut. & Condit.
choir (cadere) *to fall*				chu	
échoir *to fall due; to fall to the lot of*	échéant	il échoit (échet)	il échut	échu	il écherra il écherrait
			Imperfect.		
seoir (sedere) *to fit, to be becoming*		il sied ils siéent	il seyait ils seyaient	(sis, -e)¹⁾	il siéra il siérait
falloir	see § 96.				

1) law term: *situated.*

VERBS.

§ 103. 4ᵈ Conj.

Infinitive	Pres. Part.	Present	Imperfect	Preterite / Past Part.	Future	Conditional
braire *to bray*		il brait / ils braient			il braira / ils brairont	il brairait / ils brairaient
bruire *to war*	bruyant [2]	il bruit / ils bruient	il bruyait / ils bruyaient			2) used adjectively = *noisy*.
frire (frigere) *to fry*		je fris, n. faisons frire [3] / tu fris / il frit [etc.]		frit, -e	je frirai, etc. / je frirais, etc.	3) **The wanting** Persons and Tenses are formed with the verb **faire.**
clore (claudere) *to close*		je clos / tu clos, *no plural* / il clôt		clos, -e	je clorai, etc. / je clorais, etc.	Pres. Subs. que je close etc.
éclore *to blossom, blow*		il éclôt / ils éclosent		éclos, -e	il éclôra / ils éclôront	Conditional. il éclôrait / ils éclôraient
sourdre (surgere) *to spring, to gush*		il sourd / ils sourdent	Preterite: il sourdit		il sourdra	il sourdrait
oindre (ungere) *to anoint*	oignant	j' oins, etc.		j' oignis, etc. / oint, -e	j' oindrai, etc.	
poindre (pungere) *to prick, to dawn*	poignant	je poins, etc.		je poignis, etc. / point	je poindrai, etc.	

The Adverb (L'Adverbe).

§ 104.   FORMATION OF ADVERBS.

Adverbs are derived from Adjectives by the addition of the suffix **-ment**; as,

Adjective: facile, *easy,*   Adverb: facilement, *easily.*
-          vrai, *true,*   -   vraiment, *truly.*

If the adjective terminates in a *consonant,* -ment is added to the feminine termination: as,

Adjective: franc, *fem.* franche, **Adverb**: franchement.
-          heureux, - heureuse, -   heureusement.

Obs. 1. The adverbial suffix ment is derived from the Latin mente, abl. case of mens, *mind;* literally, *with a mind, with a manner.*

(Compare the English likewise, otherwise, and the German glücklicherweise.)

Obs. 2. The following Adverbs take an accent aigu on the e before -ment:

aveuglément, commodément, communément, comformément, confusément, diffusément, énormément, expressément, importunément, obscurément, opiniâtrément, précisément, profondément.

Obs. 3. The following have an accent circonflexe on the vowel before -ment:

assidûment, crûment, dûment, gaîment.

§ 105.   **Exceptions.**

1. Adjectives ending in ant and ent change these terminations respectively into amment, emment; i. e. they assimilate the final Consonants nt to the m of ment: as,

ADVERB. 71

  Adjective: constant, Adverb: constamment, *constantly*,
      patient,   -   patiemment, *patiently*.

Obs. lent, *slow*, *and* présent, *present*, follow the general Rule: **as**, lentement, présentement.

 2. Adjective: bon [1]   =   Adverb: **bien**
      ,,   beau [1]   =   ,, bien
      ,,   gentil   =   ,, gentiment
      ,,   impuni   =   ,, impunément
      ,,   traître   =   ,, traîtreusement
      ,,   mauvais   =   ,, mal

Obs. 1. bonnement means *simply*; bellement, *gently*.

Obs. 2. The Adj. **vite** remains unaltered; vitement is familiar.

§ 106. Many Adjectives are used adverbially without undergoing any change; as,

 sentir bon, mauvais, *to smell nice, bad,*
 parler (voir) clair,   *to speak (to see) distinctly,*
 tenir ferme,   *to hold firmly,*
 acheter (coûter, vendre) cher, *to buy (cost, sell) dear,*
 chanter faux,   *to sing out of time,*
 aller vite,   *to go at a quick pace,*
 parler bas, haut,   *to speak low, loud.*

DEGREES OF COMPARISON (LES DEGRÉS DE COMPARAISON).

§ 107. These are formed like those of Adjectives (see §§ 39—41).

Exceptions.

bien (bene), *well*, **mieux** (melius), *better*, **le mieux**, *best*,

mal (male), *badly, ill*, **pis** (pejus), {*worse, (in a moral sense)*} **le pis**,   }*worst*
         plus mal, *worse,* le plus mal,}

beaucoup, *much*, plus (plus), *more*, le plus, *most*,
peu (paucum), *little*, moins (minus), *less*, le moins, *least*.

§ 103. Adverbs may be subdivided according to their meaning into

I. Adverbs of Place:

où (ubi)? *where?*
y (ibi), là (illac) *there,*
ici (ecce hic), *here,*
ailleurs (aliorsum), *elsewhere,*
dedans (de intus), *within,*
dehors (de foras), *outside,*
devant (de + avant), *before,*
derrière (de retro), *behind,*
dessus (de + susum), *above,*
dessous (de + subtus), *below,*

d'où? *whence?*
en, de là, *thence (from there),*
d'ici, *from here, hence,*
loin (longe), *far,*
près, proche (propius), *near,*
par où? *which way?*
par ici, par là, *this (that) way,*
à gauche, *to the left,*
à droite, *to the right,*
    etc. etc.

II. Adverbs of Time:

quand? (quando), *when?*
aujourd'hui (comp^d. of .. hodie), *to-day*
maintenant (manu tenens), *now.*
à présent (ad praesentem), *at present,*
actuellement, *actually,*
alors (ad illam horam), **then,**
autrefois (altera vice), *formerly,*
hier (heri), *yesterday,*
jadis (jamdiu), *formerly,*
demain (de mane), *to-morrow,*
tôt, bientôt (tot cito), *soon,*
tantôt, { *by and by,*
         just now,
plus tôt, *sooner,* (plutôt, *rather*).

tard (tarde), *late,*
encore (hanc horam), *yet, still,*
déjà (de jam), *already,*
souvent (subinde), *often,*
jamais (jam magis), *ever,*
ne ... jamais, *never,*
toujours, *always,*
parfois (per vices), *sometimes,*
longtemps, *long,*
soudain (L. L. subitaneum), *suddenly,*
dorénavant (de hora in abante), } *hence-*
désormais (de ipsa hora magis), } *forth,*
enfin, *at last,*
    etc. etc.

III. Adverbs of Order, Manner, Degree, Quantity.

comment? (*Comp. of* comme *and* ment) *how?*
comme (quomodo), *as, like,*

bien (bene), *well,*

tant, autant (tantum), *so much, as much,*
combien? (*comp. of* comme *and* bien) *how much?*
très (trans), *very,*

ADVERB.

mal (male), *badly,*
ainsi (in sic), *thus, so,*
si (sic), aussi (aliud sic), *so,*
volontiers (voluntarie), *willingly,*
plutôt, *rather,*

peu (paucum), *little,*
assez (ad satis), *enough,*
davantage, plus (plus), *more,*
beaucoup (beau + coup), *much,*
trop, *too much,*

and nearly all those in **-ment**: as, doucement, **facilement,** etc.

IV. Adverbs of Affirmation and Negation.

oui (hoc illud), *yes,*
certes (certe), *certainly,*
vraiment, *truly,*
sans doute, *without doubt,*

non, *no,*
ne, *not,*
nullement, etc., *by no means,*
si, *yes,* answering negative questions.

    ne ... pas   (lit. no .... passum, *not a step*), *not,*
    ne ... point (ne .. punctum, *not a point*), *not (at all),*
    ne ... rien   (ne .. rem, *not a thing*), *nothing.*
    ne ... jamais (ne .. jam magis) *not ... ever, never.*

Obs. pas, point, rien, etc. were **not** originally negative adverbs, but merely substantives used emphatically to strengthen the real negation **ne;** compare the Engl. not .. a fig, not a mite, not a jot etc., the Lat. **nihil,** German **nicht.** In course of time these emphatic expressions became assimilated to the negation so as to form a regular part of it.

Obs. Très is never used before beaucoup. *Very much* is rendered simply by beaucoup, or une grande quantité.

Notice also

    I thank you *very much* = Je vous remercie infiniment.

The Preposition. (La Préposition).

§ 109. Prepositions may be divided according to their form into

I. Simple Prepositions:

à (ad), *to, at,*

après (ad pressum), *after,*
avant (ab ante), *before* (time),

avec (apud hoc), *with,*
chez (casa), *at the house of,*
contre (contra), *against,*
dans (de intus) *in,*
de (de), *of, from,*
depuis (de post), *since,*
derrière (de retro), *behind,*
dès (de ipso), *from,*
devant (de ab ante), *before* (place),
durant (Pres. Part. of durer), ***during,***
en (in), *in, by, whilst,*
entre (intra), *between,*
envers (in versus), *towards,*

hormis (comp^d. of Lat. foras et missum), *except,*
malgré (malum gratum), *in spite of,*
moyennant (Pres. Part. of Old Fr. moyenner) *by means of, on condition,*
outre (ultra), *besides,*
par (per), *by,*
parmi (per medium), *among,*
pendant (Pres. Part.), *during,*
pour (pro), *for,*
sans (sine), *without,*
sauf (from sauver), *save, except,*
selon (sub longum), *according to,*
sous (subtus), *under,*
suivant (Pres. Part.), *according to,*
sur (super), *on, upon,*
vers (versus), *towards,*
  etc. etc.

Obs. **Durant** is the only preposition which may be placed after the Noun.

II. Compound Prepositions, which govern the ACCUSATIVE case:

à travers, *through,*
d'après, *after,*

par-dessous, *underneath, under,*
par-dessus, *over, above.*
  etc. etc.

III. **Compound Prepositions** which govern the GENITIVE (de).

auprès de, *near,*
autour de, *round,*
ensuite de, *in consequence of,*
hors de, *out of,*
loin de, *far from,*
lors de, *at the time of,*
près de, proche de, *near to,*
en deçà de, *this side,*
au delà de, *beyond,*

au-dessous de, *below,*
au-dessus de, *above,*
au devant de, *against,*
le long de, *along,*
au lieu de, *instead of,*
au moyen de, *by means of,*
à propos de, *with regard to,*
au travers de, *through,*
vis-à-vis de, *opposite.*

IV. **Compound Prepositions** which govern the DATIVE case (à).

quant à (quantum), *as for, as to,*
jusqu'à, jusques à (usque ad), *as far as, until,*

par rapport à, *with regard to.*

The Conjunction (La Conjonction).

§ 110. I. Co-ordinative.

(a) *Connective:*

  et, *and,*
  et ... et, *both ... and,*
  ainsi que, *as, as well as,*
  aussi, *also,*
  ni .. ni, *neither .. nor,*

  tantôt .. tantôt, *sometimes .. sometimes,*
  au reste, du reste, *but,*
  d'ailleurs, *however, besides,*
  non-seulement .. mais encore, *not only .... but also.*

(b) *Adversative:*

  mais, *but,*
  ou, *or,* **ou ... ou,** *either ... or,*
  soit ... soit, *be it ... or, whether,*
  cependant, *however,*

  toutefois, *however,*
  néanmoins, *nevertheless,*
  pourtant, *yet, still.*

(c) *Conclusive:*

  ainsi, *thus,*
  car, *for,* **donc,** *then, therefore,*
  c'est pourquoi, } *therefore,*
  voilà pourquoi, }

  conséquemment,
  par conséquent,
  en conséquence, } *consequently,*
  partant,

II. Sub-ordinative.

A. *Requiring the Indicative or Conditional Mood.*

attendu que, vu que, *inasmuch as, whereas,*
comme, *as,*
parce que, *because,*
puisque, *since,*
lorsque, quand, *when,*
après que, *after,*
à peine ... que, *scarcely,*
aussitôt que, dès que, *as soon as,*
ainsi que, de même que, *as well as,*

à mesure que, *as, according as,*
à proportion que, *in proportion as,*
excepté que, hors que, *except that,*
selon que, suivant que, *according as,*
depuis que, *since,*
pendant que, tandis que, *while, whilst,*
tant que, *as long as,*
si, *if, whether.*

B. Requiring the Subjunctive Mood.

afin que, pour que, *in order that*,	malgré que, nonobstant, que, *for all [that]*,
avant que, *before*,	sans que, *without*,
bien que, **quoique**, *although*,	non que, non pas que, *not that*,
en (au) cas que, *in case that*,	à moins que ... ne, *unless*,
en attendant **que**, *until*,	de peur que ⎫
soit que ... où que, *whether ... or*,	de crainte que ⎭ ... ne, *lest*.

C. Requiring either the Indicative or Subjunctive.

que, *that*,	au lieu que, *whereas*,
jusqu'à ce que, *until*,	selon que, *according as*,
de façon que, de manière que ⎫ *so that*	sinon que, *except that*.
en (de) sorte que, ⎭	

D. Requiring the Infinitive Mood.

afin de, pour, *in order to*,	de crainte de ⎫ *for fear of*,
avant de, *before*,	de peur de ⎭
à moins de, *unless*,	loin de, *far from*,
au lieu de, *instead of*,	plutôt que de, *rather than*.
faute de, *for want of*,	

Interjections.

§ 111. Interjections may be divided into the following classes:

(a) Surprise: ah! oh! ô!
(b) Grief: hélas! ah! aie! **ouf!**
(c) Joy: ah! bon!
(d) Disgust: fi! fi donc!
(e) Silence: st! chut!
(f) Doubt: bah!

INTERJECTIONAL EXPRESSIONS.

bien! à la bonne heure! bravo! *well done!*
allons! courage! en avant! *come! cheer up! forwards!*
ciel! miséricorde! *O heavens! have mercy!*
au feu! au secours! au voleur! *fire! help! stop thief!*
tiens! quoi! vraiment! par exemple! *lo! what! indeed!*
gare! *mind! look out!*
silence! paix! *be quiet! silence! hush!*

Appendix I.

THE GENDER OF SUBSTANTIVES.

§ 112. I. GENDER ASCERTAINED BY THE MEANING.

Principal Exceptions.

A. Masculine: the names of **Males, Mountains, Metals, Months, Days, Seasons, Trees, Winds:**

Un homme, le Caucase, le fer, le février, le lundi, le printemps, le chêne, l'aquilon.

also **Verbs, Adjectives, Adverbs,** etc. used substantively:

le boire, le va-et-vient, le beau, le pourquoi, personne (ne), etc.

La caution,	l'ébène,
la connaissance,	l'épine,
la dupe,	l'aubépine,
la recrue,	la bourdaine,
la sentinelle,	la vigne,
la basse-taille,	la yeuse.
la flûte,	
la pratique,	la bise,
la victime,	la brise,

Names of mountains used in the plur.

les Alpes, les Pyrénées, etc.

B. Feminine: the **names of Females, Countries & Towns, Flowers, & Fruits ending in e mute; Arts & Sciences, Virtues & Vices, Holydays:**

La femme, la France, Rome, la musique, l'astronomie, la justice, la médisance, la rose, la pomme, la Saint-Barthélemy.

Besides the names of Countries, Flowers, and Fruits not ending in e mute, as, le Brésil, le Pérou, le Danemark, le lys, le raisin, l'abricot, etc., the following are Masc.:—

le Bengale, le vice, } § 113. 3.
le Hanovre, le courage, } & § 114. 1.
le Mexique, all in -isme
le Péloponèse,
le Maine,
le Caire,
le Hâvre.

C. Common: Substantives denoting both male and female: l'enfant, l'élève, l'artiste, l'esclave.

Enfant is always masculine in the Plural.

§ 113. II. GENDER ASCERTAINED BY THE TERMINATIONS.

A. Masculine: the Substantives ending in—

1) a full vowel sound or diphthong: as,

le delta, le café, un abri, le zéro, un écu, le balai, un emploi, un ennui, le noyau, le château, le feu, le trou.

Principal Exceptions.

1) Abstract nouns ending in té, tié (Lat. -tas, -tia, f.) as,

la bonté, la charité, l'amitié, etc.

la villa (L. villa), la fourmi (L. formica), la merci (L. merces), l'après-midi, la bru (O.Germ. brut, la glu (gluten, n.) Engl. bride). la tribu (L. tribus), la vertu (L. virtus) la peau (L. pellis), l'eau (L. aqua), la foi (L. fides), la loi (L. lex), la paroi (L. paries, m.)

2) a Consonant, especially b, c, d, g, h, k, l, p, q, z: as,

le plomb, le tronc, le fond, le sang, le soleil, le coup, le coq, le nez.

2) Most abstract nouns in -eur, see B. 3. (contrary to Lat. nouns in -or, -os) as,

la peur (pavor, m.) la douleur (dolor, m.), etc.

also la fleur (flos, m.), la sueur (sudor m.), la couleur (color, m.)

3) Nasal sounds (with the important exceptions mentioned in the second col.): as,

le plan, le train, le foin, le vin, le son, le serment, le gant, le pont.

la cuiller (cochleare), la souris (sorex), la chair (caro), la vis (vitis), la mer (mare, n.), une fois (vices), la tour (turris), la forêt, la cour (cohors), la nuit (nox), la brebis (vervex), la dot (dos), l'oasis, la mort (mors)

Most Nouns in -ion, çon, son (L. -tio:

la révolution, la rançon (redemptionem), la chanson, la mousson, etc.

la main (manus), la faim (fames), la jument (contr. to L. jumentum, n.), la fin la dent (contr. to Lat. m.)

4) aire (Lat. -arius, -arium): le mandataire, le dictionnaire.

acle, age, ége (L. Lat. -aculum, -aticum, -egium): l'âge, le collège, le spectacle.

ice (Lat. -itium, -icium): as, l'hospice, le vice.

-isme, -asme (Lat. -ismus, -isma, -asmus): as, le prisme.

-iste (L. -ista): as, l'ébéniste.

B. Feminine: Substantives ending in—

1) e mute preceded by a Vowel or Diphthong: as,

une armée, la vie, la rue, haie, la joie, la pluie.

2) e mute preceded by a double consonant: as,

la cuirasse, la paresse, la coulisse, la selle, la ville, la bataille, la treille, la campagne, la botte, la couronne.

3) -eur (contrary to Lat. abstract nouns in -or, -os,):

as, la peur, la candeur;
also, la fleur, la couleur, la sueur.

Principal Exceptions.

3) la chaire (cathedra), l'affaire, la circulaire, la **grammaire**, la paire.

la page (pagina), l'image (imago), la rage (rabies), la nage, la plage (plaga), les ambages (ambages), la cage (cavea).

Those nouns in **-ice** derived from Lat. in -itia, -ix; as, la notice, la justice, (but masc. as in Lat.: le calice), etc.

Some in **-iste** are common; as l'artiste, etc.

Preliminary Remarks. Names of males, and **most** Substantives derived from Lat. **nouns in** -us, -um, form, of course, a **General** exception to these Rules:

1) l'élysée (L. elysium), le périgée (περίγειον), le génie (L. genius), le parhélie (παρήγιος), l'amphibie (αμφίβιος), l'incendie (incendium), le foie (ficatum), le parapluie.

2) le carrosse, le colosse (colossus) le libelle (libellus), le polichinelle, le violoncelle, le boute-selle, le squelette (σκιλετός), le cimeterre, le verre, le lierre, le beurre, le tonnerre.

3) a few abstract nouns n -eur le bonheur (L. bonum augurium) le malheur (L. malum augurium) un honneur (honor), le labeur
all Concrete in **-eur** (Lat. -tor, -sor): (see however opposite) l'équateur, le docteur, etc. les pleurs.

APPENDIX.

Principal Exceptions.

4) -té, -tié (from Lat. abstract nouns in -tas, -tia f.):

as, la charité, l'amitié.

4) l'été (contrary to Lat. aestas, f.), le comité, l'arrêté, le pâté.
le comté (but f. in Franche-Comté), le côté, le traité.

5) -ion, -çon, -son (from Lat. abstract nouns in -io):

as, l'opinion, la leçon, la chanson.

5) **Concrete** nouns **in -ion** (Lat. concrete masc. in -io),
le bastion, le scorpion, etc.,
also le poison, le tison, un oison.
le pinson.

6) -ance, -ence (from Lat. in -antia, -entia), -ense:

as, la constance, la **patience**, la défense.

6) le silence (Lat. silentium).

7) -ace (Lat. -cies, -acia, -atio, -atca), -ade:

as, la glace, l'audace, la préface, **la place**, la parade.

7) l'espace (L. spatium).
le grade (L. gradus).

8) -ude, -une, -ure (Lat. -udo, -una, ura):

as, l'habitude, la lune, la nature.

8) le prélude.
le mercure (L. Mercurius),
le murmure (L. murmur),
l'augure (L. augurium),
le parjure (L. perjurium).

9) -ière, -oire (Lat. -aria [pl.], -or a):

as, la lumière, l'histoire.

9) le derrière,
le boire, le déboire, le pourboire,
l'ivoire (L. ebur; adj. eburneus),
le grimoire,
and those derived from Lat. nouns in -orium, -erium: as,
l'oratoire,
le cimetière (cæmeterium),

Eugène, French Grammar.

6

§ 114. III. GENDERS ASCERTAINED BY THE DERIVATION.

General Rules. 1) Words derived from **Lat. Masc.** and **Neuter** Nouns are **Masculine:** as,

le monde (mundus); le livre (liber); le temple (templum); l'animal (animal), etc.

2) Words derived from **Lat. Fem.** Nouns are **Feminine:** as,

une heure (hora), la méthode (methodus), la loi (lex), la **vertu** (virtus), etc.

Exceptions.

1) Most words in -eur, though derived from **Masc. Lat.** words in -or, -os, are Fem. in French: as,

la peur (pavor), la vapeur (vapor), la fleur (flos); etc.

Obs. honneur, labeur, pleurs are masc. according to General Rule.

2) Many French words ending in e, es, derived from **Lat. Neuter** words in -um, Plur. a, ia, are Feminine:

Obs. Most of these being frequently, and a few exclusively, used in Lat. in the Plural, their Nom. and Acc. Plur. inflections a, ia were probably the cause that in the Transition period of the formation of French, they were erroneously taken for Feminine words of the first Lat. declension: as,

la cymbale (cymbalum)	une horloge (horologium)	la pomme (pomum)
une épitaphe (epitaphium)	l'huile (oleum)	la prune (prunum)
une épithète (epitheton)	une idole (idolon)	la pointe (punctum) *but*
une étable (stabulum)		le point, *masc.*
une étude (studium)	la joie (gaudium)	la réponse (responsum)
la feuille (folium)	la poire (pirum)	la vitre (vitrium).
une arme (arma)	une enseigne (insignia)	la paire (paria)
la dépouille (spolia)	les épousailles (sponsalia)	la pécore (pecora)
	la lèvre (labra)	la voile (vela)
une écritoire (scriptoria)	la merveille (mirabilia)	la volaille (volatilia).

3) The following are **Masculine in French**, though derived from Lat. Fem. words:

un arbre (arbor)	un épi (spica)	le portique (porticus)
un appendice (appendix)	le front (frons, -tis)	le sort (sors)
un art (ars)	un orchestre (orchestra)	le soupçon (suspicio)
le dialecte (dialectos)	le paragraphe (paragraphus)	le synode (synodus)
		les thermes (thermae)
le diocèse (diœcesis)	le poison (potio)	le vertige (vertigo).

4) The following are **Feminine** in French, though derived **from Lat. Masc.** or **Neuter** nouns:

les annales (annales)	la corne (cornu)	la mer (mare)
une arche } (arcus) (but: **un** arc)	la dent (dens)	une obole (obolus)
une asperge (asparagus)	une écorce (cortex)	la paroi (paries)
la cendre (cinis)	une épigramme (epigramma)	la poudre (pulvis)
la comète (cometa)	la fin (finis)	la souris (sorex)

§ 115. SUBSTANTIVES OF BOTH GENDERS ACCORDING TO THEIR MEANING.

Masculine.	Feminine.
l'aigle (aquila), *the eagle,*	une aigle, *a standard* (female eagle),
*l'aune (alnus), *the aldertree,*	une aune (ulna), *an ell, yard,*
le crêpe (crispus), *the crape,*	la crêpe, *the pancake,*
*le foret (fr. the verb forer), *the gimlet,*	la forêt (med. Lat. forestis), **the** *forest,*
le greffe (graphium), *the registry, the rolls,*	la greffe, *the graft, the scion,*
*le **livre** (liber), *the book,*	la **livre** (libra), *the pound,* £,
le manche (manica), *the handle,*	la manche (manicae), *the sleeve,*
le mémoire (memoria), *the memorandum,*	la mémoire, *the memory,*
le mode (modus), *the mood,*	la **mode**, *the fashion,*
*le moule (modulus), *the model, the mould, pattern,*	la **moule** (musculus), *the mussel,*
*le mousse (ital. mozzo), **the** *cabin-boy,*	la mousse (Germ. moos), *the moss,*
l'office (officium), *the office, duty,*	une office, *a servant's hall, pantry,*
*le page (παιδίον), *the page,*	la page (pagina), *the page (of a book),*
le pendule (pendulus), *the pendulum,*	la pendule, *the timepiece,*
le période (periodum), *the highest pitch,*	la période, *the period,*
*le poêle (pensile), *the stove, pall,*	la poêle (patella), *the frying-pan,*
le poste, *the post, place, employment,*	la poste (Low. Lat. postus), *the post, post-office,*
*le somme (somnus), *the **slumber, nap,***	la somme (summa), *the sum,*
*le souris (from sourire), **the** *smile,*	la souris (sorex), *the mouse,*
*le tour (tornus), *the turn, trick,*	la tour (turris), *the tower,*
le vapeur (vapor), *the steamer,*	la vapeur, *the steam, vapour,*
*le vase (vas), *the vase,*	la vase (Anglo-Sax. vase), **the mud, slime,**
*le voile (velum), *the veil,*	la voile (vela), *the sail,*

Observation. (Those marked with an asterisk are not only different **in** meaning and gender, but also in origin.)

6 *

APPENDIX.

In the following words the **masc.** denotes the **agent**, the **fem.** the **action** or **instrument**.

Masculine.	Feminine.
l'aide (fr. verb aider), *the assistant,*	l'aide, *the assistance,*
le critique, *the critic,*	la critique, *the criticism,*
l'enseigne, (insignia), *the ensign,*	une enseigne, *signboard,*
le fourbe, *the knave, rogue,*	la fourbe, *the cheat, imposture,*
le garde, *the keeper,*	la garde, *watch, guard,*
le manœuvre, *workman,*	la manœuvre, *the working, manœuvre,*
le trompette, **the trumpeter,**	la **trompette,** *the trumpet,* etc.

§ 116.   PLURAL OF SUBSTANTIVES.

Substantives with a **different meaning in the Sing. and the Plural.**

l'aboi,	*the bark, barking,*	les abois (aux abois, *at bay*),	
l'arme,	*the arm, weapon,*	les armes,	*coat of arms, bear-*
l'arrêt,	*decree, judgment,*	les arrêts,	*arrest,* [*ings,*
l'assise,	*layer, stratum,*	les assises,	*assizes,*
l'auspice,	*augury,*	les auspices,	*auspices,*
la bonne grâce,	*gracefulness,*	**les** bonnes grâces,	*good graces, favour,*
le ciseau,	*the chisel,*	**les** ciseaux,	*the scissors,*
la défense,	*the defence,*	les défenses,	*tusks,*
le denier,	*the farthing,*	les deniers,	*funds,*
l'enfer,	*the hell,*	les enfers,	*infernal regions,*
l'esprit,	*spirit, ghost, mind,*	les esprits,	*senses, spirits,*
l'état,	*the state, condition,*	les états (généraux, etc.),	*parliament,*
			the states-general,
le **faste,**	*the pomp, show,*	les fastes,	*annals, records,*
le **fer,**	**the** *iron,*	les fers,	*fetters, chains,*
le gage,	**the** *pledge,* **pawn,**	les gages,	*wages,*
la grâce,	**the** *grace,* **mercy,**	les grâces,	*Graces* (mythol.),
l'honneur,	**the** *honour,*	les honneurs,	*dignities, honours,*
l'instance,	*the instance (law)*		
	lawsuit,	les **instances,**	*entreaties,*
le jour,	*the day,*	les jours,	*life,*
la lettre,	*the letter,*	les lettres,	*literature,*
la lumière,	*the sight,*	les lumières,	*intelligence, knowledge,*
la lunette,	*the telescope,*	les lunettes,	*spectacles,*
la mesure,	*the measure,*	les mesures,	*measures,*
le neveu,	*the nephew,*	les neveux,	*descendants,*

APPENDIX

Sing.		Plur.	
le papier,	*the paper,*	les papiers,	*documents, passport,*
la poursuite,	*the pursuit,*	les poursuites,	*proceedings (law),*
la pratique,	*the practice,*	les pratiques,	*intrigues, observances,*
la tablette,	*the shelf,*	**les** tablettes,	*writing-tablets,*
la troupe,	*the band,* **drove,**	**les** troupes,	*troops, forces,*
la vacance,	*the vacancy,*	les vacances,	*vacations,*
la veille,	*the watch, vigil,* **eve,**	**les** veilles,	*night labours,*

Obs. Most of these **substantives have also** in the **Plur.** the same meaning as in **the** Singular.

§ 117. The following Substantives are **not used in the Singular.**

les **alentours,**	*the neighbourhood,*	les fonts,	*font,*
les ancêtres,	— *ancestors,*	les frais,	*expenses,*
les aguets,	— *watch,*	les gens,	*people,*
les annales,	— *annals,* **records,**	**les** hardes,	*wearing apparel,*
les archives,	— *archives,* **record-offices,**	**les** intestins,	*entrails,*
		les mœurs,	*manners, morals,*
les armoiries,	— *coat of arms,*	les mouchettes,	*snuffers,*
les arrhes,	— *earnest money,*	les pénates,	*household* **gods,**
les atours,	— *attire,*	les pierreries,	*jewels,*
les balayures,	— *sweepings,*	les pleurs,	*tears,*
les confins,	— *borders,*	les proches,	*relatives,*
les décombres,	— *rubbish,*	les ténèbres,	*darkness,*
les **dépens,**	— **cost, expense, charge,**	les thermes,	*hot springs, baths,*
		les vêpres,	*vespers,*
les environs,	— *environs,*	les vivres,	*provisions, victuals,*
les entrefaites,	— *interval,*		

besides many words ending in **-ailles** (Lat. Neuter pl. **-alia**) as, fiançailles, *bethrothal;* les entrailles, *entrails;* tenailles, *pincers,* **etc.**

§ 117 (a). COMPOUND ADJECTIVES.
Formation of Feminine and Plural:

Singular:		Plural:
m. aigre-doux, } *sourish,*		{ aigres-doux.
f. aigre-douce, }		{ aigres-douces.
ivre-mort, } *dead-drunk,*		{ ivres-morts.
ivre-morte, }		{ ivres-mortes.

Thus—frais-cueilli, premier venu, sourd-muet, nouveau marié, etc.

Obs. 1. If, however, one of the components stands **in adverbial** relation to the other, **it is left** as a rule unchanged in the *fem.* and *plur.* : as,

m. nouveau-né, } *new-born,*	{ nouveau-nés.
f. nouveau-née, }	{ nouveau-nées.

Thus—clair-semé, demi-mort, léger-vêtu, mi-parti, etc. but exceptionally (like clair-semé above):

tout-puissant, } *all powerful,*	{ tout-puissants,
toute-puissante, }	{ toutes-puissantes.

Obs. 2. Compound adjectives denoting colour generally remain unchanged, like those derived from Nouns:

Des cheveux blond ardent (chatain clair, etc.). Des gants paille.

Syntax.

§ 118.   CONSTRUCTION.

Obs. In Latin the terminations of the inflected Words show their relation to each other; and the order of these may therefore be varied without affecting the sense: as, Scipio Hannibalem vicit: *or* Hannibalem Scipio vicit: *or* Hannibalem vicit Scipio, etc. In French, however, the Subject being only known by its position at **the** beginning, but one arrangement yields a certain sense.

§ 119. The French construction, **with but few exceptions, follows the logical order: as,**

SUJET.	VERBE.	RÉGIME DIRECT.	RÉGIME INDIRECT.
Les Romains,	imposèrent,	leurs lois,	aux nations conquises.

Obs. 1. When the *Acc.* (Régime **direct**) has a complement, the *Dative* (Régime **indirect**), if shorter, generally precedes it: **as,**

J'ai écrit, | à votre **frère.** | une lettre renfermant une copie du contrat.

Obs. 2. On the position **of Personal** Pronouns used objectively in the Accusat. **and Dative case see** § 188 and 189.

INVERSION.
A.   Inversion in Interrogative Clauses.

§ 120. If the Subject of an Interrogative sentence is a Substantive, this is placed *before* the Verb and repeated after it in the form of a Personal Pronoun (see §§ 74 **and** 76): as,

Mon frère ira-t-il ?   Mes frères iront-ils ?
Ma sœur viendra-t-elle ?   Mes sœurs viendront-elles ?

§ 121. If the Sentence is introduced by an Interrogative **Pronoun** *or* Adverb: as, **combien? comment? quand? où? que?** the *Noun-Subject* may be placed *before* or *after* the Verb (but with **pourquoi?** only *before*): **as,**

Quand ma sœur viendra-t-elle?	Pourquoi ma sœur viendra-t-elle?
or: Quand viendra ma sœur?	Comment se porte sa cousine?

Obs. 1. The latter construction is admissible only when the Verb is used *without an object or complement*; in all other cases the *inverted* construction is used: as,

Comment l'élève fait-il ses devoirs?
Quand ma sœur lira-t-elle ce livre?

Obs. 2. The interrogative **Pron. or Adv.** *must* always be placed *first* in the sentence:

Comment va votre frère (and *not*—votre frère comment va-t-il?)

B. Inversion in Affirmative Sentences.

§ 122. The interrogative Construction is also used **after the** following Conjunctions:

aussi, in the sense of { *consequently, accordingly,*
à peine, *scarcely, hardly,*
au moins,
du moins, } *at least,*
toujours, *at all events,*

à plus forte raison, *so much the more,*
en vain, vainement, *in vain,*
encore, *besides, even then,*
peut-être, *perhaps,*
tout au plus, *at most:* as,

Il est paresseux,	*He is lazy,*
aussi est-il dans la misère;	*Therefore he is in distress;*
aussi sa famille est-elle dans la misère.	*Therefore his family is in distress.*
À peine sait-il lire.	*He can hardly read.*
à peine cet élève sait-il lire.	*This pupil can hardly read.*

Ce mot n'est usité que dans telle science, **encore** ne l'emploie-t-on que rarement . . . . *even then it is but seldom used.*

§ 123. The *Noun-Subject* (but not the *Pers. Pron.*-Subject) *may* be placed *after the Verb*:

(a) after the Relative Pronouns **dont, lequel, duquel,** etc., **où, que,** if the Subject, on account of its complements, is longer than the Predicate: as,

Je ne sais d'**où** lui **vient** tant de confiance.

C'est là **le** mal **que devraient** prévenir l'éducation publique et l'éducation privée.

b) after **ainsi, tel, quelque . . . que, ici, là**; generally after *Adverbs* or *adverbial expressions of time and place;* also after **c'est . . . que** followed by **a** neuter Verb, after **quel** in indirect Interrogation, after the Impers. **il**, and **in Enumerations** in official documents: **as**,

Ainsi mourut ce héros! Telle fut sa fin. (German: So endete dieser Held.)
C'est à Dieppe qu'arrivent les steamers de Newhaven.
Le **médecin** demanda quel **était** l'état de sa santé.
Il lui **est** né un fils. Sont **exceptés** de cette catégorie: **les** volontaires d'un an.

Obs. In parenthetical and optative clauses the Verb must stand first: **as**,
Pourquoi, dit-il (or dit le maître), ne venez-vous pas?
Vive le roi! — Périssent les Troyens! (see also § 155, Obs.)
Thus also occasionally in **conditional or concessive** clauses (**si** being left out):
L'eût-il **voulu**, il en eût été incapable.
Dussé-je y **périr**!

§ 124. In order to give more prominence and emphasis to a word or expression in a sentence, **c'est, ce sont, c'était, ce serait**, etc., are placed before it, and a corresponding Relative **Pronoun** or **the** Conjunction **que** after it: as,

C'est mon frère qui m'envoya hier cette lettre,
C'est cette lettre que mon frère m'envoya hier,
C'est à moi que mon frère envoya hier cette lettre,
C'est hier que mon frère m'envoya cette lettre.

THE VERB.
CONCORD.

§ 125. The Verb agrees with its Subject in Number and Person: as,

Il joue, mais nous travaillons. — Je ferai ce que feront les autres.

When two or more words **form the** joint Subject, the Verb is put in **the** Plural: as,

La vertu et l'ambition sont incompatibles. —
Virgile, Pollion, Horace étaient amis.

Obs. In French the Verb agrees with the *grammatical* number of the Subject, and **not — as in** English — with the *logical* number: as,

Le peuple n'est jamais content. *The people a r e never satisfied.*
La commission a fait son rapport. *The committee h a v e made t h e i r report.*

§ 126. The Verb generally agrees with **the** *nearer* Subject only:

(a) When the different Subjects are *Synonymous*, **or form a** kind of *gradation;* **as**,

Son amitié, sa douceur nous charme.
Un seul mot, un soupir, un coup d'œil nous trahit.

CONCORD OF VERBS.

(b) When they are connected by **ou**, *or*, **ni** ... **ni**, *neither* ... *nor*, one Subject excluding the other: as,

C'est le goût, la vanité **ou** l'intérêt qui les lie.
Ni M. le duc, **ni** M. le comte ne sera nommé à l'ambassade de Rome.

(c) When the **Subjects are recapitulated by an Indefinite** Pronoun: **tout, rien, personne, chacun,** etc.: as,

Ses enfants, ses amis, **chacun l'adore.**

§ 127. When the Verb refers to several Subjects **of different persons, it agrees with the person that has the priority, the First being preferred to the Second, and** the Second to the Third: **as,**

Vous et moi **sommes** contents. (Comp. Lat. Ego et Cicero valemus.)
Si vous ou votre sœur avez le temps, ayez la bonté de venir me voir ce soir.

§ 128. When the Subject **is a** collective Substantive accompanied by another Substantive, **the** Verb agrees with **the term on which the greater stress is laid: as,**

Une faible troupe de montagnards **résista** à cette armée.
Une troupe de pauvres **montagnards résistèrent** à cette armée.
La plupart des **animaux ont** plus d'agilité que l'homme.
(Comp. Lat. **Magna pars** aut vulnerati aut occisi **sunt.**)

GOVERNMENT OF VERBS (SYNTAX OF CASES.)

§ 129. The Accusative Case.

(a) The Accusative **of the** *nearer Object* stands after *transitive* Verbs of all kinds (many of **which** take **a** preposition in English, see Appendix): as,

Dieu créa le ciel **et la terre.** Nous approuvons votre conduite.
Qu'attendez-vous? Nous attendons le train.
Qui avez-vous rencontré? J'ai rencontré le monsieur que je cherchais.

Obs. 1. The Acc. of the *cognate object* stands after some *intransitive* Verbs:

Il va toujours son chemin. Mourir une belle mort.
Jouer un jeu d'enfer. (Comp. Lat. Claudius aleam lusit.)

Obs. 2. An Acc. of *respect* frequently occurs in idiomatic phrases:

Parler politique. Causer littérature. Sentir le tabac.
Faire le grand seigneur. *To set up for a great personage.*

(b) A *double Acc.* (as in Lat. and English) stands after *factitive* Verbs nommer, élire, **faire**, déclarer, etc. : as,

On le créa **colonel** sur le champ de bataille,
Ne vous faites pas leurs **complices**.

But Verbs of *teaching* and *asking* do not take **a double Acc.** as in Lat. and English, see § 130.

(c) Time *how long* (also *time when* in dates) is generally put in the Acc. : as,

Il a plu **toute la journée**. Il restera ici **quinze jours**.
Je regrette le temps que ce travail m'a coûté.
Il partira **le premier juin**. (But see § 131. a.)

Obs. 1. An *Acc. of price* stands after **vendre**, estimer, etc.: as,
Que vendez-vous votre cheval ? Je l'estime **mille francs**.

Obs. 2. An *Acc. absolute*, answering the Lat. Abl. absolute (§ 164), or used as an Adverbial expression, is of frequent occurrence in French : as,

Mon **projet arrêté**, deux méthodes se présentaient.
Moi mort, mon fils est le légitime héritier de mon empire.
Il entra dans le monde **la tête haute**.
Déjà les divinités vengeresses, **les ailes ouvertes**, les **draperies volantes**, sont prêtes à fondre sur l'assassin tremblant.

N.B.—For list of Verbs which govern the acc. in French, but not in English, see p. 143.

§ 130. The **Dative** case, — Preposition **à** — (answering the Lat. **Dative**, Ablative, or the preposition **ad**) :

(a) **Verbs** of *giving, showing, telling*, etc., and — quite contrary to English — their *opposites, i.e.* Verbs of *taking away, asking*, etc., take a *Dative of the person* (remoter Obj.) and an *Acc. of the thing* : as,

Le général accorda une amnistie générale **aux rebelles**.
Cette langue n'a presque rien **emprunté aux** autres. '*borrowed from*'.
Je **lui** ai prêté ce qu'il **lui** fallait pour subvenir **à** ses besoins.
Est-ce que le médecin permet le café **à** ces malades?
Au contraire, il **le leur** défend. (Lat. Ne libeat **tibi**, quod nemini licet.)
Ce qu'il **donne aux** autres, il se **le refuse**.
(Lat. Quod alii donat, sibi detrahit.)
On **lui** a pris sa **bourse** et sa montre. *They took his purse and his watch from him.*

This rule also applies to Verbs of *teaching* and *asking*, which do not take a double Acc. as in Lat. and English: as,

On **lui** enseigne la géographie. *They teach him geography.*
Je **leur** demanderai une question. *I shall ask them a question.*

Obs. The Dat. of the Person is also used with **faire** followed by an *Infinitive governing an Accusative*:

Vous faites dire **à** Cicéron une chose qu'il n'a jamais dite. *You attribute to Cicero what he never said.*
Ces chants firent changer de visage **à** Atala.

GOVERNMENT OF VERBS.

But if the Infinitive has an *indirect* Object, faire governs the Accusative; — *compare* On lui fit abandonner son poste, *with* On le fit renoncer à ses prétentions.

A similar construction is used with entendre, ouïr, laisser, voir followed by an Inf.:
Je lui ai entendu **dire** cela.

(b) Words **expressing** *fitness, likeness, preference, superiority, command, obedience, trust*, etc., and occasionally their *opposites*, govern the *Dative*: as,

Cela ne sert à rien. *That is good for nothing.*
(Lat. Servit collecta pecunia **cuique**.)
Ce chapeau **vous** va à merveille. *This hat fits you to a nicety.*
Le vert plaît aux yeux. (Lat. Victrix causa **diis** placuit, sed victa **Catoni**.)
Ce fils ressemble à son père.
Louis XVI. succéda à Louis XV. Dieu créa l'homme à son image.
Ne vous y fiez pas. (§ 194.) *Don't trust him.*
Consentez-vous à cet arrangement. Non, je m'y oppose.
Il faut résister à ses passions. (Resistendum est **appetitibus**.)
Pardonner aux méchants, **c'est nuire aux** bons.
Répondez donc à mes **questions** et obéissez-moi. (Lat. Mundus Deo paret.)

With Adjectives: Conforme **à la nature.** (Congruenter naturae.)
Ardent (âpre) au gain. Utile à l'agriculture.

With Substantives: Poudre à canon, *Gun-powder.*   Vache à lait, *Milk-cow.*
Une tasse à thé, *A tea cup, but*   Une tasse de thé, *A cup of tea.*
Une salle à manger, *A dining-room.*   Une chambre à coucher, *A bed-room.*

Obs. The governing word may be understood:
C'est au maître de parler, et au disciple d'écouter. '*It is for*' (i. e. *the duty*.)

(c) *Motion towards*, or *rest at*, a place is expressed by **à** (see § 199.)

J'irai demain à Caen, en Normandie,* je n'y ai pas été depuis **longtemps.**
Il a jeté son chapeau à terre. Elle a mal à la tête (aux dents.)
J'ai chaud aux mains, mais froid aux pieds.
My hands are warm, but my feet are cold.

This rule also applies to verbs of *thinking, longing,* etc.:
Songez à vos affaires. A quoi pensez-vous donc?
Don Carlos aspire au trône d'Espagne.

* With respect to names **of** countries, à only stands before those used exceptionally in the *Plural* or in the *Masc. Sing.*:
Aller aux Pays-Bas, au Canada, au Brésil. (§ 112.) but: aller en France.

Obs. Partir, s'embarquer, faire voile take **pour**:
Partir pour Douvres. Faire voile pour les États-Unis.

§ 131. The **Dative** is further used to express

(a) *Time when* — especially if *definite* or *circumstantial:* as,
A cinq heures et demie; à minuit; à l'époque des croisades.
Au commencement; à la fin.
Le monarque, **à ce mot**, revient de son caprice.

(b) *Manner, instrument, distinctive feature:*
J'irai **à pied** et ma sœur ira **à cheval**.   'on'
Nous l'avons reconnu **à sa barbe**.   'by'
Il fut reçu **à bras ouverts**.   'with'
Jouer **aux cartes, aux échecs**, etc. (with musical instruments, see § 132)   'at'
A la mode, à la française. Peindre à l'huile.   'in'.

So also in many **adverbial expressions** and in *Compound Nouns:*
à tort, *wrongly;* à l'**unanimité**, *unanimously;* à bon marché, *cheap.*
à merveille! *capital!* etc.
un bateau à vapeur, *a steamboat.*   potage au lait,   *milk-porridge.*
un moulin à vent, *a wind-mill.*   tarte à la crème,   *cream-tart*
l'homme au masque de fer, *the man with the iron mask.* (Lat. Abl. **Senex** promissa barba, horrenti capillo.)

(c) *price, measure, estimation*, etc.: as,
Vendre au poids, à la livre. Louer **à l'heure**. *'by'.*
Le marc d'argent était, à cette époque, évalué **à cinquante francs**.

(d) the *possessor*, after the Verbs **être, appartenir:**
Ce moulin est **à moi**
Tout aussi bien, au moins, que la Prusse est **au roi**.

Also *redundantly:* J'ai **mon** caractère **à moi**.
Il a une maison à lui. *He has a house of his own.*
C'est folie **à vous** de **vouloir** entreprendre cela.

Obs. An *Ethic* **Dative is** used in French as in Lat. and German, to denote that some person feels interest in an action:
Faites-**moi** taire ces gens-là. *Pray do make these people keep silence.*
Plein d'un juste courroux, il **vous** prend sa cognée,
Il **vous** lui fend la tête.
Comp. Lat.: Quid *mihi* Celsus agit. Germ.: Ist's auch gewiss, bist du *mir* unverletzt?

For a list of **Verbs** which — **contrary to** English — govern the Dat. in French, see Appendix, p. 143.

§ 132. The **Genitive** — Preposition **de:** — (answering the Lat. Gen. and Abl. and the prepositions **de, ex, a**) is used after Verbs and Adjectives to express

(a) *Separation, privation, difference, change, deliverance,* etc.: as,
Leurs corps furent privés de sépulture. Il a changé d'avis.
L'arbre nous **garantira**-t-il de l'orage? Non, il ne vous en garantira pas.
On dirait qu'il ne sait pas **distinguer** le bien du mal.
Il **ne** saurait se passer de vin. *He cannot do without wine.*

GOVERNMENT OF VERBS.

(b) the *origin, starting-point* (in space and time) and — contrary to English — *nearness:* as,
    D'où **venez-vous**? Nous **arrivons** de Paris. Nous venons du théâtre (**de** l'école).
    Elle est originaire de Venise.   Ces vers sont de Virgile.
    Il y a trois **ans** de cela.   Nous approchons **du** champ.
      Similarly after *Nouns:* du café de Ceylon; **des vins de France**; un homme du peuple.

(c) the *cause, motive:* (expressed in English by *out of, with, from,* etc.) as,
    Ils frémirent de rage.   Ce poète mourut de faim.
    Il n'en peut plus de fatigue.   *He is worn out with fatigue.*

(d) the *agent, instrument:* (in English *with, by;* § 264) as,
    Il me fit signe de la main.   On le **ceignit** d'une écharpe.
    Le roi était suivi de ses courtisans.
    Elle **joue du** piano. (see § 131 b.)

(e) the *manner, material:* (in English *with, from, in*) as,
    Je l'aime de tout mon cœur.   Il le fit de sang froid.
    Dieu créa l'univers de rien.   **De** cette manière (façon, sorte).
      Similarly with *substantives:* Une montre d'or. Une jambe de bois.

(f) *feeling, disposition:* (in English *at, on, for*) as,
    Ayez **pitié** de ce pauvre enfant. (Lat. Gen. Misereseite *regis*).
    Ne vous **moquez-vous pas de** ses menaces? Si, nous nous en **moquons**.
    Je suis fâché de ce contre-temps. Et moi, j'en suis enchanté.
    Il est honteux de son origine.

(g) *fulness, abundance, capacity, enjoyment,* etc. and their *opposites:*
    (in English *with, of*) as,
    Ils remplirent le vase d'eau.   Ces paroles sont vides de sens.
    Les Alpes sont couvertes de neige.   Nous manquons d'argent.
    Nous jouîmes d'une vue magnifique.   Il est prodigue de son bien.
    (Comp. Lat. Abl. **Amor** et *melle* et *felle* est fecundissimus.)

(h) *perception, remembrance, information, judgment,* **occupation** etc., especially when the governing Verb is *reflective:* as,
    Vous apercevez-vous de votre erreur?   Je m'en aperçois.
    Souvenez-vous **des** pauvres.   De quoi vous occupez-vous?
    Je ne sais pas **de** quoi il **s'agit**.   *I do not know what it is about.*
    Il ne se **doute** de rien.   *He suspects nothing.*
    On l'a **traité** de fou.   *They called him a madman.*

(i) *accusation, guilt, blame, punishment,* **and** their *opposites:* as,
    Il est innocent du crime dont on l'accuse.
    (Lat. Gen. Fraterni est sanguinis insons).
    Dieu **venge** tôt ou tard les bons de l'injustice des méchants.
    Récompensez-le de sa bonne conduite.

    Obs. The Genitive is also used in answer to the question: — *in respect of what?* →
Il trembla de tout son corps. (Comp. Lat. Acc. **of** respect: Tremit artus).
Ils se sont trompés de chemin. *They have missed their way.*
Parle, ou c'est fait de toi. *Speak, or you are done for.*
For a list of Verbs which govern the Gen. in French, but not in English, see App., p. 143.

§ 133. The **Genitive** depending on a Substantive:

(a) The *Possesive* Genitive, whether used *subjectively* or *objectively*, invariably stands *after* the noun on which it depends; as,

L'amour d'une mère.   *A mother's love,* | L'amour du gain.
Les conquêtes de César. *Cæsar's conquests.*| La conquête de la Gaule.

> **Obs.** In poetry however the inverted construction is extensively used:
> Là tu verras d'Esther les pompes et les honneurs.
> De ce palais j'ai su trouver l'entrée.

(b) The *appositive* Genitive is used in **French as in Latin**: as,

Ce mot de volupté.   (Haec vox voluptatis).
Le titre de roi.   Le nom de père.

(c) The Gen. of *quality*, *quantity*, *measure*, *valuation*, etc. stands after Substantives and Adjectives: as,

Un homme de talent (de grand talent). (Vir ingeniosus. Homo magni ingenii.)
Un champ de quatre arpents.   (Ager quattuor jugerum.)
Une armée forte de dix mille hommes. Plus de vingt fois. (Appendix § 240.)
Une montagne de mille mètres de hauteur or Une montagne haute de mille mètres.
Elle est âgée de quinze ans.

> **Obs.** The Genitive may depend on a word understood (*nature, function, duty* or *token*)
> Cette action est d'un homme sage. (Lat. Tempori cedere habetur *sapientis*).

(d) The *Partitive* Genitive depends on Substantives, Pronouns and Adverbs (expressed or understood) to denote the whole of which a part is taken: as,

Un verre de vin. Donnez-moi du vin. Voici de bon vin.
Combien d'argent avez-vous? J'en ai beaucoup. (see §§ 11. 165. 170. 193.)

> Even *Adjectives or Participles* may be used *partitively:*
> Je n'ai jamais rien mangé de si bon.   Quoi de plus magnifique!
> Voilà quelque chose de beau!   Il y eut neuf cents hommes de tués.
> (Lat. Ne quid falsi dicere audeas.)
> Here observe also the use of de after *Superlatives:*
> Le plus riche négociant de la ville. *The richest merchant in the town.*

For a list of Verbs which — according to their meaning — take a different construction, see Appendix, p. 144.

MOODS AND TENSES.
INDICATIVE MOOD.

§ 134. **Present Tense.** The use of the Present Tense in French generally **coincides with that** in English: as,

Le temps s'enfuit. Nous partons demain.
L'homme propose, et Dieu dispose.

Exception. The *Present* is used in French instead of the English *Present Perfect* in sentences beginning with
depuis, voilà .. que, il y a longtemps, as,

Il y a longtemps qu'il **travaille.** *He has been working for a long time.*
Depuis quand **pleut-il?** *How long has it been raining?*
(Comp. Lat. Jam pridem *cupio* = *I have long desired.* *Cicero*.)

§ 135. Past Tenses.
The **Imperfect** and the **Preterite Definite** compared:

(a) General Rule: The **Imparfait** is the *Descriptive* Past Tense,
The **Défini** is the *Historical* Past Tense (Greek Aorist).

(b) The **Imparfait** answers the question: „*What was going on?*"
The **Défini** answers the question: „*What came to pass?*"

La famille **était** en prières, lorsqu'on entendit à la porte un homme qui **frappait.**

Harold **était** à York, quand **un messager vint lui annoncer que** Guillaume avait débarqué.

(c) The **Imparfait** is used to *describe* | The **Défini** is used to *narrate*
1. habitual or *repeated* actions, *manners* and *customs:* as, | 1. *single historical facts*, not viewed as continuing*: as

Les Romains **brûlaient** leurs morts. | Les Romains **détruisirent** Corinthe.
The Romans used to burn their dead. | *The Romans destroyed Corinth.*
(Comp. Lat. *Laudabat* quotidie virtutem.) | (Romulus urbem suam Romam *vocavit*)

2. an action *not considered as accomplished* — hence the term **Imparfait** —: as | 2. an action *fully accomplished* — hence the term **Défini** —: as

Il **mourait** de faim et de soif. | Ce poète **mourut** de faim.
He was dying (i. e. nearly dying) with hunger and thirst. | *This poet died (i. e. actually died) of hunger.*

(d) In a *narrative* the **Imparfait** expresses *accessory circumstances*, *explanatory remarks;*
the **Défini** expresses **the** *principal action* and the *progress of the narrative:* as,

Au **moment** où Guillaume, duc de Normandie, **reçut** le message qui lui **annonçait** la mort d'Edouard et l'élection de Harold, il **était** dans son parc près de Rouen, tenant à la main un arc et des flèches neuves qu'il **essayait.**

---

* The difference between these two tenses is so marked as often to affect the very meaning of the Verb:

Le général **savait** que l'ennemi approchait: — '*knew*,' or, '*was fully aware*.'
Le général **sut** que l'ennemi approchait: — '*learnt*,' or, '*became aware*.'

Tout à coup il parut pensif, remit son arc à l'un de ses gens, et passant la Seine, se rendit à son hôtel de Rouen.

(Comp. Lat. Vercingetorix copias suas, quas pro castris collocaverat, *reduxit*, protinusque Alesiam, quod *erat* oppidum Mandubiorum, iter facere *cœpit*. *Caesar.* — Jam ver *adpetebat*, cum Hannibal ex hibernis *movit*, *Liv.*)

§ 136. The **Imparfait** is besides employed to express:

(a) two or more *simultaneous* past actions: as,

Pendant que je lisais, il s'amusait à jouer.

(Lat. Catilina *erat* unus timendus tam diu, dum mœnibus urbis continebatur. *Cicero*.)

(b) a *Condition* or *Hypothesis* after the Conjunction si: as,

S'il avait du courage, il se battrait.

Obs. The Imparfait often stands, for the sake of greater vividness, instead of the Conditionnel Passé, to indicate that something was *attempted* or *intended* to be done:

Si j'avais dit un mot, on vous donnait la mort (instead of "aurait donné".)

(Comp. Lat. Gladius in pectus deferebat, ni .... etc.

„ German. Mit diesem Pfeil durchschoss ich euch, **wenn ich** mein Kind getroffen hätte. (Schiller.)

§ 137. The **Passé Indéfini** is used to describe an action as having taken place at a period which has *not yet elapsed* or which is *not distinctly specified* (hence the term Indéfini): as,

Il a fait du brouillard ce matin.
Les fruits de la terre ont été la première nourriture des hommes.

Obs. The Indéfini is frequently used instead of the English Past in *correspondence* and *conversation* to denote that which is still present to the writer or narrator, as:

Je l'ai vu l'autre jour. *I saw him the other day.*
Il n'y a pas longtemps que je vous ai écrit. *I wrote to you not long ago.*

§ 138. The **Plusqueparfait** is used to indicate that something had taken place at the time spoken of: as,

J'avais déjeuné, quand il entra.
Nous étions déjà partis, lorsque vous êtes arrivés.

§ 139. The **Passé Antérieur** is used in preference to the Plusqueparfait to indicate that an action had taken place *immediately* before the time spoken of, and is therefore generally used after the following conjunctions of time:

| aussitôt que
dès que } *as soon as* | à peine ... que, *scarcely .... when;*
ne ... pas plutôt ... que, *no sooner ... than.* |

Il partit dès qu'il eut appris cette nouvelle.
A peine eus-je prononcé ces mots, que tout le peuple ému s'écria.....

Obs. In general the Plusqueparfait corresponds to the Imparfait; the Antérieur to the Défini, from which they are respectively derived.

§ 140. The **Futur Présent** is generally used as in English (sometimes as an equivalent to the Imperative): as,

Je viendrai demain.   *I shall come tomorrow.*
Tu honoreras ton père et ta mère.   *Thou shalt honour thy father and thy mother.*

Exception. In English the Present or Perfect are often used after conjunctions of time: *when, as soon as, whenever*, in which case the Future Present or Future Perfect must be used in French: as,

Quand il viendra, dites-lui cela.   *When he comes, tell him that.*
Qu'on m'avertisse quand les chevaux seront arrivés.   *Tell me when the horses have come.*

(Comp. Lat. Profecto tunc erimus beati, quum cupiditatum *erimus* expertes. *Cicero.* De Carthagine vereri non desinam, quam illam excisam esse *cognovero*. — Romam quum *venero*, quae *perspexero*, scribam ad te. *Cicero.*)

In like manner the *Future* is used in the **following expressions:**

Faites ce qu'il vous plaira.   *Do what you like.*
On dira ce qu'on voudra.   *They may say what they like.*
Il arrivera ce qui pourra.   *Come what may.*

Obs. The Future Perfect may express *supposition:*
Vous aurez mal pris vos mesures.   *You probably took your measures wrongly.*

§ 141. The **Conditionnel** generally corresponds to the so-called English Conditional,* and is used—

(a) in *Principal Clauses* to express the conclusion based upon a *Supposition* or *Condition*, contained in a dependent clause, or merely understood: as,

J'irais, si j'avais le temps.   *I should go if I had time.*
Nous serions allés, s'il eût fait beau temps.   *We should have gone if the weather had been fine.*
S'il en était ainsi, je l'excuserais.   (Lat. Imperf. Subj.: Si ita esset *ignoscerem.*)
Quand vous auriez réussi, que vous en serait-il revenu?   *Even if you had succeeded, what would you have got by it?*

Obs. 1. *Elliptically:* Et je me laisserais tyranniser par elle?
or as a form of politeness: Voudriez-vous bien me dire quelle heure il est?

---

* Remember, however, the entirely different construction of the Condit. Past of the English auxiliary Verbs *shall (ought), can, may,* and the French devoir, pouvoir: —
Il aurait dû aller.   *He should (ought to) have gone.*
Il aurait pu venir.   *He could (might) have come.*

2. The Pluperf. Subj. is frequently used for the Condit. Past:
Si les Titans avaient chassé Jupiter, les poètes eussent chanté les Titans.

(b) in *dependent* clauses after Verbs of *thinking, knowing, saying, decreeing* etc., in a *Past Tense* (i. e. in oblique oration): as

J'espérais qu'il ferait beau temps. (*but* J'espère qu'il **fera** beau temps).*
Il me répondit qu'il ne me **rendrait** pas ce service.

(Lat. Periphr. Constr.: Ariovistus respondit, ... Aeduis **se** obsides non redditurum esse.)

Il fut convenu que nous **partirions**   *It was agreed that we should start*
le lendemain.   *on the following day.*

Obs. 1. So also after quand même, *though, even if*, expressed or implied:
Quand même je le voudrais, je ne le pourrais pas,
or Je le voudrais, que je ne le pourrais pas.

2. In *indirect statements* for the truth of which the narrator cannot vouch:
Jeanne d'Arc **faisait** à ce sujet des récits étranges: un ange **aurait** remis une couronne au roi **de la** part du ciel.

3. Si, in the sense of *whether*, may take the Verb in the Future or Conditional (Present and Past):
Nous ne savons pas s'ils **arriveront**.   *We do not know whether they will come.*
Nous ne savions pas s'ils **arriveraient**.   *We did not know, whether they would come.*

But the verb governed by **si**, in the **sense** of *suppose that*, *if*, must be used in the Present, Imperfect or Pluperfect:
S'ils le savaient, ils s'en réjouiraient.   *If they knew it, they would rejoice.*

THE SUBJUNCTIVE MOOD.

§ 142. The **Subjunctive** Mood is used to express a thing *as a conception of the mind*, and not, like the Indicative, *as a fact.* Hence it is used in Subordinate clauses (introduced by que) after Verbs and Conjunctions expressing—

(a) *a wish, command or necessity;*

(b) *doubt,* **ignorance** *or uncertainty* (Verbs of *Saying and Thinking* used *interrogatively or negatively);*

(c) **affection of** the mind, i.e. *joy, sorrow, disgust, regret, fear, surprise,* etc.;

(d) *purpose, result, concession* **or** *supposition* (see Accid. § 110 II. b.)

---

* These sentences show that the **Condit. Pres.** is strictly peaking, a **Fut. Imperf.** and the **Condit. Past** a **Fut. Pluperf.**,—witness their tense-inflections (Introd. X & § 78. Obs.)

SUBJUNCTIVE.

§ 143. (a) The **Subjunctive** after Verbs of *wishing*, *commanding*, *approving*, and their contraries:*

vouloir, *to be willing*,	demander, *to ask*,	permettre, *to permit*,
désirer, } *to desire*,	exiger, *to require*,	approuver, *to approve*,
souhaiter, } *to wish*,	supplier, *to entreat*,	empêcher, **to** *prevent*,
préférer, } *to prefer*,	ordonner, } *to order*,	défendre, *to forbid*,
aimer mieux, }	commander, } *to command*,	prier, *to beg*, etc.

Obéis, si tu **veux** qu'on **t'obéisse** un jour.
Je **désire** qu'il **aille**.   *I wish him to go.*
Je **désirai** qu'il **allât**.   *I wished him to go.*
Permettez que je vous **interrompe**.   *Allow me to interrupt you.*
Je **veux** que tu me **dises** la vérité.   *I want you to tell me the* **truth**.
     (Comp. Lat. Optavit ut in currum patris tolleretur.)

§ 144. (b) The **Subjunctive** after Verbs of *thinking*, *saying*, *perceiving* used *interrogatively*, *conditionally*, or *negatively*:

penser, *to think*,	affirmer, } *to affirm*,	soutenir, } *to maintain*,
croire, *to believe*,	assurer, }	prétendre, } *to assert*,
s'imaginer, *to fancy*,	déclarer, *to declare*,	espérer, *to hope*,
soupçonner, } *to suspect*,**	avouer, } *to confess*,	savoir, *to know*,
se douter, }	convenir, }	voir, *to see*,
dire, *to say*,		nier, *to deny*, etc.**

Croyez-vous qu'il **veuille** y consentir? Je ne **crois** pas qu'il le **sache**.
Soupçonnez-vous que ce **soit** mon frère?
Je ne me **doutais** pas que la nouvelle   *I did not suspect that the news*
     fût vraie.   *was true.*
     (Comp. Lat. Qualis sit animus, animus ipse nescit.)

     Obs. 1. Used *affirmatively*, these Verbs (except **nier**) require the dependent Verb in the *Indicative Mood*:
         Il assure que la nouvelle **est** vraie.
     Obs. 2. These Verbs may also take the *Indicative*, when no doubt is expressed by the interrogation or negation: thus
         Croyez-vous qu'il l'**ait** fait? *implies that the speaker is uncertain about the fact.*
         Croyez-vous qu'il l'**a** fait? *indicates that the speaker has no doubt about it.*

§ 145. (c) The **Subjunctive** after Verbs denoting an *affection of the mind* (*joy*, *sorrow*, *fear*, etc.):

se réjouir, *to rejoice*,	être **bien** aise, *to be glad*,
être enchanté, ravi, *to be delighted*,	regretter, être fâché, *to be sorry*,

---

    * Verbs of *decreeing* however, as: arrêter, décider, décréter, ordonner, statuer, etc., generally take the *Future* or *Conditional* (the result being considered certain):
         On résolut que les évêques **garderaient** leur autorité.
   ** Verbs of *doubting*, *denying*, etc. take the Subjunctive even if used *affirmatively*:
         Je nie que cela **soit** vrai.   Je doute qu'il l'**ait** dit.

s'étonner, étre étonné, surpris, } to wonder, to be astonished, | craindre, trembler, avoir peur, **to fear**, to dread, **to be** afraid.

Je suis bien aise **que** vous soyez venu. Je crains qu'il **ne** pleuve.
Je m'étonne qu'il ne voie pas le danger. Je regrette **qu'il soit** parti sitôt.
Je suis ravi que cela **soit** arrivé.

(Comp. Lat. *Mirari se aiebat* quod non *rideret* haruspex.)

Obs. After Verbs expressing *joy, sorrow, astonishment* (but not fear) the Conjunction **de ce que** with the Indicative may stand instead of que with the Subjunctive: as,

Je suis surpris de ce que vous le savez déjà, *instead of*
Je suis surpris que vous le sachiez déjà.

See also Synt. of the Infinitive § 152; **and ne** after Verbs of fearing, § 250.

§ 146. The **Subjunctive** after *Impersonal Verbs* (according to § 142, a, b, c):

il semble,	*it seems (as if),*	il vaut mieux,	*it is better,*
il est possible,	*it is possible,*	il convient,	*it is convenient,*
il est impossible,	*it is impossible,*	il importe,	*it is important,*
il se peut,	*it may be,*	il est temps,	*it is time,*
il ne se peut pas,	*it may not be,*	il suffit,	*it is sufficient,*
il faut, il est nécessaire, }	*it is necessary,*	il est facile, il est difficile,	*it is easy,* *it is difficult,* etc.

Il est temps que vous **partiez**. Il **convient** que vous **leur** fassiez une visite.
Il **faut** que je **parte** demain. Il fallut que je partisse à l'instant.
Il **importe** que je te **voie**. (Comp. Lat. Magni *interest ut* **te** *videam*.)

§ 147. Impersonal Verbs, however, which express *a certainty, an undoubted fact*, take the **Indicative**; and the Subjunctive only if used *interrogatively* or *negatively*:

il est certain, sûr, clair, évident, vrai, etc.; il arrive, *it happens*; il résulte, il s'ensuit, *it follows*; il paraît, *it appears*; etc.: as,

Il arrive souvent **qu'on** est trompé.

But negatively: Il n'arrive pas souvent qu'on **soit** trompé par ses amis.

§ 148. (d) The **Subjunctive** is used after the following *Conjunctions* expressing—

1. *Purpose, Result:* — afin que, *in order that*; **de façon que**, *so that*; jusqu'à ce que, *until*; etc.: as,

Dépêchez vous, afin que vous n'arriviez pas trop **tard**.
Travaillez de façon que je **sois** content de vous.

(Comp. Lat. Legibus servimus, ut liberi esse *possimus*.)

2. *Contingency, Supposition, Condition:* — en cas que, *in case that;* pourvu que, *provided that;* à moins que .. ne, *unless,* etc.: as,

Que sert d'amasser, à moins qu'on ne jouisse? Au cas que cela **soit**.

3. *Concession:* — **quoique,** *although;* quoi que, *whatever;* quelque. **que,** *however;* etc.: as,

Quoique le ciel soit juste, il permet bien **souvent** l'iniquité.
Quelque puissant qu'il soit, je ne le crains **pas**.

A list of Conjunctions requiring the Subjunctive appears § 110. II. b. c.

Obs. to 1. The conjunctions de façon que, de manière que, de sorte que, **au lieu que,** jusqu'à ce que, selon que, sinon que (see Acc. § 110 II. c.) require the *Subjunctive* when the result is considered *uncertain,* but the *Indicative* when the verb of the dependent clause expresses *a matter of fact:* as,

Comportez-vous de **manière que** vos maîtres puissent vous louer.
(Lat. Legem brevem esse oportet, quo facilius ab imperitis teneatur.)
Je me suis comporté de **manière que** mes maîtres étaient toujours contents de moi.
(On the use of que to avoid the repetition of other Conjunctions, see § 271.)

§ 149. The **Subjunctive** is used in *Relative sentences*—

1. **When** the First member of **the** sentence expresses merely a *wish* **or** an *expectation:* as,

J'habiterai **un** pays qui **me plaise,** *i. e. some country that is likely to please me.*

but, J'habiterai **un** pays qui me plaît, *i. e. a country which, I know, will please me.*

(Lat. Clusini legatos Romam, qui auxilium **a senatu** peterent, misere. *Cicero.*)

2. When the first member expresses *doubt* or *negation* with regard **to the** statement of the Relative clause: as,

Il n'y a **personne** qui **soit** exempt de défauts.

(Lat. *Nullum* est animal præter hominem, quod rationis **particeps** *sit.*)

3. After a *Superlative,* an *Ordinal number,* and **in general after** any term implying *exclusiveness:*— le seul, l'unique, etc., **especially when** the statement is merely a matter of opinion: as,

Télémaque est le plus bel ouvrage que la vertu ait inspiré au génie.
Les mouvements des planètes sont **les plus** réguliers que nous **connaissions**.
Néron est le premier empereur qui ait persécuté l'église.

(Lat. *Perpauci* equites, qui equos secum *eduxissent,* inventi sunt. *Liv.*)

§ 150. The **Subjunctive in** *Principal Clauses*:

Whenever the Subjunctive occurs in independent clauses, **it is in fact** dependent on **some** *wish, condition,* present to the mind of the **speaker or** writer, though not expressed; **as,**

Qu'il **soit** heureux! Qu'on ne croie pas connaître les poètes par les traductions!
Plût à Dieu! *Would to God!* **Puisse-t-il** réussir! *May he succeed!*

(Latin: *Valeant* cives mei, *sint* beati.
Ne *sim* salvo, si aliter scribo ac sentio. *Cicero*.)

Obs. Compare also with the Lat. *quod sciam*, the following expressions:
Que je sache. *As far I know (to my knowledge).*
Pas que je sache. *Not that I know of.*

SEQUENCE OF TENSES.

§ 151. The Tense of **a Verb in the** Subjunctive must **be in** concord with the Tense of the antecedent on which it depends, *i.e.*, the Verb **of the** *Principal* Clause in **the—**

(a) Présent
    Futur   } is followed { in the *Dependent* clause by the—
    Impératif   **Présent du Subj.** to express *a simultaneous* action,
                          Parfait du Subj. to express an *accomplished* action:

Nous regrettons
Nous regretterons   } qu'il **soit** malade, *or*
Ne regrettez **pas**   qu'il **ait** été malade.

(b) **Imparfait**
    Défini
    Indéfini   } is fol- { in the *Dependent* Clause by the
    Plusqueparfait   lowed   **Imparfait du Subj.** for a *simultaneous* action,
    Antérieur   **Plusqueparfait du Subj.** for an *accomplished*
    Conditionnel   action:

Nous regrettions, **nous** regrettâmes
Nous avons (avions, eûmes) regretté   } qu'il **fût** malade,
Nous regretterions   qu'il **eût** été malade.
Nous aurions regretté

(Compare the Latin:

Scio,   } quid agas,   Sciebam,   } quid ageres,
Audiam,   quid egeris,   Cognovi,   quid egisses.)
                                          Cognoveram,

Exception. The **Pres. Subj.** is often used after the **Indéfini**: as,
Il est parti, quoiqu'il pleuve.

Obs. The above is the *General* **Rule**, exceptions to which will frequently be found in French **authors**, but it nevertheless **may be** taken as a safe guide for the correct sequence of Tenses.

THE INFINITIVE MOOD.

§ 152. The **Infinitive used instead of the Indicative and Subjunctive.** The **Infinitive** in French is essentially a *Verbal Noun*, **and** as such **not** only stands for the Latin *Infini-*

tive but also assumes the functions of the *Gerund* and **Supine** (§§ 155, 156). On account of its conciseness and elegance, it is used in preference to the *Indicative* or *Subjunctive* in dependent clauses, *whenever the Subject of the latter is a Pronoun the antecedent of which is either the* **Subject** *or* **Object** *of the Principal clause*: as,

J'espère pouvoir revenir demain; *instead of* J'espère que **je** pourrai revenir demain.*

Je crains de tomber malade;	„	Je crains que je ne tombe malade.
Je crois l'entendre;	„	Je crois que je l'entends.
Dites-lui de venir;	„	Dites-lui qu'il vienne.

In that case the Particles

afin de, avant de,
de manière à, de façon à,
à moins de, de peur de,
sans, pour, après,
with the *Infinitive*, } *stand instead of* { afin que, avant que,
de manière que, de façon que,
à moins que, de peur que,
sans que, pour que, après que,
with the *Subjunctive* or *Indicative*: as,

avant d'aller,	*instead of*	avant que j'aille,
pour vous dire,	„	pour que je vous dise,
de manière à vous satisfaire,	„	de manière que je vous satisfasse,
Il est malade pour avoir trop mangé,	„	il est malade parce qu'il a trop mangé.

Obs. The Verbs dire (in the sense of *to assert*) répondre, répliquer, repartir, etc. always take que with the finite Verb, even if the Subjects of the two members of the sentence are identical: as,

Je vous dis que je n'irai pas.
Il nous répondit qu'il était malade.

§ 153. The Infinitive without Preposition stands

(a) *Substantively*, as *Subject* or *Predicate*:

Mentir est honteux. Végéter, c'est mourir. Attendre est impossible.

(b) **after** Verbs of *saying, thinking, wishing, causing, moving* and *perceiving*: (see Alph. List, App. II.)

1. *Saying:* — affirmer, avouer, dire, déclarer, jurer, soutenir, nier, etc.: as,
Il avoue avoir tort. Nous déclarons y adhérer.

2. *Thinking:* — penser, croire, espérer, s'imaginer, paraître, etc.: as,
Les grands ne croient être nés que pour eux-mêmes.
Il s'imagine être un grand homme.

---

* But in the sentence „J'espère que Charles (or qu'il) pourra revenir demain" the Infinitive construction is not admissible, because the subject of the *dependent* clause (Charles or il) is not contained in the *Principal*.

3. *wishing* and *causing:* — vouloir, souhaiter, désirer, préférer, oser, faire, laisser, etc.: as,
   Je voudrais bien voir cela. Il préfère rester.
   Il fait bâtir une maison. Laissez-le faire.

4. *motion:* — aller, courir, envoyer, **venir**, etc.: as,
   Ils allèrent demeurer à Paris. M. N. vient souvent **nous voir**.
   Ne vas pas l'irriter. *Mind you do **not** irritate him.*

5. *perception:* — voir, apercevoir, écouter, entendre, sentir, etc.: as,
   Nous l'avons entendu parler. Je te regarderai travailler.

Many of these Verbs may take de or à, see Alphab. List. App., p. 144.

Obs. The Infinitive is often used *elliptically* in interrogative sentences and exclamations:
Pourquoi ne pas écrire !
Moi, trahir le meilleur de mes amis! (i. e. je pourrais trahir...)

§ 154. **Faire, followed by** another Verb **in the Infinitive,** is equivalent to the Verbs *to order*, *to get*, *to cause*, **to have**, etc. and, contrary to English construction, this **Infinitive** is always in the *active* Voice: as,

Je vous ferai punir. *I will have you punished.*
Vous ne le ferez pas **faire**. *You will not get it done.*
Il est plus facile de se **faire aimer** *It is easier to make one's self*
que de se faire haïr.   *beloved than hated.*
On les fit conduire en prison. *They were ordered into custody.*
Je me **ferai** faire une paire de bottes. *I shall order **a** pair of boots to be made.*

§ 155. The **Infinitive** *preceded by* **de** stands—

(a) *Substantively*, joined to a *Substantive or Adjective* requiring a complement in the *Genitive* Case (see §§ 132. 133. 181.), generally instead of an *English Present Participle* (Lat. Gerund): as,

1. L'art **d'écrire**. *The art of writing* (Ars scribendi).
   Le **désir de** vous plaire. *The desire of pleasing you.*

2. Curieux **d'entendre**. *Desirous of hearing* (Cupidus audiendi).
   Digne de **commander**. *Worthy of commanding.*

(b) **after** most Verbs denoting *command, entreaty, praise, recollection, affection of the mind*, *action*, and *their opposites:* —

ordonner de, commander de, enjoindre de, empêcher **de**, défendre de, etc.
prier de, conjurer de, supplier de, menacer de, etc.
louer de, féliciter de, blâmer de, accuser de, se souvenir de, oublier de, etc.

INFINITIVE.

se réjouir de, s'affliger de, se repentir de, craindre de, soupçonner **de**, etc.
se dépêcher de, se hâter de, s'abstenir de, résoudre de, oublier **de**, etc.,
(see Alphab. List. App., p. 145.)

Je vous ordonne de partir.   Empêchez-le de le faire.
Nous vous prions de rester.   Vous réjouissez-vous de revenir?
Hâtez-vous de le dire.   Ne négligez **pas** d'y aller.

(c) after most *Impersonal* Expressions:— il me tarde, *I long;* il importe, **il suffit,** il est difficile, il est nécessaire, etc.

Il me tarde de vous voir.   *I long to see you.*
Il n'est pas aisé de bien écrire.   *It is not easy to write well.*

Obs. An **Infinitive** standing Subjectively, preceded by its **Predicate, takes de:**
Il est honteux de mentir.   *Lying is shameful.*
(On the Infinitive with de after other Prepositions and Conjunctions, see § 152.)

§ 156. The **Infinitive** *preceded by* à stands after **(a)** *Substantives*, **(b)** *Adjectives* and **(c)** *Verbs* to express—

Destination, tendency, fitness, exhortation, possibility, necessity, consent, habit, and their *opposites:* — (§§ 130. 131. 181.) as,

(a) Une maison à louer. Une **salle** à manger. Une machine à coudre.
Une distinction à faire. Les formalités à remplir.
(Compare the English Infinitive **Passive:** *A house to be let;* and the Lat. **Gerundive:** Diligentia est colenda.)

(b) C'est facile à faire. *It is easily done.*
Ce banc de sable est impossible à passer.
La raison n'est pas difficile à trouver (see Synt. of Adj. § 181).
(Compare the Lat. Supine in u: Nefas *visu* est; and **Dative of Gerund:** Par est *disserendo*.)

Obs. But any of these Adjectives used *impersonally:* as, il est facile, aisé, difficile, etc., **takes** the Preposition **de,** see § 155 (c):—
Il est facile de faire cela.
Il est impossible de passer ce banc de sable.
Il n'est pas difficile d'en trouver la raison.

(c) **Nous cherchons** à louer une maison. Il apprend à dessiner.
Le vrai courage **consiste** à **résister.**
Vous m'avez autorisé à **faire** cette démarche.
Les études contribuent à nous procurer le bonheur.
See Alphabetical List, Appendix, p. 145

Obs. The **Infinitive** stands *elliptically,* in various Idiomatic Expressions:
À le voir, on dirait qu'il est malade.   *To see him one would say he is ill.*
À vous entendre ...   *From what you say.*
À vous en croire ...   *If we are to believe you.*
Un conte à dormir debout.   *A tale that would send you to sleep.* (§ 130. b.)
C'est à n'en jamais finir.   *There is no end of it.*
Un homme à pendre.   *A man who deserves to be hanged.*
Elle est laide à faire peur.   *She is a fright,* etc.

PARTICIPLES.

§ 157. The **Present Participle** (Gérondif, **always** ending in **-ant**) must be carefully distinguished from the **Verbal Adjective**:

(I) The **Present Participle**, used to denote a *transitory action*, is **indeclinable**;

(II) The **Verbal Adjective**, describing *a state, a permanent quality*, is **declinable**, i.e. it agrees in Gender and Number with the Noun to which it relates.

(For Pres. Participles the *Adjectival* form of which differs from the *Verbal* form, see p. 145.)

§ 158. (I) The Verb in **-ant** is the **Present Participle** and therefore **indeclinable**—

(a) when preceded by the Preposition **en** *(which is the only Preposition requiring the Pres. Part.):* as,

En disant ces mots, elle pleura. L'avarice perd tout, en **voulant** tout gagner.

(b) when it has a *direct Object (Acc.):* as,

Une figure **tenant un sceptre** à la main.
On entendit les coups des marteaux **frappant** l'enclume.

(c) generally when it is followed by an *Adverb:* as,

J'ai vu ces personnes **souffrant cruellement**.

(d) **when** used as equivalent to **comme, puisque, parce** que, **quand:** as,

| Les animaux, **vivant** d'une manière plus conforme à la nature, sont sujets à moins de maux. | As animals *live more conformably to nature, they* **are** *subject to fewer evils.* |

but, Tous les **animaux vivants**. *All living animals.*

§ 159. (II) The **Verb in -ant** is the **Verbal Adjective**, and therefore **declinable**, when it is used as an *Attribute* or *Predicate:* as,

Les chevaliers **errants**.   *The knights-errant.*
Elle paraît **souffrante**.   *She looks poorly.*

Remember that in French the **Pres. Part.** is *never* a Verbal Noun, as in English, but either a **Verb** or an **Adjective, and** accordingly cannot be used as an Appositive Complement (Gen. Case). The English Pres. Part. (Gerund) must be rendered either **(a)** by a *Substantive*, **(b)** by a *dependent clause*, or **(c)** by an *Infinitive*, which is the Verbal Noun in French (§§ 152-155):

(a) La chasse au renard. La pêche à la ligne.   *Fox-hunting. Angling.*
Le chant des oiseaux.   *The* **singing** *of birds.*

(b) J'approuve que vous alliez.   *I approve of your going.*
Je le vois qui vient.   *I see him coming.*
(c) Je commencerai par vous dire que ...   *I must begin by telling you that ...*
Il finit par **me dire** des injures.   *He ended by insulting me.*

PAST PARTICIPLE.

§ 160. The **Past Participle** *used without* **an** *auxiliary Verb* agrees with the word it qualifies: as,

Que de palais **détruits**, que de trônes **renversés**!
Peu de **richesses ménagées** avec soin valent mieux que de grands **trésors** mal **employés**.

§ 161. The **Past Participle** *construed with* **être** (Reflective Verbs excepted, see § 163.) agrees with its *Subject* in *gender* and *number:* — but construed with **avoir** it never agrees with the *Subject* —: as,

Les temps **sont passés**.   Les temps ont fui.
Les fleurs **étaient fanées**.   Les roses avaient fleuri.

§ 162. The **Past Participle** *construed with* **avoir**, and the Past Part. of Reflective Verbs, agree in gender and **number** with the *nearer Object* or *Accusative* (régime direct), *when this object precedes the Participle*:

(a) *Agreement with the Object preceding:*
Que de livres nous avons **lus**!
Voici **les lettres** que j'ai **écrites**.
On nous a **trompés**.
Où **sont** mes sœurs? **Les avez-vous vues?**

No agreement with the Object following:
Nous avons lu les livres.
Avez-vous écrit vos lettres?
On a trompé nos amis.
Non, mademoiselle, je n'ai pas **vu** vos sœurs.

(b) *Agreement with the* **Direct** *Object only:*
Je les ai **loués**.
Où sont les **pommes** que j'ai ap**portées**? Je les ai **mangées**.
Que de fautes vous avez **faites**, et que vous n'avez pas **corrigées**!

No agreement with the **Indirect** *object:*
Je leur **ai** parlé.
Je vous avais apporté des pommes; en avez-vous mangé?
Vous avez fait des fautes dont vos amis **ont** profité.

§ 163. The Past Participle of Reflective Verbs agrees with the Reflective Pronoun *only* when the latter is the *Nearer* object (Accusative); but it *does not agree* when it is the *Remoter* object (Dative):

Agreement with the Pronoun in the **Accusative** :—

Elles se sont réjouies.
They have enjoyed themselves.

Mes **cousines se sont présentées.**
My cousins have presented themselves.

No Agreement with the Pronoun in the **Dative** :—

Elles se sont **proposé** un plus noble but.
They have proposed a more noble object to themselves.

Mes cousines se sont procuré une bonne place.
My cousins have procured a good situation for themselves.

It is therefore **all important to** ascertain which case the Reflective Verb governs.

§ 164. **Participle absolute.** Analogous to the Latin Ablative absolute the French language **has what may be called** a Nominative or Accusative absolute: as,

Le **pouvoir** vaincu, il **fallait le** restituer. (Lat.: potestate **victâ.**)
Cela dit, je m'éloignai. *Having said that, I withdrew.*
Le **cas échéant.** *The case occurring.* Dieu aidant. *God helping.*

SPECIAL RULES.

The Past Part. construed **with *avoir* does not agree** with its object:—

(a) When the object **answers the** question: *how long? how much?*: as,
Les années que j'ai vécu. Les **cent** louis que ce cheval a coûté.

(b) When the Verb is *impersonal:* as,
Les grandes chaleurs qu'il **a fait.** (*Because* chaleurs *is logically the Subject.*)

(c) When the Object depends on the *verb in the Infinitive,* **and** not on the Past Participle: as,
Étudiez la **leçon** que vous avez **oublié** d'apprendre; *i. e. forgot to learn,* leçon *is the object to* apprendre.
but: Étudiez la **leçon qu'on** vous a **donnée.**

(d) With the Verbs **voir** and **entendre** (followed by an Infinitive) taken in a *Passive* sense: as,
La femme que j'ai vu peindre; *i. e. whom I saw being painted* (Passive).
La **femme que** j'ai **vue** peindre; *i. e whom I saw painting* (Active).

ARTICLES AND SUBSTANTIVES.

It follows that when the French Infinitive can be rendered **in English by the** Infinitive *Passive*, the Past Part. preceding it *does not agree.*

(e) The Past Part. fait followed by **an Infinitive** never agrees (see c): **as,**
On les a **fait** sortir, *because* **les** *is the object to* fait sortir *and* **not** to fait.

(f) After the Partitive Pronoun en (in the sense of *some, any*): **as,**
Voici de belles fleurs; en avez-vous cueilli? *because* **en** *is an indirect Obj. (Genitive).*

(g) **cru, dû, voulu** do not agree when the preceding object **depends on a** verb in the Infinitive *understood:* as,
Il a rendu tous les **services** qu'il a pu. (rendre *understood, to which* que *is the object.*)

(h) When the objective pronoun **le relates to** an *adjective* or a *whole sentence:* as,
Cette femme est plus **instruite** que je ne l'avais cru. (le *refers to* instruite.)

Obs. 1. The following Past Participles, being used elliptically as Prepositions, **do not agree** when they stand *before* the Substantive:
attendu, vu, *inasmuch as, whereas, seeing;* compris, *including;* supposé, *supposing;* excepté, *excepted, as,*
Vu votre légéreté. Il **a vendu** son château, y **compris sa** ferme.

Obs. 2. Ci-inclus and ci-joint, do not agree with the noun following, when used without an article: **as,**
Vous trouverez **ci-joint copie de ce** que vous demandez.

ARTICLES AND SUBSTANTIVES.

§ 165. General Rule. A Substantive may be used —

(I) in **a** *General* Sense; i. e. expressing the *whole species*, or — if abstract — the *whole idea;*

(II) **in** an *Individual* or *Particular* sense, i. e. expressing one or more particular *individuals* or *kinds* — either definitely or indefinitely —;

(III) in an *Indeterminate* sense: i. e. expressing neither the whole species (idea) **nor any** Single individual, but merely a *quality* or *material;*

(IV) **in a** *Partitive* sense, i. e. expressing a certain *quantity*, *number* or *fraction* of a whole: as,

(I) *General:*		(II) *Individual* or *Particular:*
L'homme.	*Man.*	L'homme au masque de fer.
Les hommes.	*Men. Mankind.*	*The man with the iron mask.*
Le génie.	*Genius.*	Le génie de la peinture.
		The genius of painting.
L'argent.	*Silver. Money.*	L'argent qu'il me doit.
		The money he owes me.

(III) *Indeterminate:*
Habits d'homme. *Men's clothing.*
Un poète de génie.
A poet of genius.
Une montre d'argent. *A silver watch.*
Un sac à argent. *A money bag.*
Ils sont Anglais.
Le ciel se couvre de nuages.

(IV) *Partitive:*
Il **y a des** hommes qui ....
Il **a du** génie.
He has of genius.
Vous doit-il de l'argent ?
Does he owe you any money?
Des Anglais sont arrivés ce soir.
Il y a des nuages à l'horizon.

Compare also —

(I) **General**, (II) *Individual*,   with   (III) *Indeterminate*,
    on one hand,   on the other :—
L'amour de la vertu.   **Un** acte de vertu.
The love of virtue.   *A virtuous action.*
Les jeux **de** l'enfant.   Un jeu d'enfant.
The plays of the child.   *A child's play.*
Le plaisir du roi.   Un plaisir **de** roi.
The king's pleasure.   *A kingly sport.*
L'appartement de la reine.   Un port **de** reine.
The apartment of the queen.   *A queenly bearing.*
Le pot **au** lait.   Un pot à lait.

Special Rules. I. The *Definite Art.* is used in French, but not in English :

(a) **before** Substantives taken **in a** *General* sense, especially before *Abstract*, **Common** and *Collective Nouns ;* except after the preposition **de : as,**

    L'homme est mortel. L'amour, l'espérance **et la** foi.
    L'eau est composée d'hydrogène et d'oxigène.

(b) before names of *Countries, Provinces, Mountain peaks,* **large** *Islands, Cardinal Points* used in the Singular : as,

La France, le Brésil, l'Angleterre, la Normandie, le Poitou, **le** Mont-Blanc, la Corse, le Nord.

(c) before names of *Dignities, Titles, Professions:* as,

Le roi Théodore ; le prince Jérome ; **le** docteur Nelaton ; le major Dalghetti ; monsieur le baron ; madame **la** comtesse.

    (See also Suppl. Notes on Synt. Appendix, p. 146.)

Obs. When governed by the preposition en, or by a Verb of *motion,* as aller, venir, retourner, partir de, etc., names of Countries are used *without* the Article : as,

    en France, en Angleterre ; **but dans** la France méridionale (see Synt. § 255).

The same rule holds good with feminine names of countries preceded by de when the country is not taken as a whole, but only as expressing *origin, extraction* (generally when *used adjectively*) : as,

    Les vins de France (*French wines*), *but,* Les malheurs de la France.
    Les ducs de Lorraine.   L'annexion de la Lorraine.
    Les côtes d'Afrique (*The African coasts*),   L'étendue de l'Afrique.
    Une lettre m'est arrivée de Suisse.   Les frontières de la Suisse.

§ 166. The **Definite Article** is used in French instead of the **Indefinite Article or a Preposition** in English—
(a) before names of *measure, price, weight,* etc., as,
   Cinq francs **la** livre. *Five francs* **a** *pound.*
(b) generally in describing a *part of a person, animal or plant:* **as,**
   Elle **a le** pied petit. *She has* **a** *small foot.*
   Cet arbre a l'écorce dure. *This tree has* **a** *hard bark.*
   (See also § 201. Obs.)

   Obs. The Definite Article is often used instead of the English Possessive Pronoun:
   Il s'est cassé le bras.   *He has broken his arm.*
   Donnez-moi la main.   *Give me your hand.*
   J'ai mal à la tête.   *My head aches.*
   Il s'est coupé au doigt.   *He has cut his finger.*

§ 167. The Definite Article is omitted in French, but not in English, before *Cardinal* and *Ordinal Numbers* in apposition to names of sovereigns, quotations, pages, chapters etc.: as,
   Louis quatorze . François premier . **Livre premier** . **Tome** quatre.

II. § 168. The **Indefinite Article is omitted in French,** but **not** in English, before names of *Nations, Professions,* etc., (a) in Apposition, (b) after the Verbs **être, devenir, croire, créer, nommer, rester, paraître,** etc., (c) after **quel** and **en** (see also Appendix, p. 146) : as,
   (a) Aristote, célèbre philosophe grec.   *Aristotle,* **a** *celebrated Greek philosopher.*
   (b) Je suis Anglais.   *I am* **an** *Englishman.*
   Il **est** devenu catholique.   *He has become* **a** *Roman Catholic.*
   Il s'est montré honnête homme.   *He has shown himself* **an** *honest man.*
   Je le crois honnête homme.   *I believe him to be* **an** *honest man.*
   (c) Je vous conseille en ami.   *I advise you* **as** *a friend.*
   Quel coquin d'intendant !   *What* **a** *rascal of* **a** *steward.*

   But after **c'est, ce sont, voici, voilà, or when the noun is qualified by an Adjective** or complement, the Article is used as in English : as,
   C'est **un** Anglais de qualité. — Voilà **un** honnête homme.

III. REPETITION OF **THE** ARTICLE.

§ 169. In French the Article is generally repeated before any singular Substantive : as,
   Le cœur, **l'**esprit, **les** mœurs, tout gagne à la culture.

Generally also before two or more adjectives which qualify different objects of the same kind: as,

Les nouveaux **et les vieux** livres. *but* Le sage et pieux Fénelon; *because* **both** *adjectives qualify the same person.*

IV. THE PARTITIVE ARTICLE.

§ 170. Instead of the Partitive Articles du, **de la, de l'**, des, the Preposition de alone is used—

(a) when the Substantive taken in a Partitive sense is preceded by an **Adjective**, unless this Adjective forms a kind of Compound Substantive with it: as,

De bon lait,   *good milk;*   *but,* du petit-lait,   *some whey.*
De petits enfants, *little children;*   ,, des petits enfants, *grand-children.*

(b) After Substantives and Adverbs expressing *measure, quantity,* or *negation:* as, **nombre, quantité,** une livre, une bouteille, etc. assez, autant, tant, beaucoup, combien? moins, plus, **trop,** ne ... pas, ne ... point, etc. — except if qualified by a Noun or by a Relative clause: as,

Il y a beaucoup de fruits; *but,* Il reste peu des fruits qu'on a cueillis.
Donnez-moi un verre de vin; ,, Donnez-moi un verre du vin que M. a envoyé.
A-t-il de la prévoyance?   ,, Non, il n'a pas de prévoyance.

Obs. After la plupart, *most,* and bien, in the sense of beaucoup, *many,* the Partitive Article is used; as, La plupart des gens; *most people.* Bien des fautes, *but:* Beaucoup de fautes. (See *b.*)

(c) After Verbs and **Adjectives** which take **de** before their complement (see §§ 132 and 181); compare—

On a versé du sang,   Un tigre altéré de sang.
Il y **a de** la neige.   Les Alpes sont couvertes de neige.
Voici **de** l'argent.   Je manque d'argent.
           (See also Appendix, p. 146.)

THE ADJECTIVE.
A. PLACE OF ADJECTIVES.

§ 171. Preliminary Remark. The majority of Adjectives are placed *after* the Substantive; some are generally placed *before;* others are placed indifferently *before or after;* **and lastly** there **are** Adjectives which are placed either ***before* or** *after,* but *with different meanings.*

ADJECTIVES.

§ 172. After the Substantive are *generally* placed:

(a) Adjectives denoting *colour, shape, taste:* as,
Un drapeau **blanc**; une table ronde; des fruits **doux**.

(b) Adjectives derived from *Proper names (nations, religions, dignities, sciences):* as,
La langue **anglaise**; la religion catholique; le théâtre **royal**; le règne végétal.

(c) *Participles used Adjectively:* as,
Un fer tranchant; une vie assurée; un **point élevé**.

(d) *Adjectives* used *Substantively*, and *Substantives* used *Adjectively;* as,
Le maître **tailleur**; un garçon menteur; un homme **philosophe**.

(e) *Ordinal Numerals* used without the Article: as,
Tome premier; scène **troisième**.

(f) Adjectives *with a Complement:* as,
Un homme digne d'envie; *but* Un digne homme.

(g) *Polysyllabic* Adjectives qualifying *monosyllabic* Substantives: as,
Un roi généreux; une vue grandiose; la paix éternelle;

(h) Adjectives terminating in **al, el, if, il, ique**, able, ible, érieux, eur, eresse: as,
L'amour conjugal; un traité **méthodique**; un écolier attentif.

§ 173. Before the Substantive are *generally* placed:
Adjectives denoting an *essential* quality; as,

bon, digne, méchant, mauvais, sot: — un bon chien; un **sot** orgueil.
grand, gros, petit: — un grand livre; un petit enfant.
beau, joli, vilain: — un beau visage; un joli garçon.
jeune, vieux (vieil): — un vieil homme; une jeune femme.

Also *Ordinal Numerals*, if used with the definite Article: as,
Le **troisième** volume. La dixième année.

§ 174. The Place of an Adjective before or after the Substantive depends on three circumstances: *Meaning, Emphasis, Euphony:*

Place of an Adjective according to MEANING AND EMPHASIS:

(a) The Adjective is generally placed before the Substantive, when it forms with the latter one single term, expressing *habitual* or *permanent quality*, or a *quality pertaining to the whole Class* and not to a single individual only: as,

(a) The Adjective is placed after when it merely expresses an *accidental*, and not an essential, *quality* of the noun modified, or a quality *pertaining only to a single individual* and not to the whole class: as,

Eugène, French Grammar. 8

un fidèle ami,
un cruel tyran,
un adroit fripon,
une basse intrigue.

un homme fidèle,
un roi cruel,
un ouvrier adroit,
une action basse.

(b) an Adjective taken in a *figurative* or *derived* sense is generally placed before the Substantive: as,
les **noirs** chagrins,
de tendres sentiments,
la sombre jalousie,
une étroite liaison,
de mûres réflexions,
un aveugle désir,
un assuré **menteur**.

(b) the same Adjective, taken in its *literal* meaning is generally placed after: as,
les cygnes noirs,
du beurre tendre,
une forêt sombre,
un chemin étroit,
une pomme mûre,
un homme aveugle,
un asile assuré. (See also § 172. f. g. h.)

§ **175.** Adjectives of different meaning according as they are placed before **or after** any Substantive:—

une certaine nouvelle (Lat. quidam), *certain news,*
mon cher frère, *my dear brother.*
différentes ⎱ choses, *sundry things,*
diverses ⎰
une fausse clef, *a skeleton key,*
un honnête homme, *a good man,*
un malhonnête homme, *a dishonest man,*
un pauvre poète, *an indifferent poet,*
un plaisant conte, *an absurd tale,*
son propre habit, *his own coat,*
son seul enfant, *his only child,*
un vrai coquin, *an arrant (notorious) rogue*

un mal certain (Lat. certum), *a positive evil,*
un livre cher, *an expensive book,*
des objets ⎰ différents, *different, various,*
⎱ divers, *ous objects,*
une clef fausse, **a** *wrong key,*
un homme honnête, *a polite man,*
un homme malhonnête, *a rude man,*
un poète pauvre, *a needy poet,*
un conte plaisant, *an amusing tale,*
un habit propre, *a clean coat,*
un enfant seul, *a child alone,*
une nouvelle vraie, *true intelligence.*

§ **176.** Adjectives **which change their** meaning only before **or after** certain Substantives:

un brave homme, *an honest* **man,**
un grand homme, *a man of genius,*
un petit homme, *a little (short)* **man,**
d'une **commune voix, unanimously,**
une grande dame, *a* **lady** *of rank,*
une méchante épigramme, *a poor epigram,*
de méchants vers, *poor verses,*
la dernière année, *the last year (of any period).*

un homme brave, *a brave man,*
un homme grand, *a tall man,*
un homme petit, *a mean man,*
une voix commune, *a vulgar voice,*
une dame grande, *a tall lady.*
une épigramme méchante, *a wicked epigram,*
des vers méchants, *wicked verses,*
l'année dernière, *last year.*

Observe: un habit neuf, *a newly made coat,*
un nouvel habit, *another coat,*
un habit nouveau, *a new-fashioned coat.*

B. AGREEMENT OF ADJECTIVES.

§ 177. Principal Rule. An Adjective agrees with its **Substantive** or Pronoun in Gender and Number: as,

    Ces jolies maisons sont bien situées.
    Ils sont attentifs ; elles sont attentives.

§ 178. When an Adjective **relates** to **two** or more Substantives, it is **put in** the *Plural :* as,

    Le blé et le vin nécessaires.

Obs. 1. If the Substantives are of different genders, the Adjective is put in **the *Masc.* Plural:**   L'orgueil aveugle se suppose une grandeur et un mérite parfaits.

Obs. 2. An Adjective agrees with the *nearest* Substantive only :

(a) when the Substantives are Synonymous or form a kind of gradation :
    Il a une aménité, une douceur enchanteresse.

(b) when the Substantives are connected by ou, or ni .. ni, so that one **excludes** the other :
    Servez-vous d'une plume ou d'un crayon bien taillé.

§ 179. When two or more Adjectives refer to a Substantive which denotes several objects of the same kind, they may be construed in the following different ways : as,

    La littérature espagnole et la littérature italienne.
    La littérature espagnole et italienne.
    Les littératures espagnole et italienne.

§ 180. The Adjectives **demi** and **nu** are—

(a) *invariable before* the Substantive : as, Il était nu-tête et nu-jambes.
    Je viendrai dans une demi-heure.

(b) *variable after* the Substantive : as, Il marchait pieds nus.
    Je viendrai dans une heure et demie.

Obs. The Adj. feu, *late,* agrees only when *preceded* by a Def. Article :
    La feue reine. *but* Feu la reine. *The late queen.*

On excepté, supposé, ci-inclus, ci-joint, etc. see § 164, Obs. 1. 2. On Adjs. used adverbially, § 106.

C. GOVERNMENT OF ADJECTIVES.

§ 181. The Complement of an **Adjective** is always preceded by a Preposition.

(a) The Preposition de is used after Adjectives signifying—

    1. *an Affection of the mind:* fâché, triste, heureux, content, malheureux, ravi, étonné, confus, honteux, fier, orgueilleux, jaloux, etc.
    2. *Desire:* affamé, altéré, avide, curieux, désireux, etc.

3. *Capacity, Plenty:* plein, fort*, **riche*** (* see also **d**), comblé, capable, couvert, etc., *and their opposites,* vide, faible, pauvre, incapable, privé, dénué, etc.: as,

Il est fâché de ne vous avoir pas rencontré. (*but:* Il est fâché contre vous. *He is angry with you.*)
Qui vit content de rien, possède toute chose.
Seriez-vous capable d'une telle action?
Le peuple romain était jaloux de sa liberté. Un discours vide de sens.
Il est plein de lui-même. *He is self-conceited.*

(b) The Preposition à is used after Adjectives signifying:

1. *Similarity, Equality:* conforme, semblable, etc. *and their opposites:* contraire, étranger, opposé, etc.
2. *Preference, Precedence:* préférable, supérieur, antérieur, etc. *and their opposites:* inférieur, postérieur, etc.
3. *Aptness, Fitness, Inclination:* âpre, ardent, assidu, enclin, prompt, attentif, sensible, facile, agréable, etc. *and their opposites:* inaccessible, impénétrable, inattentif, insensible, difficile, sourd, rebelle, etc.
4. *Utility:* utile, avantageux, favorable, propre, salutaire, etc. *and their opposites:* inutile, nuisible, funeste, défavorable, impropre, etc.: as,

La copie est conforme à l'original. Cela est contraire à la vérité.
Un trépas glorieux est préférable à une vie honteuse.
Un homme ardent et âpre au gain.
La jeunesse est prompte à recevoir toutes sortes d'impressions.
L'astronomie est utile à l'agriculture et à la navigation.
La bataille de Pharsale fut fatale à la république romaine.

Obs. A few adjectives require à in French, but *of* or *in* in **English: as,** adroit, habile, patient, zélé, exact, etc.

(c) The Preposition envers is required after Adjectives denoting—

Feeling, Disposition: affable, bon, libéral, généreux, juste, etc.: as,
Il est bon d'être charitable: Mais envers qui? c'est là le point.

(d) The Preposition en is required after Adjectives denoting—

Fulness, Abundance: riche, fort, fertile, fécond, **etc.:** as,
La France est riche en vins et en fruits. Une armée forte en infanterie (d'infanterie).

Obs. 1. Fort also takes à or sur: Elle est très forte sur le piano, aux échecs.
Obs. 2. Versé, *versed,* takes dans: as, C'est un homme versé dans les affaires de finance.

D. DEGREES OF COMPARISON.

§ 182. The Comparative of *Equality* is formed as follows:

In *Affirmative* Sentences: | In *Negative* Sentences:
before *Adjectives* and *Adverbs*:
aussi ... que, *as* ... *as*; | aussi or si ... que, *so* ... *as,*

DIMENSIONS. 117

before *Substantives* and *Verbs*.

autant .. que, *as much ... as ;* | autant *or* tant ... que, *so much .. as.*
Je suis **aussi** habile que vous. *I am a s clever a s you.*
Je ne suis pas si (aussi) habile **que** vous. *I am not so clever as you.*
Je travaille **autant** que lui. *I work as much as he.*
Je ne travaille **pas** tant (autant) que lui *I do not work so much as he.*

Obs. Tant que also means *as long as :*—Tant que je vivrai. *As long as I live.*

§ 183. To express the degree of *intensity* **and not** of comparison, **si** and **tant** (tellement) must be used: as,

Il marchait si vite que je ne pus l'atteindre.

Obs. 1. On davantage, instead of plus, see § 240.
Obs. 2. Verbs depending on a *comparative* must be preceded by the negation ne, except when the Verb of the principal clause is interrogative or negative: (§ 252. Obs. 1.)
Il est plus riche que vous ne croyez.
but, Il n'est pas plus riche que vous croyez.

§ 184. In using the terms **of** comparison

plus ... plus, *the more ... the more* | moins ... moins, *the less ... the less*
plus ... moins, *the more ... the less* | moins ... plus, *the less ... the more*

the **Adjective,** instead of following immediately after **plus** or **moins** as in English, must always be separated from these adverbs by another word: as,

Plus on est vertueux, plus on est aimé.
The more virtuous one is, the more beloved one is.

Obs. 1. *By,* expressing *how much* one thing exceeds another, is rendered by de: **as,** Plus haut de deux pieds. *Higher by two feet.* (§ 133. c.)

Obs. 2. The Definite Article, which forms part of the Superlative, remains invariable, when not different objects, but different degrees of quality of **one** or more objects are compared: as,

Quels sont les pays où la terre est le mieux cultivée ?
La terre la mieux cultivée produit quelquefois des ronces et des épines.

Obs. 3. When only two Persons or Things are **compared,** the **Superlative** is used in French, instead of the English **comparative** :

De ces deux poires, celle-ci est **la plus douce.** *Of these two pears this is the sweeter one.*

E. DIMENSIONS.

§ 185. **Dimensions** may be expressed either by an *Adjective* or by a *Substantive* : **as,**

Cette montagne est **haute** de dix mille pieds.
This mountain is 10,000 feet high.

or, Cette montagne a dix mille pieds de hauteur, *or* de haut.

Obs. In Relative Proportions the English *by* or *and* is expressed in French by **sur:**
Un jardin de cinquante pieds de longueur sur quarante de largeur.

§ 186. **Age** is expressed either by the auxiliary verb **être** followed by the adjective **âgé**, or by **avoir** without **âgé**: as,

Elle **est** âgée de douze ans, *or* Elle a douze ans. *She is twelve years old.*

PERSONAL PRONOUNS.

A. CONJUNCTIVE PERSONAL PRONOUNS. (See Accid. § 49. 50.)

§ 187. The **Conjunctive** Personal Pronoun used as the Subject stands before **the Verb**, except (a) in *Interrogative, Elliptic* and *Parenthetical* Clauses; (b) after some *Adverbs* and *Conjunctions* (see §§ **121**, 122): as,

Suis-**je** le bienvenu? Sans doute, répondit-**il**.
Dussé-**je voir mon palais en** cendres! *Though I should see my palace reduced to ashes!*
A peine fut-**il** parti que... *Hardly had he started when...*

Obs. In English the 3d p. of the Personal Pron. is also used *demonstratively* either as an antecedent to a Relative Pron. or followed by a complement, in which case celui or an appropriate Substantive is employed in French:—

Celui qui est content est riche. *He who is contented is rich.*
L'homme à la balafre. *He with the scar.*

§ 188. The **Conjunctive** Pronoun used as **Object** (both *nearer* **and** *remoter*) stands *before the Verb*, in Compound tenses *before the Auxiliary:* as,

	Sing.	1ˢᵗ Person.	*Plural.*
Nom.	je réponds		nous écrivons
Acc.	il me regarde		il nous aime
Dat.	il me répond		il nous parle.
		2ᵈ Person.	
Nom.	tu travailles		vous observez
Acc.	il te voit		il vous amuse
Dat.	il te donne...		il vous écrit.
		3ᵈ Person.	
Nom.	il, elle se promène		ils, elles sortent
Acc.	je le, la punis		je les (m. & f.) assiste
Dat.	je lui (m. & f.) réplique		je leur propose.

NB. The Genitive case of the 1st and 2d Person is wanting; it is supplied by the corresponding Disjunctive Pron. governed by **de**; as also in the 3d pers., when the Pronoun refers to a person and not to a thing:—

Gen. de moi, de toi, de lui, d'elle, de nous, de vous, d'eux, d'elles.

Obs. The Objective Personal Pronoun must be *repeated*—

(a) **if used before** Verbs in a simple Tense; (b) if used in a different **case** (Acc. and Dat.): **as, Il les loue et les** admire. Il m'a vu (Acc.) et m'a parlé (Dat.).

PERSONAL PRONOUNS.

3ᵈ Person of Pronouns referring to things.

Nom. Lisez ce vers (cette fable), **il** (**elle**) est facile. ... *it is easy.*
Acc. Ce vers (cette fable) est facile, je veux **le** (**la**) lire. ... *I will read it.*
Gen. Nous **en** lirons le commencement. *We will read the beginning of it.*
Dat. Nous **y** regarderons. *We will look to it.*

In Compound Tenses:

Il	**m'**	a	regardé.	Il	**nous** a	trompés.
Elle	**t'**	avait	écrit.	Elle	**vous** eut	répondu.
Je	**l'**	aurai	lu (lue).	Je	**les** aurai	vus.
Nous	**lui**	aurions	donné.	Nous	**leur** aurions	parlé.

Negatively.

Il *ne* me parle *pas*.   Il *ne* m'a *pas* parlé.

Interrogatively.

Me répondra-t-il?   M'avait-il répondu?

Interrogatively and Negatively.

Ne me punira-t-il *pas*?   *Ne* m'aura-t-il *pas* puni?

Exception. With the 1ˢᵗ and 2ᵈ p. of the *Imperative affirmative* the Pronoun stands *after* the Verb as in English, and me and te are strengthened into moi and toi:

Donne-moi,	*but negatively*:—	Ne me	donne pas.
Souviens-toi,	,,	Ne te	souviens pas.
Rendez-lui,	,,	Ne lui	rendez pas.
Parlez-en,	,,	N'en	parlez pas.
Songez-y,	,,	N'y	songez pas.

§ 189. When a Verb has *two different Conjunctive Personal Pronouns* for Objects, one in the *Accusative* and the other in the *Dative*, they both precede it in the following order:

The Dat. Pron. of the **1ˢᵗ** and **2ᵈ** pers. stand before the Acc. Pr. of the **3ᵈ** p. :

me $\begin{cases} le, \\ la, \\ les, \end{cases}$ te $\begin{cases} le, \\ la, \\ les, \end{cases}$ nous $\begin{cases} le, \\ la, \\ les, \\ en, \\ y, \end{cases}$ vous $\begin{cases} le, \\ la, \\ les, \\ en, \\ y, \end{cases}$

m' $\begin{cases} en, \\ y, \end{cases}$ t' $\begin{cases} en, \\ y, \end{cases}$

If both are of the 3ᵈ p., the **Accusative** stands before the **Dative**:
(**Se**, however, always stands first)

le $\begin{cases} lui, \\ leur, \end{cases}$ la $\begin{cases} lui, \\ leur, \end{cases}$ les $\begin{cases} lui, \\ leur, \\ en, \\ y, \end{cases}$ but se $\begin{cases} le, \\ la, \\ les, \end{cases}$

l' $\begin{cases} en, \\ y, \end{cases}$ l' $\begin{cases} en, \\ y, \end{cases}$ s' $\begin{cases} en, \\ y, \end{cases}$

Il me *le* (*la, les*) montre. Je te *le* (*la, les*) donne.
Il ne nous *le* (*la, les*) montre pas. Charles vous *le* (*la, les*) donne.
Il nous *les* a donnés. Ils ne vous *les* ont pas donnés.
Je *le* lui (leur) promets. Nous *les* lui (leur) offrons.
Me *le* donnera-t-il? Ne vous *l'*offrira-t-il pas?
Il se *le* rappelle. Elle se *les* approprie.

Exception. With a Verb in the *Imperative Affirmative* both Pronouns follow the Verb; **me** and **te** become **moi** and **toi**; and the Accusative precedes the Dative (y, however, stands before moi, toi, le, la):

Montre-*le*-moi.   *but negatively,*   Ne me *le* montre pas.
Montre-*les*-leur.   ,,   Ne *les* leur montre pas.
Menez-y-*moi*.   ,,   Ne m'y menez pas.

§ 190. The Pronominal Adverbs en (*of it, of them, from it,* etc.) and y (*to it, to them, there,* etc.), stand after the other Objective Pers. Pronouns (see however Exception to § 189): as,

Il m'en donne.   Vous les y obligez.
Donne-m'en.   Obligez-*les*-y.

Obs. If en and y occur in the same sentence, y stands first: as, Nous y en avons vu.

§ 191. Two Obj. Pers. Prons. cannot stand before the same Verb, unless at least one of them is either en, y, or le, la, les: as,

Je le (la, les) lui recommandai. Je *lui* en parlerai. Il m'y a conduit.

If one *Obj.-Pron.* is in the 1st p. and the other in the 2d p.:—He recommended *me to you*; or if the 1st or 2d P.-Pron. is in the *acc.,* and the 3d P.-Pron. in the *dat.*:—He recommended *us (you) to him (to them)*;

then the *acc.* only can stand before the Verb, whilst the *dat.* Pr. must stand *disjunctively* (i.e., with à) after the Verb:

Il *me* recommanda à vous.   Il *nous* (vous) recommanda à lui (à eux.)

This rule especially applies to *Reflective* Verbs: Il se fie à moi (à toi, etc.).

LE, LA, LES.

§ 192. Le is either—

(a) a *Conjunctive* Personal Pronoun, and declinable: **le, la;** *he, she, it;* **les;** *they;*

i.e. it agrees in gender and number with its antecedent, if the latter is

(1) a *Substantive,* (2) an *Adjective* used substantively, taken in a determinate sense to establish the identity of a person: as

(1) Êtes-vous la mère de cet enfant?
Oui, je la suis. *Yes, I am* (*the mother*).
Êtes-vous les héritiers du défunt?
Non, nous ne les sommes pas.

or (b) a *Neutral* Pronoun, and indeclinable: **le,** *it, so;*

i.e. it does not agree with its antecedent, if the latter is

(1) an *Adjective,* (2) a *Substantive* used *adjectively* or in an indeterminate sense, (3) a *whole clause:* as,

(1) Êtes-vous mère?
Oui, je le suis. *Yes, I am* (a *mother*).
Êtes-vous héritiers?
Non, nous le sommes pas.

PERSONAL PRONOUNS. 121

(2) Sont-ils les malades qui m'ont fait appeler? Oui, ils **les** sont.
Croyez-vous **les médecins**? Non, je ne les crois pas.

(2) Sont-ils malades?
Oui, ils le sont.
(3) Ont-ils obtenu un prix? **Je ne le** crois pas. *I do not think so.*

EN AND Y.

§ 193. **En** is used as a Pronoun in the *Genitive* case:

(a) instead of **de lui, d'eux, d'elle, d'elles, de ceci, de cela**, generally with reference to *things* (sometimes also, though less frequently, with reference to persons): as,

On accorde souvent sa confiance à des personnes qui en sont indignes. *One often puts one's trust in* **persons** *who are unworthy of it.*
C'est **un** événement bien triste, j'en suis affligé. *It is* **a very sad** *event, I am grieved at it.*
Son récit m'enchante, quoique je n'**en** comprenne pas toute la sagesse. *I am pleased with his narration, though I do not comprehend* **all its** *wisdom.*

Compare also

Parlez-vous de mon oncle (de ma tante)? Oui, nous parlons **de lui (d'elle).**
Parlez-vous de la guerre? Oui, nous **en** parlons.

(b) with reference to a Substantive used *partitively*, in the sense of the English *some* or *any*, expressed or understood: as,

Voulez-vous du vin? Oui, j'**en** veux. *I will have some.*
J'ai de l'argent; **en** avez-vous aussi? *I have some money; have you any?*

(c) *redundantly*, with an Adjective, an Adverb of quantity or a Numeral, *referring to a Substantive mentioned before*, in which case it is generally not expressed in English: as,

Avez-vous une pomme? Oui, j'**en** ai une. *Yes, I have* **one** *(of them).*
A-t-il des protecteurs? Il **en** a de très-puissants. *He has* **some** *very influential* **ones**.

(d) with reference to a *place mentioned before*, and in answer to the question *whence?*: as,

Vient-il de la **ville**? **Oui, il en vient.** (Comp. Lat. inde.)

§ 194. **Y** is used as a Pronoun in the *Dative* Case:

(a) instead of **à lui, à eux, à elle, à elles, à ceci, à cela**, especially with reference to *things*: as,

Cette règle est impérieuse, il faut vous **y** conformer. *This rule is imperious, you must conform to it.*
Quant à vos conditions, j'**y** consens. *As for your conditions, I consent to* **them**.

Obs. With the Verb **se fier, penser, songer,** and **croire** (*to believe in*) **y** is often used with reference to Persons; as,

   Cet homme est faux, ne vous y fiez pas.

(b) with reference to a **place mentioned before**, answering the question, *where? whither?* (conformably to **its** derivation from the Latin **ibi**).

 Est-il à l'école ? Oui, il **y** est. *Yes, he is there.*
 Est-il allé à l'école ? Oui, il y est allé. *Yes, he has gone thither.*

Remember that en and y are not only the equivalents of *of it* and *to it*, but of any other English preposition coupled with a pronoun of the 3d p., if the governing Verb **or** Adjective in *French* takes the preposition de or à respectively: as,

Êtes-vous content de cet habit?	*Are you satisfied with this coat?*
Oui, j'en suis très content.	*Yes, I am very satisfied with it.*
Ne vous moquez pas de mes remontrances.	*Do not laugh at my remonstrances.*
Je ne m'en moque **pas.**	*I do not laugh at them.*
Avez-vous pourvu **à ses** besoins?	*Have you provided for his wants?*
Oui, j'y ai pourvu.	*Yes, I have provided for them.*

§ 195. En *and* Y *used idiomatically:*

Où **en** sommes nous?	*Where did we leave off? How far have we got?*
Il en est de cela, comme de la plupart des choses du monde.	*It is with that as with most concerns of this world.*
Quoi qu'il en soit.	*However that may be.*
Croyez-m'en.	*I can assure you. You may take my word for it.*
C'en est **fait** de lui. (Lat. actum est de ..)	*He is done for. It is all over with him.*
Il est temps d'en finir.	**It is time to** *put a stop to it, .. to have done with it.*
Je n'en puis mais.	*It is not my fault. I cannot help **it**.*
Ils en sont venus aux mains. (aux coups.)	*They have come to blows.*
Je m'en prends à vous.	*I lay the blame on you. I make you responsible.*
Je m'en rapporte à vous.	**I refer the matter** *to you. I leave it to you.*
Il faut **en** passer **par** là.	**One** *must submit to it.*
En croirai-je mes yeux?	*Can I believe my eyes?*
Nous n'**en** pouvons plus.	*We are exhausted. (worn out, knocked up.)*
Je ne vous en veux pas.	*I bear you no malice. I owe **you** no grudge.*
On n'y voit plus.	*One cannot see any longer.*
On **y** va, monsieur!	*Coming, Sir!*
J'y suis. Vous y êtes.	*I have got it. You have hit it.*
Vous n'y êtes pas.	*You are wide of the mark.*
Il y va de mon honneur. (Lat. agitur.)	*My honour is at stake.*
Monsieur n'**y** est pas.	*Master **is** not at home, etc.*

B. DISJUNCTIVE PERSONAL PRONOUNS. (See Acc. § 52.)

§ 196. The **Disjunctive** Personal Pronouns **moi, toi, lui,** elle, nous, vous, eux, elles, and the *refl.* soi, are used—

(a) after *Prepositions,* **or standing alone** as Subject or Object to a Verb understood; as,
  Viens avec moi. Il est chez lui. Elles sont retournées chez elles.
  C'est pour toi. Ils ont eu querelle entre eux.
  Qui a fait cela? Lui. (*Subj.*)   *Who has done that? He.*
  Qui avez-vous invité? Lui. (*Obj.*)   *Whom have you invited? Him.*
  Il est plus appliqué que toi. Ni toi, ni lui.

(b) before a *Relative Pronoun:* as,
  Moi, qui suis content. C'est **toi** qui l'as fait.

(c) *Emphatically,* in **the sense of** *as for me, thee,* etc., or with **même, seul, aussi:** as,
  Moi, je ne le crois pas. **Toi, tu** oserais le faire?
  J'irai moi-même. Eux **seuls** sont coupables. Moi **aussi je** partirai.

(d) with the Verb être, (1) as an equivalent to a *Possessive Pronoun,* (2) used *impersonally* after ce: — c'est, ce sont, etc.: as,
  (1) Ces effets sont à moi (à toi, à lui). *These things are mine, (thine, his).*
  (2) C'est nous qui l'avons fait. Ce sont eux qui ont commencé.
    Obs. In this case être is used in the *Plural* before the Pronouns of the *third Person* (eux, elles) *only:* as,
    Ce sont eux (elles). *It is they;* but, c'est nous, c'est vous.

(e) *Coupled to a Noun* or *to another Pronoun* (see also § 127): as,
  Votre frère et moi, nous sommes de vieilles connaissances.
  Nous avons, vous et moi, besoin de tolérance.
  Il vous a invités, toi et lui.

§ 197. **Disjunctive Pronouns** are *generally* used with reference to *Persons* only; in speaking of *Things*—
  en stands for the *Genitive* de lui, d'elle, etc. (see § 193.) —
  Voilà une plume, servez-vous-en. *There is a pen, make use of it.*
  y for the *Dative* à lui, à eux, etc. (see § 194.)—
  Quant à la raison que vous m'alléguez, je m'y rends . . *I yield to it.*

(See also *Appendix,* p. 147.)

§ 198. **Soi** is used as a **Reflective Disjunctive** Pronoun (corresponding to the Refl. **Conjunctive** Pron. se) with reference to *Indefinite Pronouns, Things,* and *Animals:*—chacun, aucun, quiconque, tout, personne, etc.: **as,**

> La franchise est bonne de soi.
> Le chat ne paraît sentir que pour soi.
> Aucun n'est prophète chez soi.
> On a souvent besoin d'un plus petit que soi.

§ 199. With the following **Verbs**, *to* not being strictly the **sign** of the *Dative* case, the Régime indirect of Personal Pronouns must be expressed by **Disjunctive** Pronouns preceded by **à**, and not by the Dative of **Conjunctive** Pronouns:—

accoutumer à,	*to accustom to,*	penser à }	*to think of,*
en appeler à,	*to appeal to,*	songer à }	
courir à,	*to run to,*	renoncer à,	*to renounce,*
être à,	*to belong to,*	venir à,	*to come to:* as,

> Nous pensons à lui. Je songe à vous. Il accourut à moi.
> J'en appelle à eux. Il vint à nous tout effrayé.

POSSESSIVE PRONOUNS.

§ 200. Possessive Adjectives and Pronouns agree in Gender and Number with the *Noun which they qualify*; and *not with the Possessor*, as in English: **as,**

> Elle a perdu son argent, sa bourse, et ses effets.
> *She has lost her money, her purse, and her luggage.*
> Il a revu son père, sa mère, et ses sœurs.
> *He has seen his father, his mother, and his sisters again.*
> Sa Majesté, le roi de Suède. *His Majesty, the king of Sweden.*

(**See also** Appendix, p. 147.)

§ 201. The English **Possessive** Pronoun predicated of the Verb *to be* is equivalent to the French Disjunctive **Personal** Pronoun preceded by **à**: (§ 131. d.) as,

> Ce cheval-ci est à moi, celui-là est à eux.   *This horse is mine, that one is theirs.*
> Je suis tout à vous.   *I am yours truly.*
> Ce cahier est-il à lui ou à elle ?   *Is this copy-book his or hers?*

Obs. 1. In like manner the Engl. *Possessive* Pronoun is often expressed in French by the Conjunctive *Personal* Pronoun and the Def. Art. in speaking of *parts of the body* (also of goût, esprit, vie):—

> Vous me marchez sur le pied.   *You tread upon my foot.*
> Il s'est cassé le bras.   *He broke his arm.*
> Le cœur me fend de le voir souffrir.   *It breaks my heart to see him suffer.*

DEMONSTRATIVE PRONOUNS.

Compare also (§ 166)—
Il a le front haut. *His forehead is high.* Elle a l'esprit lourd. *Her understanding is dull.*

Obs. 2. The English *Personal* Pronoun stands for the French *Possessive* in many Idiomatic Expressions:

Avez-vous eu de ses nouvelles?   *Have you heard of h i m ?*
Il vint à ma rencontre.   *He came to meet me.*
Saluez-les de ma part. Bien des **amitiés de ma** part. *Remember me to them.*
Pour ma part. À mon égard.   *As for me. With regard to me.*

(See also Appendix, p. 147.)

§ 202. The English **Possessive** Pronouns of the third Person (sing. and pl.) are generally rendered in French by **en** and the Definite **Article**, when they **refer to** *inanimate* Objects in a preceding sentence or member of a sentence : **as,**

Le soin qu'on apporte au **travail**, empêche d'en sentir la fatigue.
The care bestowed upon work prevents our feeling i t s wearisomeness.
Le temps fuit, la perte en est irréparable.

Obs. Son, sa, ses, with reference to Things, and **en** for Persons, are less frequently used.

§ 203. But the **Possessive** Adjectives **son, sa, ses, leur, leurs,** *must* be used instead of **en,** if the thing possessed stands in the same sentence, or if it is governed by a preposition, **as,**

Chaque travail a sa fatigue.
Le temps fuit, je regrette la rapidité de son vol.

DEMONSTRATIVE PRONOUNS. (See Accid. §§ 56—61.)

§ 204. **Ceci** and **cela** (contracted **ça**) **are** used with reference to things *pointed at, but not mentioned, or to whole* **sentences :**

Ceci *t h i s ,* **denotes** *this near me,* or *this here,*
Cela *t h a t,* denotes *that near him,* or *that, yonder :* as,
Ceci est difficile, cela est encore plus difficile.

When not standing in opposition to each other,

Ceci denotes something that is *following,*
cela something *mentioned before* or *indetermined :* as,

Retenez bien ceci.   *Bear this in mind.*
Après **cela** il prit son chapeau et se retira. *After that he took his hat and withdrew.*
Cela ne me plaît pas. Pourquoi faites-vous **cela ?** (See also p. 148.)

§ 205. **Ce** (*neuter* Demonstrative Pronoun) **is** used—

(a) before the Relative Pronouns **qui** (Subj.), **que** (Obj.) **dont** (gen.) corresponding to the Engl. *that which, what* (Latin: **id quod**) (see Synt. of Relat. Pron.): as,

Ce qui est amer à la bouche, **est** doux au cœur.

(b) before the Verb **être** in **the** Third **Person**; as,

C'est lui qui l'a fait. C'est vrai.
C'est à savoir. *That remains to be seen.* (See also p. 148.)

§ 206. **Ce is used** *emphatically* before **the** Verb **être** in the third Person—

(a) as a Correlative to **ce qui** (nom.), **ce que** (acc.), **ce dont** (gen.): as,

Ce qui me plaît, c'est sa candeur. Ce que je crains, ce sont les ennemis.

Obs. 1. If the Predicate after the verbs **être** is in the Plural, **ce** *must* be used, but its use is optional with a Predicate in the Singular.

Obs. 2. If the Predicate is an *Adjective* or a *Participle,* **ce is** not used: as, Ce qui est beau, n'est pas toujours utile.

(b) before a Verb in the *Infinitive* Mood used predicatively: as,

Végéter c'est mourir, beaucoup penser c'est vivre.

(c) to recapitulate **the Subject: as,**

Le plaisir d'un bon cœur, c'est la reconnaissance.
La vraie noblesse, **c'est d'être vertueux.**

§ 207. On the **different** uses of **c'est** and **il est:**

ce is used—

(a) when the Predicate is (1) a Substantive *qualified by an Article,* a *Possessive* or *Demonstrative Pronoun;*

C'est **un** Anglais. Ce sont des Anglais.
It is an Englishman. They are Englishmen.
C'est mon père. *It is my father.*
C'est cet homme qui ... *It is this man who ...*

(2) a Personal Pronoun:
C'est moi qui le dis.
Ce sont eux qui se trompent.

il is used—

(b) when the Predicate is a Substantive *used indeterminately* or *Adjectively:*

Il est Anglais. Ils sont Anglais.
He is an Englishman. They are English.
Il est père. *He is a father.*
Il est homme à faire cela.
He is a man capable of doing that.
(Obs. In such sentences as "il est malade" il is, of course, a personal pronoun, without any demonstrative meaning.)

(c) when the Predicate is an Adjective referring to something mentioned *before:*

Vous vous trompez, c'est incontestable.

Je lis et relis Lafontaine; c'est mon **auteur** favori; il est **admirable.**

(d) when the Predicate is an Adjective referring to something mentioned *after:*

Il est incontestable que vous vous trompez.

(e) as an **antecedent** to the conjunction **que,** or to a *Relative Pronoun:*
C'est pour m'amuser que je fais cela.
Obs. See however (d) when the Predicate is an Adjective.

§ 208. **Même** (Demonstrative Adj.) *the same, the very,* (which must be carefully distinguished from the indeclinable Adv. **même,** *even*) takes **the sign of the Plural:**

(a) if preceded by the Article and followed by a Substantive or Pronoun in the Plural: as,
Ce sont les **mêmes** gens. *They are the same people.* (Lat. idem, eadem, etc.)

(b) after a Substantive or Pronoun in the Plural: as,
Les enfants **mêmes** (*or* eux-mêmes) sont venus. *The children themselves have come* (Lat. liberi ipsi.);

but without s: Ils immolèrent les femmes **et même** les enfants (*and even the children.*)

RELATIVE PRONOUNS (see Accid. §§ 62—64).

§ 209. The **Relative Pronoun** agrees with its Antecedent in *Gender, Number,* and *Person:* **as**

Est-ce ta sœur **qui** est venue? (§ 161.)
Non, ce sont mes cousines **qui** sont venues.
Est-ce vous **qui** avez fait cela? Oui, c'est **moi** seul **qui** ai fait cela.
Vous avez des habitudes **auxquelles** il faut renoncer.

But in *Case* it depends on the construction of its own clause:

Nom. Où est l'homme **qui** m'a demandé?
Acc. La plante **que** l'on ne cultive pas, dégénère.
Gen. La dame **de qui (dont)** je tiens cette nouvelle est une personne sûre
Dat. Votre frère est l'homme **à qui** j'ai le plus d'obligation.

Obs. In French the Relative pron. cannot be omitted as in English:
The man I saw. L'homme que j'ai vu.

§ 210. **Qui** (Nom.) and **que** (Acc.) refer to Persons and Things of *both genders* and *numbers:* as,

L'homme **qui** travaille. La rose **qui** fleurit. Les écoliers **qui** jouent.
Nous **qui** vous parlons. Vous **qui** travaillez. Elles **qui** s'amusent.

§ 211. **Qui,** if governed by a Preposition, is used of Persons (or personified things) only; and **lequel, laquelle,** etc. (§ 63) *must* be used whenever the Relative Pronoun, *governed by a Preposition,* refers to **Things** or **Animals**:

L'homme à **qui je** me suis adressé. Le travail **auquel** je me suis appliqué.
L'écolier **avec qui** j'ai étudié. La patience **avec** laquelle j'ai étudié.

Obs. **Qui** is often used *absolutely* instead of **celui qui,** quiconque: as,
Aimez qui vous aime. *Love him who loves you.*
Qui ne fait pas des heureux, n'est pas digne de l'être.
He who (whoever) does not make other people happy is not worthy of being so himself.

§ 212. **Lequel,** instead of **qui,** is used to avoid ambiguity, whenever the Relative does not refer to the **nearer** word in the first member of the sentence: as,
C'est un **effet** de la divine Providence, **lequel** est conforme à ce qui a été prédit.
La **femme** de votre oncle, **laquelle** est très charitable.

On lequel instead of dont, see § 215.

§ 213. **Dont,** *Gen. of* **qui** (Lat. de unde); *whose, of whom, of which,* refers to Persons and Things, and depends either—

(a) on a *Substantive* (which, contrary to English construction, is always preceded by the *Definite Article*): as,
C'est un **homme dont le** mérite égale la **naissance.**
He is a man whose merit is equal to his birth.

or, **(b)** on a *Verb* requiring the Preposition de: as,

L'homme dont je parle est estimé. '*of whom I am speaking*' ....
Votre vie n'est-elle pas à Dieu **dont** '*from whom*' ....
vous l'avez reçue?
Étonné de l'air tranquille **dont** son '*with which*' ....
frère l'avait accueilli.
Un morceau de pain sec dont j'avais '*on which*' ....
déjeuné.

The observation on the use of en (§ 194.) also applies to dont:
L'habit dont je suis content. Les remontrances dont je me moque, etc.

§ 214. When the Substantive, on which **dont** depends, is used *objectively* or *predicatively,* this Substantive is, contrary to English, placed *after* the Verb: as,

La nature, dont nous ignorons les *Nature whose secrets we ignore.*
secrets.
Les orphelins **dont** vous êtes **le** *The orphans whose protector you*
protecteur. *are.*

---
* Je pardonne à *la main* par qui Dieu m'a frappé.

§ 215. When a Relative Pronoun in the *Genitive* case depends on a *Word governed by a Preposition*, **duquel, desquels, de laquelle, de qui**, etc. must be used instead of **dont**: as,

L'homme à la probité duquel (de qui) je me fie est estimé.
The man in whose honesty I trust is esteemed.
but C'est un homme dont la probité est à toute épreuve.
He is a man whose honesty is incorruptible.

§ 216. **Quoi** (Lat. quid); *what, which*, is only used with a Preposition, and refers to *indefinite* antecedents, (especially to **ce, voici, voilà, rien**) and to *whole sentences:* as,

Il n'y a rien sur quoi l'on ait tant disputé.
Voilà de quoi je voulais vous parler.
Vous avez cité Cicéron, en quoi vous vous êtes trompé. (See also p. 148.)

§ 217. **Ce qui** (*Nom.*), **ce que** (*Acc.*), **ce dont** (*Gen.*), do not refer to a Determinate Substantive, but to a *sentence* or an *Indefinite Pronoun*, and signify *that which, what:* as,

Faites ce qui vous plaira.   *Do what you like.*
Faites ce que vous avez à faire.   *Do what you have to do.*
Faites ce dont vous êtes capable.   *Do what you can (are capable of).*
Il disparut, ce qui diminua mon revenu. (See also p. 148.)   *He absconded, which reduced my income.*

§ 218. **Où**, (adverbial Relative Pron., from. Lat. ubi) *where*, generally denotes a relation of *time* or *place*, and stands often, for the sake of brevity, instead of **lequel** governed by a preposition: **auquel, duquel, dans lequel, chez lequel, dont**, etc.: as,

L'instant où nous naissons est un pas vers la mort.... *in which....*
Le péril d'où l'on m'a sauvé. *The danger from which ....*

INTERROGATIVE PRONOUNS. (see Accid. §§ 65—67.)

§ 219. **Qui?** (Lat. quis?) *who?* refers to *Persons* only, and is used in direct and indirect questions, both as subject and object: as,

Nom.   Qui va là?   *Who goes there?*
Acc.   Qui voyez-vous?   *Whom do you see?*
„   Dites-moi qui vous aimez?   *Tell me whom you love?*

Obs. 1. Qui est-ce qui? (*Nom.*) and Qui est-ce que? (*Acc.*) are **used** for the sake of emphasis instead of qui?: as,

Qui est-ce qui va là? Qui est-ce que vous voyez?

Obs. 2. *What?* in indirect questions is translated by ce qui (*Nom.*) ce que (*Acc.*) ce dont (*Gen.*) ce à quoi (*Dat.*): as,

Dites-moi ce qui vous inquiète?
Dites-moi ce que vous allez faire? (on *what?* before an Infinit. see § 221. b).

§ 220. The English Interrogative **Pronoun** *whose?* is rendered in French—

(a) by **quel?** when coupled with a Substantive *not taken predicatively*: as,
Quel cheval avez-vous loué? *Whose horse have you hired?*
but, De qui êtes-vous le protégé? (Predicate) *Whose protégé are you?*

(b) by **à qui?** when used as a Possessive Pronoun with the Verb être: as,
À qui est la faute? *Whose fault is it?*

§ 221. Que? (Lat. quem) *what?* refers to *Things*, and is used—

(a) as a *Grammatical Subject* to *Impersonal Verbs only*: as,
Qu'importe? *What does it matter?*
Que vous en **semble?** *What do you think of it?*

(b) **as a** *Predicate* to the Verbs être, devenir, paraître, *or* as an *Object:* as,
Que sommes-nous? Que dis-je? Que faites-vous?
Nous ne savons pas que dire.

Obs. When used subjectively with other verbs than **Impersonal**, *what?* is rendered by the emphatic qu'est-ce qui? qu'est-ce que c'est?
Qu'est-ce qui vous alarme? Qu'est-ce que c'est **que de mourir?**
Qu'est-ce que c'est que cela? *What is that?*

§ 222. Lequel? laquelle? *which?* are used *absolutely,* not adjectively, and are followed by a Genitive, either expressed or **understood: as,**

Voilà **trois** chevaux; lequel **est** le vôtre?
Laquelle de ces deux villes **est** la plus illustre, d'Athènes ou de Rome?

§ 223. Quel, quelle? (Lat. qualis?) *which? what?* are used *adjectively*: as,

Quel temps fait-il? Quelle heure est-il?

Obs. Quel is sometimes used absolutely before the verb être, in the sense of *who? what?*
Quel est cet homme? Quel est votre plan?

§ 224. **Quoi?** (Lat. quid?) *what?* is used—

(a) after a *Preposition*, instead of **que**, which is *never used with a preposition*: as,

    A **quoi** pensez-vous?   *What are you thinking of?*
    De **quoi** vous plaignez-vous?   *What do you complain of?*

(b) *absolutely*, either standing by itself, or followed by a Comparative: as,

    Quoi! Vous voilà déjà de retour?   *What! Back again already?*
    Quoi de plus beau que cette première page?   *What can be more beautiful than this first page?*

INDEFINITE PRONOUNS. (see Accid. §§ 68—71.)

§ 225. **Quelqu'un, quelques-uns,** *somebody, some, some one, any, anyone,* are used substantively of Persons; but of Things only with reference to a preceding or following **Substantive**: as,

    Quelqu'un est venu. Quelques-uns assurent le contraire.
    Ces livres sont curieux, j'en ai acheté quelques-uns.

§ 226. **Personne,** *no one, no body, not anybody,* and **rien,** *nothing, not anything,* **when used with a** verb require the negative particle **ne**: as,

    Personne ne vient. Je ne vois personne.
    Rien ne lui plaît. Cela ne vaut rien.

When used without the verb, ne is suppressed: as,
    Que faites-vous?—Rien. Qui est venu?—Personne. (see also § 244 & p. 118.)

§ 227. **Aucun, nul,** and the more emphatic **pas un,** *not a single one,* are used both absolutely and adjectively, and require the Verb with **ne**: as,

    Aucun n'est prophète chez soi. **Nul** n'est exempt de mourir.

Obs. Either aucun or nul must be **used instead of pas de,** point de, before a Substantive taken as *Subject or Indirect* Object; **as,**
    Je ne le veux en aucune **manière.**
but, Il n'a nulle amitié pour vous, *or* .. **point d'amitié (Direct Object).**

§ 228. **Autre** (Lat. alter), *other,* **is** used—

(a) *Adjectively:* un autre homme; l'autre vie. Autre temps, autre usage,
    Autre chose est tenir, autre chose est promettre.   *It is one thing .... and another ...*

(b) *Substantively:* d'autres, *others;* bien d'autres, *many others;* etc.

(c) as an *ordinal Number*, in the sense of *a second*: as,

C'est un autre Attila. Un autre moi-même. (Alter ego.)

Obs. The Preposition which governs l'un l'autre, *one another, each* **other**, is placed between **l'un** and **l'autre**: as,

Ils médisent les uns des autres. *They speak evil of one another.* (See also p. 148).

§ 229. Autrui (Lat. alterius), *others, other people*, is most commonly used in **the general sense of** *our neighbours*: as,

Vivre aux dépens d'autrui. *To live at other people's expense.*

§ 230. Tout, tous, (Lat. totus) *every, any, all*, are used *collectively*—

either *without* article: as, tout homme, *every, any man*; toute ville, *any town*; tout autre, *any other*; etc. (See also p. 149.)

or *with* the article: as, tous les hommes, *all men*; toutes les villes, *all towns*; tout le monde, *everybody*; tous les deux (tous deux) *both.*

§ 231. Chaque (Lat. quisque) masc. and **fem.**, no plural; *every, each*, is used *distributively*, and **thus** differs from tout, which is used *collectively* **(just as aucun,** *distributive*, differs from **nul,** *collective*)**:** as,

Chaque homme a sa marotte. *Every man has his (own) hobby.*
(*but* Tout homme est mortel. *All men are mortal.*)
Chaque homme **a son génie.** *Every man has his peculiar genius.*
(Comp. Lat.: Sibi **quisque** maxime consulit.)

§ 232. Chacun (Lat. quisque unus); **no** plural; *each one, every one;* is used *Substantively* **with** reference to *Persons;* but *Adjectively* only with **reference to** *Things:* as,

Chacun pour soi. *Every one for himself.*
Ces oranges coûtent un sou chacune. *These oranges cost a halfpenny each.*

§ 233. Qui que (Lat. quisquis) *whoever;* **quoi** que (Lat. quidquid) *whatever,* **are often strengthened by ce soit,** *it be:*— Qui que ce soit, quoi que ce soit: as,

Qui que ce soit qui l'ait fait, il sera puni. (See also p. 149.)

§ 234. Quelque .. que; *whatever, however,* is used—

(a) *Adjectively* (Lat. quantuscunque): as,
Quelques efforts que vous fassiez... *Whatever efforts you make...*

(b) *Adverbially* (Lat. quamvis **or** quantumvis), in which case si may be used:
Quelque (or si) puissants qu'ils soient. *However powerful they may be.*
Quelque adroitement que les choses soient faites. *However cleverly the things may be done.*

(See also **p.** 149.)

INDEFINITE PRONOUNS.

§ 235. **Quel que**, *whoever, whatever*, agrees with the **Substantive to** which it refers: as,

Quelles que soient les lois, il faut **toujours les suivre.**
Quels que soient les humains, il faut vivre **avec eux.**

§ 236. **Quiconque (Lat. quicumque),** *whoever,* is used *substantively;* **Quelconque (Lat.** qualecumque)**,** *any, whatever,* is used *adjectively,* after the noun only; as,

Quiconque résiste à la loi, est indigne d'être citoyen.
Deux points quelconques étant donnés. *Any two points being given.*

§ 237. **On, l'on (Lat.** hominem), *one, some one, we, they, people;* is **used** in the *Nominative only;* as,

On appelle. *Some one is calling.*
On court (Lat. curritur), *There is a running.*
On n'est point des esclaves pour endurer de si mauvais **traitements.** —
We are not such slaves as to submit to such bad treatment.
On les laissa seuls. *They were left alone.*

Obs. 1. In most cases on is best rendered in English by using the Verb in the *Passive Voice:* as, On entendit un bruit immense. *A tremendous noise was heard.*

Obs. 2. The Adjective or Verb predicated of on **is often** made to agree in Gender and Number with the person understood by on: as,
Aujourd'hui on est amis, demain rivaux. *To-day they (we) are friends, to-morrow rivals.*

ADVERBS. (see **Accid.** §§ 104—108.)

§ 238. *Place of Adverbs.* The Adverb generally stands—

(a) *after* the Verb in simple Tenses: **as,**
Je l'admire toujours. *I always admire him.*

(b) *between* the Auxiliary **and the Past** Participle with the Verb in a Compound Tense: as,
Je l'ai toujours admiré. *I always admired him.*

Exceptions: 1. **The** laws of Euphony generally require the longer **Adverb** *after* the shorter Participle: **as,**
Je l'ai dit expressément.

2. The following Adverbs of Time and Place generally stand *after* the Participles or Infinitives, or, if used emphatically, at the beginning of a sentence: **aujourd'hui,** hier, demain, **tôt,** tard, autrefois, ici, là, partout, nulle part: as,
Nous serions partis aujourd'hui. Il a été puni hier.
Demain nous partirons. Il doit arriver demain.

§ 239. *Adverbs of Quantity* require the Preposition **de**: as,

Assez d'éloquence, mais peu de sagesse. (**Lat.** Satis *eloquentiae, sapientiae parum.*)

Bien in the sense of beaucoup requires the Partit. Articles **du, de la, de l', des**:—

Bien des hommes. *Many men.* Bien du monde. *Many people.*

On Adjectives used adverbially, see **Accid. § 106.** See also Partitive Gen. § 133 and p. 149.

§ 240. The following Adverbs must not be confounded:

plus .. que (modifying *adjectives* and *verbs*) *more .. than*, which is followed by the **second term** of comparison;

davantage (modifying *verbs* only), *more of it, more so;* which is *never* followed by que with the second term of comparison; as,

La paresse est plus dangereuse que la vanité.
Idleness is more dangerous than vanity.
La vanité est dangereuse, la paresse l'est davantage.
Vanity is dangerous, idleness is more so. (See also p. 149.)

§ 241. Plus tôt signifies *earlier;* plutôt *rather;*
tout à coup „ *suddenly;* tout d'un coup, *with one blow:*
Vous auriez dû revenir plus tôt.
Plutôt souffrir que mourir, c'est la devise des hommes.

§ 242. Comment? *how?* is used in **direct** and indirect questions, or standing by itself: as,
Comment cela se fait-il? Je ne sais pas comment cela se fait.

Comme, *how, as,* is used in comparisons, also in exclamations as an equivalent to combien; but *never interrogatively:* as,

Comme (or qu') elle est jolie!   *How pretty she is!*
Comment vous portez-vous?   *How are you?*
Comme vous voyez.   *As you see.*
Voyez comment il travaille!   *See in what manner he works!*
Voyez comme il travaille!   *See how hard he works!*

ADVERBS OF AFFIRMATION AND NEGATION. (see § 108. IV.)

§ 243. Si must be used instead of **oui** in an affirmative answer to **a** *negative* question: as,

Est-ce que vous allez à Paris? Oui, monsieur, j'y vais.
but Est-ce que vous n'allez pas à Paris? Si,* j'y vais.

---

* Or si fait, emphatical, but hardly polite.
See also § 270:— Vous dites que non, je dis que si.

NEGATIONS.

§ 244. **Ne** can only be used in connection with **a Verb**. In elliptical sentences, in which the Verb is understood, only the second part of the negation must be used: as,

Point de bonheur sans vertu. Qui est venu?—Personne.
Que faites-vous?—Rien.

Obs. When rien, personne, jamais, etc., are used *affirmatively* (according to their original meaning) ne is, of course, not used: as,

Qui vous reproche rien? *Who reproaches you with anything?*
Personne oserait-il me contredire? *Should any body dare to contradict me?*
Si vous venez jamais me voir... *If ever you come to see me....*

§ 245. **Ne** pas and **ne point** compared:

(a) ne point, according to its derivation, is more emphatic than ne pas: as,
Il ne travaille pas. *He does not work (just now.)*
Il ne travaille point. *He does not work at all.*

(b) in Interrogative sentences—
ne point implies doubt; as, N'avez-vous point été là? *Have you not been there?*
ne pas implies no doubt: as, N'avez-vous pas été là? *You have been there, have you not?*
(Compare Latin, nonne = **ne** pas: Canis nonne similis lupo?
num = ne point: Num negare audes?)

§ 246. **Pas** must stand instead of point—
(a) before *Adverbs of quantity and quality*: pas beaucoup; pas moins; pas plus; pas si; etc.
(b) before *Numerals*: as,
Avez-vous de l'argent? Pas trop.
Il n'y a pas un mot qui ne soit à propos.

§ 247. From the Examples given above it will be seen that in *simple* tenses—

ne is placed *before* the Verb, and pas, point, jamais, etc. *after* it: as,
Je ne veux pas. Cela n'arrivera jamais.

In *compound* tenses most frequently *between* the **Auxiliary** and the Past Participle: as,
Je ne l'ai jamais vu. Ils n'ont point dormi.

With a Verb in the *Infinitive*, however, the two negations need not be separated: as,
Vous avez tort de **ne pas** y aller; *or* Vous avez tort de **n'y pas** aller.

§ 248. Ne *may* be used without pas or point with the verbs savoir, pouvoir, oser, **cesser**, especially when these are followed by another verb in the Infinitive: as,
Je ne puis (je ne saurais) me taire. On n'ose l'aborder.
Il ne cesse de gronder. Je ne sais que faire.

Obs. After savoir in the sense of *to have learnt*, pas *must* be used: as,
Il ne sait pas le grec. Ne savez-vous pas nager?

§ 249. **Pas** and **point** *must not be used,* **if the** Verb be already negatived by **rien, personne, plus, aucun, jamais, guère, que, ni,** etc.:

Ne le dites à personne. — *Do not mention it to anybody.*
Ils ne travaillent guère. — *They work but little.*
Il **ne** travaille plus. — *He no longer works.*
(but Il **ne** travaille pas plus que vous. — *He does not work more than you.*)
Il **ne** travaille pas non plus. — *He does not work either.*
Elle n'a que douze ans. — *She is only twelve years old.*
Je n'ai que le plaisir de la lecture. — *I have no other pleasure but reading.*

§ 250. **Ne used in French — contrary to** English construction—:

(a) After words which express *fear* or *anxiety*—
ne expresses the apprehension that something *will* occur,
ne pas „ „ „ „ *will not* occur: as,
Je crains qu'il ne vienne. *I fear he will come.* (Lat. Timeo ne veniat.)
Je crains qu'il ne vienne pas. *I fear he will not come.* (Timeo ut veniat.)
De peur qu'il ne perde son procès. *Lest he should lose his law-suit.*

If, however, the principal clause is *interrogative* or *negative,* or followed by **de** with the *Infinitive* (§ 152) ne is not used: as,

Je ne crains pas qu'il vienne. *I do not fear that he will come.*
Nous craignons de le faire. *We are afraid of doing it.*

§ 251. (b) Words which express *preventing* or *avoiding:* **empêcher, éviter, se garder, prendre garde,** etc. follow the same rule as words of *fearing:* as,

Prenez garde qu'on **ne** vous voie. *Take care lest one should see you;*
but *with the Infinitive:* Prenez garde de tomber. *Mind you don't fall.*

Also after il s'en faut used negatively (generally with peu): as,
Il s'en est peu fallu qu'il n'ait été tué. *He was near being killed.* See also p. 149.

§ 252. (c) Verbs of **doubting** and *denying:* douter, nier, contester, désespérer, etc. used *negatively* generally require **ne** in the dependent clause (Comp. Lat. Non dubito quin ... See also p. 149): as,

Je ne doute pas que cela ne soit ainsi. *I have no doubt it is so.*
but Je doute que cela soit ainsi. *I doubt if it is so.*

Observe also the use **of ne after** (1) *comparatives* employed *affirmatively,* and after autre, autrement, followed by **que,** (2) **à moins** que, depuis que, il y a .. **que,** etc.:

(1) Il est plus habile que vous ne croyez. Il agit autrement **qu'il** ne parle.*
but negatively Il n'est pas plus habile que vous croyez.
Il n'agit pas autrement qu'il parle.

---

* The negation implied is easily found by inverting the sentence: *He does not speak as he acts.*

2) A moins que vous ne lui parliez. *Unless you speak to him.*
Il s'est passé de bien grandes choses depuis que je ne vous ai vu. *Great events have happened since I saw you last.*
Ce n'est pas qu'il ne soit aimable. *Not but that he is amiable.*
Est-il quelqu'un qui ne le sache? *Is there anybody but knows it?*
Qui l'a fait si **ce** n'est lui? *Who but he has done it?*
Il ne viendra **pas** si vous ne l'en priez. *He will not come unless (except) you ask him.*

PREPOSITIONS.

Lists of Prepositions are given in the Accid. § 109.

§ 253. **A** (Lat. ad), *to, at, in, with, from, for*; used of *place, motion, time, manner, destination*; equivalent to the Latin *Dative* case especially, but not unfrequently also to the *Genitive, Accusative* and *Ablative*. See Dat. Case §§ 130. 131. and Synt. of Adj. § 181 (b).

§ 254. **De** (Lat. de), *of, from*; denotes **origin**, *separation, affection, quality, price, quantity, motive, object,* etc. and is equivalent to the **Latin Prepositions de, ex, a,** and to the Latin *Genitive* and *Ablative* cases. See Gen. Case § 132 and Synt. of Adj. § 181. a.

§ 255. **Dans** *and* **en** *compared*:
  dans is used in a *determinate* and *special* sense,
  en, in a *vague* and *general* sense (see also § 165.):—

Hence dans is always followed by an *Article or Pronoun*, whilst **en** is generally used *without* Article or Pronoun (except: en l'honneur, en l'air, en l'absence):

dans	**en**
Place: Être **dans** la prison de Newgate.	Être **en** prison.
Demeurer **dans** la France méridionale.	Demeurer **en** France.
Dans la vie des camps.	Être **en** vie.
Dans la bataille de Waterloo.	Rangé **en** bataille.
Dans notre voyage en Suisse.	Être **en** voyage.
Dans la ville de Paris.	Être (dîner) en ville.
Time: **Dans** la même année.	En 1871.
Dans l'hiver de 1812.	En hiver.
Je finirai ce travail **dans** huit jours .. *Within a week.*	Je finirai ce travail **en** huit jours. *It will take me a week to finish this work.*
Manner: Il est **dans** son secret.	En secret. En repos. En fureur.
Tomber dans la disgrâce du roi.	Être en disgrâce.

Obs. en = *as a*: agir— en roi; se costumer en Turc, etc.

§ 256. Dans *and* à *compared*:

dans implies *inside, within*:
Dans cette ville il y a trois églises.
Il y a cinquante chambres dans l'hôpital.

à, implies *presence at, attendance at:*
Il n'est pas à la ville, il est à la campagne.
Il est mort à l'hôpital.

Obs. The prepositions à, de, en are *generally* (other prepositions *frequently*) repeated **before two** or more words governed by them; à pied et à cheval; de jour et de nuit; **pour vous et pour** lui.

§ 257. Avant and devant:

avant denotes *time, priority, precedence:*
Nous arriverons avant midi.
L'adjectif grand se met avant le substantif.

devant implies *place, presence:*
Devant la maison.
Il jura devant témoins.

Obs. The opposite of avant is après, the opposite of devant is derrière (de retro).

§ 258. Entre (inter) and parmi (per medium):

entre nous, *between ourselves.*
entre eux, *among themselves.*
Rester entre les mains, *in the hands.*

parmi nous, *among us.*
parmi le peuple, *among the people.*

§ 259. Chez, (Lat. casa), *to (in, at) the house of, at home, with, among, at .... 's, to .... 's:*

at the house of, at .... 's (Lat. domi): Il est chez Monsieur B. Vous trouverez cela chez l'horloger. Chacun est maître chez soi. Est-il chez lui?

home (Lat. domum): Il retourne chez lui. Allons-nous-en chacun chez nous.

from .... 's (Lat. domo): Je viens de chez le libraire.

among: Chez nous les modes changent vite. Chez les Grecs. (Apud Graecos).

with: C'est chez lui une habitude.

(*Substantively:* Un chez-soi, *A home:* — Quand j'aurai un chez-moi, j'y recevrai mes amis.)

§ 260. Près de, auprès de, proche (Lat. proximus):

near: près de l'église; près de mourir, *near dying.*
close by, hard by: auprès de l'église.
with: Je suis heureux auprès de vous. Son influence auprès du prince.
to: Ambassadeur auprès de la cour de Suède.
attending on: Il a auprès de lui un excellent médecin.
in comparison with: La terre est un point auprès du reste de l'Univers.
near, hard by: Proche de la ville. C'est ici proche.

PREPOSITIONS.

§ 261. **Sur** (super), **au-dessus de** (Compound of Lat. *sursum*):

sur: *on, upon:* Sur la terre. Sur le Rhin. Sur ma parole. Boulogne-sur-mer.
over, above: L'oiseau plane sur la rivière. Pâlir sur les livres.
concerning: Faire des réflexions sur sa conduite.
towards: Tourner sur la droite. Sur les dix heures.
about: Je n'ai pas assez d'argent sur moi.

au-dessus de: *above:* Dix degrés au-dessus de zéro.
beyond: Cela est au-dessus de nos forces.
upwards: Les enfants de douze ans et au-dessus.

§ 262. The same distinction applies also to **sous** and **au-dessous de**:

under: Sous le ciel. Sous vos auspices. Sous le règne de Henri quatro. Au-dessous de cinquante ans.
by: sous tel nom; *in:* sous ce rapport; sous silence.
on: sous condition.

§ 263. **Envers** (Comp. of Lat. in and versus), **vers** (Lat. versus), **contre** (Lat. contra); *towards, against*:

envers: *towards, to;* (Lat. erga, in) *denotes feeling, disposition, behaviour:*
Charitable envers les malheureux.
Pieux envers Dieu.
(Lat. Pietas justitia adversus deos.)
Traitre envers la patrie.
Redundantly: envers **et contre tous**, *against all comers.*

vers: *towards, to:* (Lat. versus, in) Lever les yeux vers le ciel.
(Lat. Arpinum versus.)
about, towards (Lat. circa, circiter), *denoting time:* Vers les quatre heures, *towards* four *o'clock.* Vers la fin du quatorzième siècle.

contre: *against:* (Lat. contra, in) Marcher contre l'ennemi.
contrary to: Contre l'attente générale. Parler contre sa pensée.
close to: Sa maison est contre la mienne.
in exchange for: Échanger contre de l'or.
In compound words: Contre-amiral, *rear-admiral*.
Contre-maître, *foreman*.

§ 264. De and par, *by*; denoting the agent after *Passive* Verbs:

de denotes a *general indeterminate* relation, and is used especially after verbs, expressing *affection of the mind:*
Il est aimé de tous ses camarades.

Similarly: honoré de; estimé de; haï de; etc.
A few verbs of motion also take de: as,
suivi de, précédé de, accompagné de.

par denotes a *special, determinate* relation, and is used after verbs expressing *physical action:* as, La Gaule fut conquise par les Romains.
Similarly: battu par, persécuté par, écrit par, fondé par, etc.

§ 265. Par, à travers, au travers de, *through, by:*

par (Lat. per) *through, viâ:* Sauter par la fenêtre. Passer par Calais.
by: Voyager par mer. Prendre par les bras. Gravé par Desnoyers. Commencer par ... Finir par ...
out of, for: Par crainte. Par malice. Par cette raison.
into: Diviser par chapitres.
on, in: Par une belle matinée de printemps. Ne sortez pas par cette pluie.

Obs. Trois fois par semaine, *three times a week.* Par ici, *this way;* par là, *that way,* par où? *which way?*

à travers, (Lat. transversus) au travers de; (*the latter more energetic*) *through, across, athwart:* Passer le fil à travers l'aiguille. Se faire jour au travers des ennemis. *To cut one's way through the enemy.*

§ 266. D'après, selon, suivant, *after, according to, conformable to, from:*
d'après: *after, from:* Dessiner d'après nature.
selon: *according to:* Selon la loi. Évangile selon Saint-Matthieu.
Selon moi, *In my opinion.*
idiomatically: c'est selon, *that depends on circumstances.*
suivant: *in pursuance of:* Suivant vos ordres.

CONJUNCTIONS. (See Accid. §§ 110.)

§ 267. Que. Besides the constructions in which que corresponds to the English conjunction *that,* the following deserve notice:

CONJUNCTIONS. 141

§ 268. **Que** *must be* **used** in French — whereas the Conjunction *that* is generally **omitted** in English — after Verbs **of** *saying, hearing, perceiving,* **knowing** (i. e. Verbs which in Lat. take the Acc. and Infinitive): **as**,

Il dit qu'il est malade.   *He says he* **is** *ill.*
Je crois **qu'il a** raison.   *I think he* **is** *right.*
Nous **savons** que cela **est vrai**.   *We know it is* **true**, etc.

§ 269. After the same Verbs the English *Acc. and Inf.* construction **is** generally rendered in French **by** que followed by the *finite* **Verb**: **as**,

Je crois qu'il est **honnête**.   *I believe him to be honest.*

Obs. **Que** may after some Verbs be omitted, **but** then **the Dependent** Verb must be suppressed: as, Je le crois honnête. (See also § 152.)

§ 270. **Que is used emphatically—**

(a) before Adverbs of affirmation and negation: oui, si, non: as,

„Ils ne le feront pas." „Je vous dis que si." „Et moi, je vous dis que non."
„Et qu'en dites-vous, Monsieur?" „Je crois que oui." (See also p. 149.)

(b) to strengthen **the Subject**, when it is placed at the end of the sentence: as,

C'est une chose honteuse que de mentir = Mentir est une chose honteuse.
C'est une belle montre que la vôtre = Votre montre est belle. *Yours is a fine watch.*

(See also § 141, Obs. 1.)

§ 271. **Que is** used instead **of comme, quand, lorsque, parce que, puisque, pendant** que**, tandis** que**, dès** que**, depuis** que**, si**, etc., to avoid the repetition of these conjunctions in the second and consecutive members of one sentence: as,

Lorsqu'on a des dispositions et qu'on (*instead of* **lorsqu'on**) étudie, on **fait** des progrès.

Si les hommes étaient sages, et **qu'ils** (*instead of* **s'ils**) suivissent les lumières de la raison . . .

Obs. 1. **Que** standing thus for **si** requires the Verb in the Subj. Mood, though si itself does not.

Obs. 2. **Que** is also used after an Imperative, **especially** in the familiar style, for the following Conjunctions: **afin** que, de peur que, avant que, jusqu'à ce que, si bien que, sans que, et néanmoins (after a Conditional clause), etc.: as,

Approchez, que (*instead of* afin que) je vous parle.
Attendez que (*instead of* jusqu'à ce que) mon frère revienne.
Je le voudrais, que (*instead of* et néanmoins) je **ne le pourrais pas.** (See § 141 (b) Obs. 1 & p. 150.)

§ 272. Si signifies both *if* and *whether*: **as**,

Si tu vis, je vivrai, si tu meurs, je mourrai.
Je ne sais pas si cela est vrai.

§ 273. Par ce que signifies *by what, from what,*
        Parce que   „   *because:*

Par ce que j'apprends, il est malade.   *From what I learn, he is ill.*

On me loue, **parce que** j'apprends mes leçons.   *I am praised, because I learn my lessons.*

§ 274. Quoi que, *whatever;* quoique, *although:* as,

Quoi que je fasse, je ne réussis pas.   *Whatever I do, I cannot succeed.*
Quoique je fasse mes devoirs.   *Although I do my duty.*

§ 275. **Pendant que,** *while,* implies *simultaneousness;*
        tandis que both *simultaneousness* and *contrast:* as,

Pendant que j'écrivais, il lisait.   *Whilst I was writing, he was reading.*

Il s'amusait, **tandis que** moi, je travaillais.   *He amused himself, whilst I, on the contrary, was working.*

Appendix II. (to Syntax.)

(SUPPLEMENTARY NOTES, OBSERVATIONS, EXCEPTIONS, ALPHABETICAL LISTS.)

THE VERB: CONCORD, GOVERNMENT, MOODS AND TENSES.

(to § 129.) Verbs which in French govern the Accusative, but which in English take a Preposition:

accepter	*to accept of*	résoudre	*to resolve upon*	envoyer chercher	*to send for*
admettre	*to admit of*	attendre	*to wait for*	espérer	*to hope for*
approuver	*to approve of*	chercher	*to look for*	fournir	*to supply with*
considérer	*to look upon*	désirer	*to wish for*	rencontrer	*to meet with.*

(to §§ 130 & 131.) Verbs which govern the Dative (à), but which in English require a different Preposition, or no Preposition:

arracher à	*to snatch from*	se soustraire à	*to escape from*	coopérer à	*to co-operate in*
emprunter à	*to borrow from*	penser à	*to think of*	pourvoir à	*to supply with*
prendre à	*to take from*	songer à		présider à	*to preside at, over*
voler à	*to steal from*	rêver à	} *to dream of*	croire à	*to believe in*

commander à	***to** command*	ordonner à	*to order*	résigner à	*to resign*
conseiller à	***to** advise*	pardonner à	*to forgive*	résister à	*to resist*
défendre à	***to** forbid*	parvenir à	*to attain, reach*	ressembler à	*to resemble*
dire à	***to** tell*	permettre à	*to allow*	subvenir à	*to relieve*
se fier à	***to** trust*	persuader à	*to persuade*	succéder à	*to succeed*
importer à	***to** concern*	plaire à	*to please*	survivre à	*to survive*
nuire à	***to** injure*	remédier à	*to remedy*	toucher à	*to touch*
obéir à	***to** obey*	renoncer à	*to renounce*		

also reprocher quelque chose à quelqu'un, *to reproach some **with** something.*

(to § 132.) Verbs which, differently from English, **govern the Genitive,** i. e. which take the Preposition de:

avoir besoin de	*to need*	s'approcher de	*to approach*	médire de	*to slander*
avoir pitié de	*to pity*	se défier de		se passer de	*to do without*
s'acquitter de	*to discharge*	se méfier de	} *to mistrust*	se souvenir de	*to remember*
s'apercevoir de	*to perceive*	jouir **de**	*to enjoy*	se tromper de	*to mistake*

armer de	***to** **arm** with*	couvrir de	*to cover with*	se mêler de	*to meddle with*
brûler de	***to** burn with*	envelopper de	*to surround with*	munir de	
charger de	} *to load with*	faire présent de	*to present with*	pourvoir de	} *to provide with*
combler de		fourmiller de	*to swarm with*	remplir de	*to fill with*
se contenter de	*to be content with*	honorer de	*to honour with*		

s'affliger **de**	*to be sorry for*	se moquer **de**		dépendre de	*to depend on*
punir de	*to punish for*	rire de	} *to laugh at*	féliciter de	*to congratulate on*
récompenser de	*to reward for*	se réjouir de	*to rejoice at*	vivre **de**	*to live on*
remercier de	*to thank for*	sourire de	*to smile at*	**triompher** de	*to triumph over.*

APPENDIX.

(to §§ 129—133.) Verbs with different Constructions — according to **their** meaning:

	Accusative	Genitive (de)	Dative (à)	
abuser	to deceive	to misuse		
appeler	to call	to appeal against	en...., à, to appeal to	s'...., to be called
applaudir	to praise			s'...., to congratulate one's self
approcher	to approach	to come near to		s'...., to come nearer to
assister	to help		to be present at	(§ 132. b)
changer	to exchange, alter	to change, alter, modify		
commander	to order, be in command of, enjoin		to have authority over	
convenir		to agree, own to	to suit, be convenient	
croire	to believe (a person or thing)		to believe in something	(Obs. croire en Dieu)
demander	to ask for (§ 130)		to ask (from)	
imposer	to enjoin, to tax		to command respect	
insulter	to insult, abuse		to deride, to scorn	
jouer	to play for, stake, dupe	to play (on a musical instrument)	to play (at cards etc.) (§ 131—2)	intrans.: to gamble; so .... de: to trifle with
manquer	to miss	to be deficient, to fail in	to break, neglect	
parer	to adorn, parry		to guard against	
répondre		to be responsible for	to reply to, answer	
rêver (songer)	to dream, fancy	to dream of	to meditate on	
satisfaire	to content		to fulfil (duties to)	
servir	to wait on, serve	to serve as	to be good for	se .... de, to make use of
user	to wear out	to make use of		

(to § 153.) VERBS WHICH REQUIRE THE INFINITIVE WITHOUT PREPOSITION.

affirmer, to affirm,
aimer mieux, to prefer,
aller, to go,
assurer, to assure,
avouer, to confess,
compter, to reckon,
croire, to believe,
courir, to run,
daigner, to deign,
déclarer, to declare,
désirer (de), to wish, to want,
devoir, to be obliged, to have to,
dire (de), to say,
entendre, to hear,

envoyer, to send,
espérer (de), to hope,
faillir (de, à), to fail, to be well [nigh,
falloir, to be necessary.
faire, to make,
il faut, it is necessary,
s'imaginer (de), to fancy,
jurer, to swear,
laisser (de), to let, to **allow**,
nier (de), to deny,
oser, to dare,
paraître, to appear,
penser, to think,
préférer, **to prefer**,

prétendre, to pretend,
pouvoir, to be able,
reconnaître, to acknowledge,
savoir, to know,
sembler, to seem,
sentir, to feel,
souhaiter (de), to wish,
soutenir, to assert,
témoigner, to testify,
valoir mieux (Impers.), to be better,
venir (de, à), to come,
voir, to see,
vouloir, to be willing.

APPENDIX. 145

(to § 155.) VERBS WHICH REQUIRE THE INFINITIVE PRECEDED BY DE.

s'abstenir de, *to abstain from,*
s') accuser, *to accuse,*
achever, *to finish,*
affecter, *to affect,*
s'affliger, *to grieve,*
s'applaudir, *to congratulate one's self,*
avertir, *to inform,*
s'aviser, *to imagine,*
blâmer, *to blame,*
cesser, *to cease,*
se) charger, *to undertake,*
commander, *to command,*
conjurer, *to conjure,*
conseiller, *to advise,*
se contenter, *to be satisfied,*
convenir (à), *to agree; to suit,*
craindre, *to fear,*
dédaigner, *to disdain,*
défendre, *to forbid,*
se défier, *to distrust,*
désespérer, *to despair,*
*désirer, *to wish,*
différer, *to delay,*

* dire, **to tell,**
dispenser, *to dispense,*
dissuader, *to dissuade,*
écrire, *to write,*
empêcher, *to prevent,*
entreprendre, *to undertake,*
s'étonner, *to wonder,*
essayer, **to try,**
éviter, *to avoid,*
s'excuser, *to apologize,*
* faillir (à), *to be well-nigh,*
feindre, *to feign,*
féliciter, *to congratulate,*
se flatter, *to flatter one's self,*
(se) hâter, *to hasten,*
*jurer, *to swear,*
manquer, *to neglect,*
menacer, *to threaten,*
mériter, *to deserve,*
négliger, *to neglect,*
*nier, *to deny,*
offrir, *to offer,*
omettre, *to omit,*
ordonner, *to order,*
oublier, *to forget,*

(se) permettre, *to permit,*
(se) persuader, *to persuade,*
se plaindre, *to complain,*
prescrire, *to prescribe,*
presser, *to urge,*
prier, **to beg,**
promettre, *to promise,*
(se) proposer, *to propose,*
se rappeler, *to remember,*
recommander, *to recommend,*
refuser, *to refuse,*
regretter, *to regret,*
se réjouir, *to rejoice,*
remercier, *to thank,*
résoudre, *to resolve,*
risquer, *to risk,*
sommer, *to summon,*
*souhaiter, *to wish,*
soupçonner, *to suspect,*
se souvenir, *to remember,*
supplier, *to entreat,*
tâcher, tenter, *to attempt,*
trembler, *to tremble,*
se vanter, *to boast.*

Obs. Those marked * are also used without **de.**

(to § 156.) VERBS WHICH REQUIRE THE INFINITIVE PRECEDED BY THE PREPOSITION À.

s'abaisser, *to lower one's self,*
aboutir, *to lead to, to end in,*
s'accoutumer, *to accustom,*
aider, *to assist,*
*aimer, *to like,*
s'amuser, *to amuse one's self,*
s'appliquer, *to apply, to devote one's self to,*
apprendre, { *to learn, to teach,*
aspirer, *to aspire,*
s'attacher, **to stick to,**
s'attendre, *to expect,*
autoriser, *to authorise,*
se borner, *to limit one's self,*
chercher, **to endeavour,**
concourir, **to co-operate,**
condamner, **to condemn,**
consister, **to consist in,**
consentir, **to consent,**
conspirer, **to concur,** *to tend,*

contribuer, *to contribute,*
(se) décider, *to decide,*
déterminer, *to determine,*
dévouer, *to devote,*
(se) disposer, { *to dispose, to prepare,*
(s') employer, *to employ, to exert one's self,*
(s') encourager, *to encourage,*
(s') engager (de), *to engage,*
enseigner, *to teach,*
exercer, *to exert one's self,*
(s') exposer, *to expose one's self,*
(s') habituer, *to accustom,*
hésiter, **to hesitate,**
inviter, **to invite,**
se mettre, *to begin,*
montrer, *to show,*
s'obstiner, } *to persist in,*
s'opiniâtrer, }
parvenir, *to succeed in,*

*penser (de), *to think of,*
persister, *to persist in,*
se plaire, *to be pleased,*
(se) préparer, *to prepare,*
prendre plaisir, **to delight in,**
réduire, *to reduce,*
renoncer, *to renounce,*
*répugner, *to feel repugnance,*
se résigner, *to resign,*
se résoudre, *to resolve,*
réussir, *to succeed in,*
*servir (de), *to serve,*
songer, *to think of,*
suffire, *to suffice,*
*tarder (de), *to delay,*
travailler, *to work,*
viser, *to aim,*
(se) vouer, *to devote.*

Obs. For those marked *, see the preceding lists.

(to § 159.) **Obs.** There are some Verbs, **the Present Participle of** which differs in spelling from the Adjective derived from them:

différant, *differing,* — différent, *different,* | intriguant, *intriguing,* — intrigant, *meddling,*
excellant, *excelling,* — excellent, *excellent,* | négligeant, *neglecting,* — négligent, *careless,*
fatiguant, *tiring,* — fatigant, *tiresome.* | sachant, *knowing,* — savant, *learned,* etc.

Eugène, French Grammar. 10

APPENDIX.

(to § 165.) THE ARTICLE.

The Definite Article is also used in *French*, but *not in English*—

(d) before the Names of some of the most renowned Italian (and **a few** French) Artists and Poets, (analogous to Italian): as,

Le Corrége; le Titien; les Carrache; le Tasse; l'Arioste; le Poussin, etc.

(e) after **tous**, *all*, followed by a Substantive or Numeral; also after **dont**, *whose*, between two nouns:

Tous les hommes. Tous les **deux**.

L'homme dont vous connaissez la probité.

(f) in many *Idiomatic Expressions:*

À la maison; à la hâte; à la vérité (en vérité); c'est aujourd'hui la foire. Soyez le bienvenu; il est arrivé le premier; je n'ai pas le temps; il n'a pas le sou; garder le silence; faire (demander) l'aumône; sentir le brûlé; savoir le français, etc.

(h) before most names of *Holydays:* — La Saint-Jean; la Toussaint; la Chandeleur.

The Definite Article is omitted in *Proverbs, Enumerations*, for the sake of brevity: as, Contentement passe richesse. Tombeaux, trônes, palais, tout périt, tout s'écroule.

(to § 168.) The Indefinite Article **is also omitted in French**

(a) before the Collective Nouns quantité, nombre, force (*in sense of many*):

Nombre de fois: — Nombre d'historiens l'ont ainsi raconté.

also before **cent and mille**: — Cent francs. Mille écus.

(b) in *Titles of Books*: — Grammaire latine; Histoire de France.

(c) **in** many *Idioms* and *Proverbs:*

Prêter serment. *To take an oath.* Faire signe, présent. *To make a sign, a present.* Avoir envie. *To have a mind.* Ne dire (souffler) mot. *Not to say a word.* Rendre visite. *To pay a visit.* Mettre fin à .. *To put a stop to ..* etc.

Obs. The Indef. Art. is placed *before the Adjective* in French, but *after it* in English with—

tel, *such*; **si**, *so:* — Un **tel** homme, *Such a man.* Un si beau spectacle, *So beautiful a sight.*
demi, *half;* **quart**, *quarter:* — une demi-heure. *Half an hour.*
trop, *too much:* — Vous avez un trop grand feu. *You have too great a fire.*

(to § 170.) Obs. In like manner **de** is used instead of du, des, etc.:

after **ne ... pas**, **ne ... point**, when the Verb itself and not another member of the sentence is negatived: as,

Je ne vous ferai **pas de reproches.** *I shall not make you any reproaches,*

but Je ne vous ferai **pas des reproches** frivoles. *I shall make you reproaches, but not frivolous ones.*

The Partitive Article is generally omitted

(a) after **ni ... ni**; **soit ... soit**; as,

Ni conseils, ni prières, **ni menaces** n'ont pu le faire changer **d'avis.**

(b) after the Prepositions avec, par, pour, sans, sur, etc., taken in an indeterminate sense, and forming an *Adverbial Expression* with the following Noun: as,

Attaquer avec courage, *i. e. Courageously;* but Attaquer avec de la cavalerie. Jean sans peur. — Par amitié. — Massacrer sans pitié, (*pitilessly*).

APPENDIX.

THE ADJECTIVE.

(to § 178.) Obs. An Adjective agrees with the nearest Substantive only:

(a) when the Substantives are Synonymous or form a kind of gradation:
 Il a une aménité, une douceur enchanteresse.

(b) when the **Substantives are connected** by ou, or **ni .. ni**, so that one **excludes** the other:
 Servez-vous d'une plume ou d'un crayon bien taillé.

(to § 180.) Obs. The Adj. feu, *late*, agrees only when *preceded* by a Def. Article:
 La feue reine. *but* Feu la reine. *The late queen.*

On excepté, supposé, ci-inclus, ci-joint, etc. see § 164, Obs. 1, 2.
Obs. Tant que also means *as long as:* — Tant que je vivrai. *As long as I live.*

(to § 184.) When only two Persons or Things are compared, the Superiative is **used** in French, instead of the English comparative:
 De ces deux poires, celle-ci est la plus **douce.** *Of these two pears this is the sweeter one.*

THE PRONOUNS.

(to § 191.) Obs. The Objective **Personal** Pronoun must be repeated

(a) if used before Verbs in a simple Tense; (b) if used in a different case (**Acc.** and Dat.): as,
 Il les loue **et** les admire. Il m'a vu (Acc.) et m'a parlé (Dat.).

(to § 197.) Obs. In like manner ce l'est, **ce** les sont, etc., stand for **c'est lui, ce sont** eux, etc., which **latter** are only used with reference to Persons:
 Est-ce là **votre livre?** Oui, ce l'est. *Is that your book? Yes, it is.*
 Sont-ce là **vos habits?** Oui, ce les sont. *Are those your clothes? Yes, they are.*

(Ces réponses sont grammaticalement correctes, mais on évite de les employer, parce qu'elles ont quelque chose d'affecté, de bizarre; on dit simplement: oui, ou, oui, ce sont mes livres. Académie).

Obs. If the Disjunctive Pronoun depends on other Prepositions than de or à, then **the** Adverbs corresponding to those Prepositions are used: as,
 dessous instead of sous lui, sous elle, sous eux, etc.
 dessus instead of sur lui, sur elle, sur eux, etc.: —
  Ce livre n'est pas **sur** la table, il est dessous. (*under it; underneath.*)

In like manner are used dehors, dedans, à côté, derrière; etc.
(Compare the German: darunter, draussen, darinnen.)
Disjunctive **Personal** Pronouns are, however, frequently **used** with reference to things, especially if there **is no** corresponding Adverb: as,
 J'aime la vérité au point que je sacrifierais tout pour elle.

(to § 200.) Obs. The Possessive Adjective must be repeated:

(a) before two or more Substantives in the same sentence:
 Ma mère et mon frère. Ses amis et ses connaissances.

(b) before two or more Adjectives qualifying different Objects of the same species:
 Je lui ai montré mes beaux et mes vilains habits. *I showed him both my fine and my ugly clothes.*

But they are not repeated if the Adjectives refer to the same **Object:**
>Je lui ai montré mes beaux et riches habits.

Obs. A French Possessive Adjective before a Substantive **in the Plural**, is frequently rendered by the Engl. Possessive Pronoun:
>Une de mes amis. *A friend of mine.*
>Votre langue. *That tongue of yours.*

(to § 201.) Obs. 1. The Engl. Possessive Adjective is generally rendered in French by **de** after the Verbs changer, redoubler: as,
>Nous redoublons d'efforts. *We redouble our efforts.*
>Il a changé d'état. *He has changed his profession.*

Obs. 2. The English *my own, thy own,* etc., is rendered in French either by le mien propre, le tien propre, etc., or simply by le mien, le tien, etc.
>Il regardait leur maison comme la sienne (propre).

Or also by the Dative of the Disjunctive Pronoun: as,
>**Il a un cheval à lui.** *He has a horse of his own.*

(to § 204.) **Obs. Cela (or ça) with reference to Persons has a** familiar *or* contemptuous meaning: as,
>Cela danse, cela rit, etc. *They dance, they laugh,* etc.

The contracted form ça is only used in the familiar style: as,
>C'est ça! *That is it.* Comment ça va-t-il? *How are you?*

(to § 205.) Obs. Ce sometimes occurs before the Verbs devoir, pouvoir, sembler, dire: as,
>Ce doit être vrai. *It must be true.* Ce me semble. *Methinks.*
>Ce dit-il. *Quoth he!* Voyons ce que ce peut être.

(to § 211.) Obs. Qui is often used *absolutely* instead of celui qui, quiconque: as,
>Aimez qui vous aime. *Love him who loves you.*
>Qui ne fait pas des heureux, n'est pas digne de l'être.
>*He who (whoever) does not make other people happy is not worthy of being so himself.*

(to § 216.) Observe also the following Idiomatic uses of quoi:
>Il n'a pas de quoi vivre. *He has not enough to live upon.*
>Donnez-moi de quoi écrire. *Give me writing materials.*
>Il n'y a pas de quoi. *It is not worth while.*

(to § 217.) Obs. Qui instead of ce qui is used in the following Expressions:
>**Qui pis est.** *What is worse.* — Voilà qui est fait. *That is done.*

THE ADVERB.

(to § 226.) Obs. **1.** Ne is suppressed after Verbs of *doubting* and *forbidding* and after the Preposition sans, because the negation is implied in the very meaning of these words: as,
>Je doute que personne soit venu.
>Il m'a défendu de rien dire. Sans rien faire.

Obs. 2. When qualified by an Adjective, these Indefinite Pronouns take the Preposition de: — Rien de plus beau.

(to § 228.) Obs. Autre is also used emphatically: as,
>Nous autres Français. *We French people.*

APPENDIX. 149

(to § 230.) **Obs.** Tout, though used adverbially in the sense of quite, agrees in Gender and Number with a following feminine Adjective beginning with a consonant (evidently for the sake of euphony): as,

Ma sœur est **toute triste**; *but:* Ma sœur est **tout** affectionnée.

(to § 233.) **Obs.** When used in a negative sentence, **qui que ce soit** and **quoi que ce soit**, are equivalent to personne and rien respectively; as,

N'en dites mot à qui que ce soit. *Do not mention it to anybody.*
Il ne se soucie de quoi que ce soit. *He does not care for anything.*

(to § 234.) **Obs.** Quelque is also used as an Adverb in the sense of *about:*

Il y a quelque cinquante ans. *About fifty years ago.*

(to § 239.) **Obs. 1.** The Adverbs bien, mieux, mal, are employed *adjectively* after the Verb être and other Verbs which denote a state or mode of *existence:* devenir, rester, paraître, etc., (Verbs which take the Nomin. in Latin): as,

Prenez cette place, **vous y serez bien (mieux)**. *Take this seat, you will be (more) comfortable there.*

Obs. 2. A few *Adverbs* derived from Adjectives take the Preposition required by the corresponding Adjective: — Conformément à la loi.

Indépendamment de ces deux variétés.

(to § 240.) **Obs.** *Than,* between two terms of comparison is rendered by

plus que, before a Noun used *Subjectively*, plus de, before a Noun used *Objectively:* as,

Ce cheval peut traîner **plus que** quatre mulets.
Ce cheval peut traîner plus **de** vingt quintaux.

Observe also the following uses of plus and moins:

Plus … plus: *the more … the more:* — Plus je le regarde, plus je l'admire.
Plus … *besides, moreover:* — Une table, **plus** six chaises et un fauteuil.
Ni … non plus, *nor .. either:* — Ni moi non plus. *Nor I either.*

Cela coûte au moins huit francs. *That costs at least eight francs.*
J'aurai du moins l'honneur de l'avoir entrepris. *I shall have, at any rate, the honour of undertaking it.*

(to § 251.) After empêcher used *negatively* or *interrogatively*, the use of ne is optional: as,

Je n'empêche pas qu'il sorte (*or*, qu'il **ne sorte**.)

(to § 252.) Compare also—

Doutez-vous que cela soit? *You do not doubt of it, do you?*
Doutez-vous que cela ne soit? *You do doubt of it, do you not?*

The best authorities, however differ on the use or omission of ne after these Verbs used *interrogatively*.

THE CONJUNCTIONS.

(to § 270.) **Obs. 1.** Que is also used in some Adverbial Expressions: as, voici que, voilà que, heureusement que, malheureusement que, etc.

Comme nous étions à la promenade, **voilà qu'une** ondée vint à tomber. *Whilst we were walking all at once there came on a shower.*

Obs. 2. Que is used in the sense of *when,* if the principal clause begins with à peine, pas plutôt, and adverbial Expressions of time: as,

A peine fut-il arrivé qu'il repartit.
Un matin que je regardais par la fenêtre, j'entendis des cris perçants.

11

Obs. 3. Que si (Lat. quodsi) is equivalent to si cependant, *but if: as,*
Que si vous alléguez telle raison, je répondrai **que** ...

(to § 272.) Obs. 1. *Even if* **is** generally rendered by quand même or lors **même que:**
Quand même cela serait vrai. *Even if that were true.*

Obs. 2. Si ce n'est **is** equivalent to *except. only. were it not, but for:*
Il vous ressemble, si ce n'est qu'il est plus petit. *(except that.)*
Si ce n'était la crainte de vous déplaire. *Were it not for fear of displeasing you.*

———

INDEX.

NB. *The numbers indicate the sections; those in brackets are contained in the Appendix.*

à, elided, 7.
à, after Adj. 181 b, after Verbs 130. 131, 253 (p. 143. 4 App.).
about to, how rendered 92.
absoudre, conj. 99 B.
abstract nouns, with article 165 a.
abuser, conj. (p. 144).
accents 5.
accusative, after transit. verbs 129, absolute 129 Obs., double 129 b, cognate 129 Obs., of respect 129, verbs with acc. in Fr. but not in English (p. 143), of pers. pron. 189, with infinitive 269.
acquérir 93 C.
adjectives, fem. of, 27—37, plural of, 38, comparison of, 39—41. 182, possessive 53, 200. 3, demonstrative 56. 57, used adverbially 106, with *à* 130 b, used partitively 133 d, verbal 159, position of, 171—176, agreement of, 177—9 (p. 146), government of, 181.
adverbs, formation of, 104—5, compared 107, classified 108, of negation 108 IV, 243—52, (p. 148), of quantity 107 b, 239, of place 238.
afin de and *afin que* 141. 1, 152.
age, how expressed 186.
agent, how expressed 132 d.
aïeul, plural of, 21.
aimer, conj. 80. 84.
ainsi, with inversion 122 b.
aller, conj. 92, with infinit. 153. 4.
alphabet 1.
amour, gender of, 23. 1.
anomalous Verbs 91—99.
antérieur, see Past Anterior.
any, how rendered 11, 193 b, anything 244 Obs.
apostrophe 7.
appeler, construction of, (p. 144).
applaudir,   "   "
approcher,   "   "
après and *après que* 152.
article definite, decl. 9, contracted 10, derivation 12 Obs., used in French and not in English 165 a (p. 146), for the Indef. art. 166, for English Possess. Pron. 166 Obs., omitted 167, repeated 169, invariable 184 Obs. 2.

article indefinite, decl. 12, omitted in Fr. but not in English 168 (p. 146), placed before adjectives (p. 146).
article partitive, decl. 11. 14, omitted 15. 133 d, 170 (p. 146).
arts, gender of names of, 112 B.
as, how translated 182.
asking, verbs of, 130 a.
assaillir, conj. 94.
asseoir,   -   97.
asservir,   -   93 A.
asses 170 b.
assister, constr. (p. 144).
astonishment, how rendered 145.
astreindre, conj. 99 A.
atteindre,   -   "
attendu, agreement of, 164 b, Obs. 1.
au, aux 10. 11.
aucun 227.
au-dessous de and *sous* 262.
au-dessus de and *sur* 261.
auprès de and *près de* 260.
aussi, inversion after, 122 a.
aussi and *si*, compared 182.
autant and *tant*, compared 182.
autre 228, followed by *ne* 252, emphatic (p. 143)
autrui 229.
avant and *devant* 257, *avant de* and *avant que* 152.
avoir, conj. 72. 74—75.

Battre, conj. 99 D Obs.
beau, bel, fem. of, 37, *il fait beau* 89.
beaucoup, compared 107, with *de* 170 b, 239.
before, how rendered 152, 257.
bénin, feminine of, 39.
béni and *bénit* 84, 7.
bétail, plural of, 20.
bien, compared 107, for beaucoup 239, used adjectively (p. 149).
blâmer, with Genit. 132 c.
boire, conj. 98 c.
bon, compared 41.
bouillir, conj. 93 a.
braire,   -   103.
brave 176.

152 INDEX.

bref, feminine of, **33**.
bruire, conj. 103.
by, how rendered 131 b. c, **132 d, 262—5**.

Ça, contracted from *cela* (p. 148).
cause, how rendered 132 c, 153 b.
ce 56, 205, emphatic 206, before devoir (p. 148).
c'est and *il est*, distinguished 207, with article 168 c.
ce l'est (p. 147).
ce n'est pas que 252. 2.
ce qui, decl. 64. 3, construction of, **217**.
ceci and *cela* 58, 204.
cedilla, 7 II.
ceindre, conj. 99 a.
cela and *ceci* 58, 204.
celui and *celui-ci*, distinguished **59—61**.
celui = he 187 Obs.
cent 42.
chacun 68, **232**.
changer, construction of, 132 a (p. 144. 148).
chaque 68, **231**.
chaud, constr. with *faire* 89, with *avoir* 130 c.
cher, place **of, 175**.
chez 259.
choir 102.
chose, gender of, 23. 6.
-ci, demonstr. suffix 57.
ci-inclus and *ci-joint*, agreement of, 164 h, Obs. 2.
ciel, *cieux* 21.
ci-inclus, agreement of, 164 Obs.
ci-joint, - -
circumflex 6 III.
clore, conj. 106.
cognate acc. 129 Obs.
combien and *comment* 121.
commander, **constr.** of, 130 b (p. **144**).
comme and *comment* 242.
commun, place of, 176.
comparative of equality 182.
comparison of Adjectives 39—41.
 — of adverbs 106.
compound nouns, plural of, 22.
conclure, conj. 98 C.
concord, rules of, 125—128.
condition, with subjunct. 148. 2.
conditional, formation of, 78, 91, in principal clauses 141 a, in dependent clauses, after *quand même*, *si* 141 b, Obs.
conduire, conj. 98 a.
confire, - **98 B**.
conjunctions, classified 110, with Subj. or Indicat. 148 Obs., Syntax of 267—275 (p.149).
conjunctive pronouns 49. 50. 51, 187—195.
connaître, conj. 99 C.
consonants 2.
construire, conj. 98 a.
construction of sentences 118—124.
contingency, with subjunctive 148. 2.
contraction of Definite Art. 10.
contraindre, **99** a.
contre, envers, **263**.

contrevenir, with *avoir* 86.
convenir, constr. of, (p. 144).
coudre, conj. 99 B.
countries, art. with **names of,** 165 b, gender of, 112 B.
couple, gender of, **23. 7**.
courir, conj. 93 B.
couvrir, - 94 a.
craindre, conj. 99 a, constr. 145 c, with *ne* 253.
croire, conj. 98 C, constr. of, 144 Obs. 2 (p. 144).
croître, - 99 C.
cru, agreement of, 164 g.
cueillir, conj. 94 B.
cuire, - 98 A.

Dans and *à* 256; *dans* and *en* 255.
d'après, selon, suivant 266.
dative, before the accus. 119 Obs., of remoter object, with verbs of taking, asking, teaching 130 a, with *faire* 130 Obs., of advantage 130 b, of place 130 c, of time 131 a, of manner, instrument 131 b, of price, measure 131 c, of possessor 131 d, ethic 131 Obs., after Adjectives 131 b, of pers. pron. 189, List of Verbs governing the Dat. (p. 143.)
davantage and *plus que* 240.
de, instead of Part. art. 170 (p. 146. 148) = by how much 184. 185, see also Genitive 132-4. 254, compared with *par* 264.
de ce que, after Verbs of joy, etc. **145** Obs.
de peur que ... **ne 250**.
déchoir 97.
dedans for *dans lui* (p. 147).
défini, see Preterite.
dehors for *hors lui* (p. 147).
demander, constr. of, 130 a (p. 144).
demi, agreement of, 180, article with **(p. 146)**.
demonstrative adjectives 56. 57, 208.
 — pronouns 58—61, 204—207.
dentals 3, denying, verbs of, with *ne* 252.
depuis, tense used with, 134 Exc.
depuis que, followed by *ne* 252.
dernier, place of, 176.
dessous for *sous lui* (p. 147).
dessus - *sur lui* (p. 147).
devant and *avant* 257.
devoir, conj. 82 Obs. **2**.
diaeresis 7 II.
différent, place **of, 175**.
dimensions 185.
diphthongs 4.
dire, conj. 98 B, **constr.** 152—3 (p. 144).
disjunctive pers. pronouns, for Conjunctive 193.
distraire, conj. 98 B.
divers, place of, 175.
dormir, conj. 93 a.
dont, 162, 213—215 (p. 146).
douter, with subjunct. 144, with *ne* 252 (p. 149).
doux, fem. of, 34.
du 10, 11, agreement of, 164 g.
duquel for *dont* 215.
duty, how rendered 130 b Obs.

E, elided **7**.
écrire, conj. 98 A.
échoir, - 102.
éclore, - 103.
either, how rendered (p. 149).
élire, conj. 98 C.
elision 7.
elle 196.
empêcher, with *ne* 251, constr. of, (p. 149).
en, after adjectives 181 d, position of, 188—190, use of, 193, idiomatic 195, for disj. pers. pron. 197, for possess. pron. 202, 203.
en (prepos.) and *dans* 255, with names of countries 130 c.
encore, inversion after, 122 a.
enfant, gender of, 238.
enfreindre, conj. 99 A.
enseigner, constr. of, 130 a.
entendre, constr. 153. 5 (p. 144).
entre and *parmi*, 258.
envers, *vers* and *contre* 263, after Adjectives 181 c.
envoyer, conj. 92.
est-ce que 74. 79, 121 Obs.
estimation, dative after verbs of, **131** c.
éteindre, conj. 99 A.
être, conj. 73—76, intrans. verbs with *être* 86. 87, agreement of past part. with, 161.
-eur, feminine of adjectives in, 36.
eux 196.
éviter, with *ne* 251.
excepté, agreement of, 164 Obs.
exclusiveness, subjunct. after terms of, 149. 3.
expectation, - - - 149. 1.

Facile, with *à* or *de*, 156 b.
de façon à or *que* 141, 152.
faillir, conj. 101, constr. of (p. 144).
faire, conj. 98 I. B, constr. of, 130 a, with infinitive 154, *il fait chaud, froid*, etc. 89.
fait, agreement of, 164 e.
falloir, conj. 96, impersonal 90.
faux, fem. of, 34, place of, 175.
favori, fem. of, 34.
fearing, constr. of Verbs of, 145, with *ne* 250 (p. 148).
feeling, verbs of, with genit. **132** f.
feindre, conj. 99 a.
férir, conj. 101.
feu, late, agreement of, **147**.
finir, conj. 81.
fleurir, conj. 84. 8.
flowers, gender of names of, **112** B.
fois = times 48.
foudre, gender of, 23. 8.
fou, fol, fem. of, 37.
franc, franche, franque **35**.
frais, fem. of, 33 c.
frire, conj. 103.
froid, with *avoir* 89.
fuir, conj. 93 B.
future, formation of, 78 a, 9₁, use of, 140.

Eugène, French Grammar.

Garde, plur. of compounds of, **22** Obs. **2**.
se garder, with *ne* 251.
genders, names of both, **23**, determined by derivation 114, by meaning 113, by termination 112.
genitive, after adjectives 181 a, of accusation 132 i, of agent 132 d, appositive 133 b, of cause 132 c, of feeling 132 f, of fulness **132** g, of manner, material 132 e, of origin **132** b, of perception, remembrance 132 h, partitive 133 d, possessive 133 a, of quality 133 c, of separation 132 a, list of verbs governing the g. (p. 143. 144).
gens, gender of, **23**.
gentilhomme, plural of, **22** a.
-ger, verbs in, 84 *β* **1**.
gésir, conj. 101.
gerundive 156 b, 157.
government of Verbs 120—133 (p. 143—145).
grand, place of, 173, 176.
guère ... *ne* 249.
gutturals **3**.

Haïr, conj. 84. **6**.
haut, hauteur, constr. of, 185.
he who, how rendered 187 Obs.
hearing, verbs of, 153. 5.
holydays, gender of names of, **112** B.
honnête, place of, 175.
how, how rendered 242.
hyphen 7 IV.

Il and *lui* 49 a. b.
il est and *c'est*, distinguished 207.
il y a 90, with present tense 134.
imperative, formation of, 79 d, with pronouns 188 Exc.
imperfect indicative, formation of, 78 b, distinguished from Preterite 135, to express simultaneous actions 136 a, expressing condition 136 b, after *si*, if 141 b, Obs.
imperfect subjunctive, formation of, 79 e, sequence of, 151.
impersonal Verbs, conj. 89—90, Subjunctive or Indicative with, 146—7, Infinitive with, 155 c.
imposer, constr. of, (p. 144).
indéfini, see past indefinite.
indefinite pronouns 69—71, 225—237, after *de ce que* 145 Obs., after impers. Verbs 147, for the English Infinitive 269.
indicative, tenses of, 134—141.
infinitive, tenses derived from, 78 a, after Conjunctions 110 d, 152, instead of Indicat. or Subjunctive 152, with *à* 156 (p. 145), with *de* 155 (p. 145), elliptically 156 Obs., with *faire* 154, instead of the English Pres. Part. 159 e.
insulter, constr. of (p. 144).
instrument, how expressed 131 b, 132 i.

interjections 111.
interrogative conjugation 74, 76, 84 a.
     adjectives and pronouns 65—67, 219—224.
     - construction 187 a.
inversions 120—123, 187.
intransitive verbs, conj. 86 c.
intensity, degrees of, 183.

Jamais 249, without *ne*, 244 Obs.
jeter, conj. 84 β 3.
joindre, conj. 99 a.
jouer, constr. with à 131 b, with *de* 132 d (p. 144).
jouir, - *de* (p. 143).
jusqu'à ce que, 148. 1.

-là, demonstr. **suffix 57**.
labials, 3.
le, la, les, neutral pronouns 192.
lequel, decl. of, 63, *lequel?* 66, for *qui* 212.
liquids 3.
lire, 98 C.
long, fem. of, 30. 3.
lors même que (p. 149).
lorsque, elision of *e* in, 7 I.
lui, disjunct. pron. 49 b, 196. 197.
lui, dat. of conjunct. pron. 50, 187—189, 191.
luire, conj. 98 A.
l'un ... l'autre, 228 Obs.

Mal, **compared** 107, used **adjectively** (p. 149).
malin, **fem.** of, 34.
manger, conj. 84 β 1.
de manière à or *que*, 152.
manquer, constr. of (p. 144).
many, how rendered 170 b.
maudire, conj. 98 B.
mauvais, compared 41, place **of, 173**.
measure, with dative 131 c.
méchant, place of, 176.
même 58, 208.
mener, conj. 84 β 4.
mentir, - 93 A.
mettre, - 99 D.
mieux, used adjectively (p. 149).
mil, mille, million 42, Obs. 3. 4.
mine, how rendered 201.
moi, disjunctive pron. 49 b, 196, *à moi* 201.
  - dat. of conj. pron. 188 Exc.
moi-même **52** Obs.
moins ... moins 184.
au moins, inversion after, 122.
à moins de, infinitive after, 152.
du moins and *au moins* (p. 149).
months, gender of names of, 112 A, days of, **44.**
more, how rendered 40. 41, 107, 240.
mou, mol, fem. of, 37.
motion, how expressed 130 c.
motive, - - 132 c.
moudre, **conj. 99 B.**

mourir, conj. **93 C.**
mouvoir, - **95.**
mutes 3.

Naître, conj. 99 C.
ne 108 IV, after comparatives 183, 252, after *à moins que, depuis que* 252, suppressed (p. 148), used with verbs only 244, after verbs of denying, doubting 252, after verbs of fearing 250, after verbs of preventing 252.
nearness, how expressed 132 b.
necessity, verbs of, with Subjunct. 143 **a, 146.**
negations 149, 244—52.
ne pas and *ne point* 245, 257, followed by *de* (p. 146).
ne que 249.
neuter verbs, see intransitive verbs.
ni ... non plus (p. 149).
nier, constr. of, 252.
nouns, see substantives.
nous, disjunct. pron. **49 b**, 196.
nouveau, nouvel, fem. **of, 37, place of**, 176.
nu, agreement of, **180.**
nuire, conj. 98 A.
nul ... ne, 226.
numerals 42—48, **cardinals used** for English ordinals 44.

Obedience, verbs **of, 130 b.**
occupation, how **rendered 132 b.**
œil, plural of, 21.
œuvre, gender **of, 23. 4.**
offrir, conj. 94 A.
oindre, - 103.
on, l'on, 237.
onze, onzième, vowel not elided before, 42.
optative clauses, construction of, 122 c.
où, inversion after 121, relat. pron. 218.
ouïr, conj. 101.
ouvrir 94 A.
own, how rendered 131 d (p. 148).

Paître, conj. 99 C.
pâques, gender of 23. **3.**
par and *de* 264, *par* **and à** *travers* 265.
paraître, conj. 99 C.
parce que and *par ce que* 273.
pardonner, with **dative** 130 b.
parenthetical clauses 122 c.
parer, constr. **of** (p. 144).
parfait du Subj., sequence of, **151.**
parmi and *entre* 258.
partir, conj. 93 A.
partitive article 11, 14, 15, 133 d, 170 (p. 146).
participle, used partitively 133 d.
participle past 79 c, 91, agreement of, 160-164.
    - present 78 b, 91, distinguished from Verbal Adjective 157, declinable 159 II, indeclinable **159 I**, spelt differently from the corresponding Adjective (p. 144).
pas, for *point* 246, omitted 248. 249.

INDEX. 155

pas un 246.
passive voice, conj. 85 B, rendered by *'on'* 237 Obs. 1.
past anterior, formation of, 79 c, use of, 139.
— indefinite 137.
pauvre, place of, 175.
pécheur, fem. of, 25 Obs.
à peine, inversion after, 122 (a).
pendant que and *tandis que* 275.
peindre, conj. 99 A.
penser à 130 c.
perception, verbs of, with genitive 130 h.
periphrastic construction 124.
— interrogation 74, 76.
personal pronouns, see pronouns.
personne, gender of, 235, with *'ne'* 226, 249.
petit, compared 41, place of, 175.
peu, compared 107.
de peur que ... ne 250, *de peur de*, with infinitive 152.
peut-être, with inversion 122 a.
place, how rendered 130 c.
plaire, conj. 98 C, with dative 130 b.
plaisant, place of, 175.
pleonastic use of *'le'* 192
pleuvoir, conj. 95.
la plupart, concord of, 128.
pluperfect, formation of, 79 c, use of, 138, 139 Obs.
pluperfect subjunctive, for conditional past 141 a, **Obs**.
plural, formation of, 16—21, of Adjectives 38, of Substantives 116—117.
plus 40, *plus .. plus* 184 (p. 149), *plus que* and *davantage* 240, *plus que* and *plus de* (p. 149), *plus ... ne* 249, *plus tôt* and *plutôt* 241.
poindre, conj. 103.
point 244, *point* and *pas* 246.
possessive adjectives 54, 200, 166 Obs., repeated (p. 147).
possessive pronouns, see pronouns.
pour, **with infinitive**, and *pour que*, **with subj.** 152.
pourvoir, conj. 97.
pourvu que, with **subjunct. 141. 2.**
pouvoir, conj. 95.
preference, verbs of, with dative 130 b.
prendre, conj. 99 D, constr. of, 130 a.
prendre garde with *ne* 251.
prepositions, contracted with article 10, classified 109, **use of,** 253—266, infinitive with, 155—156.
près de, auprès de 260.
presque, elision of *e* in, 7 I.
present indicative 79 d, for **the English perfect** 134 Exc., English **pres.** for **French future** 140 Exc.
present subjunctive, formation of, 79 d, Sequence of, 151.

preterite (défini), compared with Imperfect 135.
prévaloir, conj. 96.
prévoir, conj. 97.
price, accusat. of, 129 Obs., 166 a.
privation, how constr. 132 a.
pronouns demonstrative 56-61, 204-208 (p. 148).
— indefinite 68—71, 225—237.
— interrogative 65. 66, 219—224.
— personal 49—52, 187—199 (p. 147).
— possessive 53 — 55, 166, 200 — 203 (p. 147—8).
— reflective 51.
— relative 62—64, 209—218 (p. 148)
proche 260.
proper nouns, plural of, 21 Obs. 1.
propre, place of, 175.
proverbs, article omitted in, (p. 146).
puisque, elision of *e* in, 7 I.

Quand, constr. of, 121, *quand même* (p. 150).
quatre-vingts, *s* dropped in, 42. 2.
que, interrog. pron. 221.
que, conjunction, emphatic 270, for other conjunctions 271, never omitted in French 268, denoting time (p. 149), *que si* (p. 149).
quel, rel. pr. 65, interrogatively 220, 223.
quelconque 236.
quelque (p. 149).
quelque ... que, 141. 3, 234.
quel que 235.
quelqu'un 68, 71, 225.
qu'est-ce qui (*que*)? emphatic 221 b.
quérir, conj. 93 C.
qui, relat. pron. 62, 210, 211, for *ce qui* (p. 148), for *celui qui* and *quiconque* (p. 148), interrogative 65—67, 219.
qui est-ce qui, emphatic 67, 219 Obs.
quiconque 236 (p. 148).
qui que ce soit 233.
quoi, interrogative 66, 224.
— relative 216, idiomatic (p. 148).
quoi que ce soit, for *rien* (p. 148).
quoi que and *quoique* 141, 3, 274, elision of *e* in, 7 I.

Recevoir, conj. 82.
reciprocal verbs 88.
redoubler, constr. of (p. 148).
reflective pronouns 51—52.
— verbs, conj. 88, agreement of past part. 163, construct. 191.
régime direct 162.
relative pronouns, see pronouns.
remembering, verbs of, 132 h.
repartir and *répartir* 93 C.
se repentir, conj. 93 A.
repondre, constr. 130 (p. 144).
resemblance, verbs of, 130 b.
résoudre, conj. 99 B.
ressortir, - 93 A.
rêver, constr. of (p. 144).

rester, conj. with *être* or *avoir* 87.
rien . . *ne* 226, 249, without *ne* 244.
rire, conj. 98 B.
roux, fem. of, 34.

Saillir conj. 94 B, 101.
same, how rendered 208.
sans, with infinitive 152, *ne* omitted after (p. 148).
satisfaire, constr. of (p. 144).
savoir, conj. 95.
sciences, gender of names of, 112 B.
se, **reflect.** pron. 51, place of, 189.
seasons, gender of names of, 112 A.
selon que, subjunct. or indicat. after, 148 **Obs.**
selon, d'après and *suivant* 266.
sentir, conj. 93 A.
seoir,   -   102.
sequence of tenses 151.
servir, conj. 93 A, constr. of, 130 b (p. 144).
seul, place of, 175, subjunct. after, 149. 3.
si, adv., compared with *aussi* 182—3, for *oui* 243, for *quelque* 234 b, *si fait* 243.
si, conj., 141 b, 272, imperfect after, 136 b, replaced by *que* with subjunct. 271 Obs. **1.**
si ce n'est que (p. 149).
sibilants 3.
sis, sise 102.
so, how rendered 182. 183, 192. **3.**
soi, **refl. pron.** 52, 198.
some, how rendered 11, 14, 170, 193, 225, 237.
songer à 130 c. (**p.** 143).
sortir, **conj.** 93 A, with *avoir* 86.
souffrir,   -   94 A.
sourire 103.
sous and *au-dessous de* 262.
starting point, how rendered 132 b.
strong verbs 91—99.
subject, placed after the Verb 120—123.
subjunctive mood, formation of, 78. 79, in dependent clauses 142—149, in principal clauses 150, after *si* 271 Obs. 1.
substantives, compound 130 b, 131 b, plur. of, 22, declined 13, gender of, 23—26, gender determined by meaning, termination and derivation 112—114, of both genders 115.
•   partitive 11, 14, preceded by adjectives 170 a.
•   plural of, 16—22, with different meaning in plural 116, not used in Singular 117.
•   used in a general, individual, indeterminate or partitive sense 165.
subvenir à, with *avoir* 86, constr. of (**p.** 143).
suffire, conj. 98 B.
suivre,   -   99 D.
superlative 40. 107, subjunct. after, 149. 3, for English comparative (p. 146).
supposé, agreement 164 Obs. 2.
supposition. Subjunct. after verbs **of, 148. 2.**

sur = **by** 185, *sur* and *au-dessus de* 261.
surseoir, conj. 97.
suivant, selon, 266.

Taire, conj. 98 C.
taking away, verbs of, 130 a.
tandis que and *pendant que* 110.
tant and *autant* 182. 3 (p. 147).
teaching, verbs of, 130 a.
teindre, conj. 99 A.
tel, with inversion **122 b (p. 146).**
tenir, conj. 93 C.
tenses, formation of, 77—79, use of, 134—141, sequence of, 151.
than, how rendered (p. 149).
thinking, verbs of, 130 c, 144 b.
time, how long 129 c, definite 131 a.
tiret 7, **IV.**
toi, disjunct. pron. 49, 196.
tout, tous 230 (p. 146 & 148).
towns, gender of names of, 112 B.
traire, conj. 98 B.
trait d'union 7 IV.
travail, plural of, 21.
à *travers* and *au travers de* 265.
tréma 7 II.
trees, names **of,** 112 A.
trop (p. 146).
trust and distrust, dative after verbs of, 130 b.

Unique, subjunct. **after, 149** 3.
user, constr. of (p. 144).

Vaincre, conj. 99 D.
valoir,   -   96.
venir,   -   93 C.
verbs,   -   72—103, syntax 125—164.
verbs, envers, contre 263.
the very, how rendered **203.**
vêtir, conj. 93 B.
vieux, vieil, feminine of, 37.
virtues and vices, gender of, 112 B.
vivre, conj. 99 D.
voici que, voilà que (p. 149).
voir, conj. 97.
vouloir, conj. 98.
voulu, agreement of, 164 g.
vous, disjunct. pron. 196.
vowels 2.
vrai, place of, 175.
vu, agreement of, 164 h, Obs. 1.
What! which! whose! how rendered 213-223
when, Future after 140, = *que* (p. 149).
winds, gender of names of, 112 A.
wishing, verbs of, **149.** 1.

Y, **place of, 188—194**, for disjunct. pron **197.**
-yer, verbs **in,** 84 β 5.
yeux 21.

14, *Henrietta Street, Covent Garden,* **London**; *and*
20, *South Frederick Street,* **Edinburgh.**

WILLIAMS AND NORGATE'S
LIST OF
French, German, Italian, Latin and Greek,
AND OTHER
SCHOOL BOOKS AND MAPS.

French.

FOR PUBLIC SCHOOLS WHERE LATIN IS TAUGHT.

Eugène (G.) **The Student's Comparative Grammar** of the French Language, with an Historical Sketch of the Formation of French. For the use of Public Schools. With Exercises. By G. Eugène-Fasnacht, French Master, Westminster School. 11th Edition, thoroughly revised. Square crown 8vo, cloth. 5s.

Or Grammar, 3s.; Exercises, 2s. 6d.

"The appearance of a Grammar like this is in itself a sign that great advance is being made in the teaching of modern languages. . . . . The rules and observations are all scientifically classified and explained."—*Educational Times.*

"In itself this is in many ways the most satisfactory Grammar for beginners that we have as yet seen."—*Athenæum.*

Eugène's French Method. Elementary French Lessons. **Easy** Rules and Exercises preparatory to the "Student's Comparative French **Grammar.**" By the same Author. 9th Edition. Crown 8vo, cloth. 1s. 6d.

"**Certainly deserves** to rank among the best of our Elementary French Exercise-books."—*Educational Times.*

Delbos. **Student's Graduated French** Reader, for the use of Public Schools. I. First Year. Anecdotes, Tales, Historical Pieces. Edited, with Notes and a complete Vocabulary, by Leon Delbos, M.A., of King's College, London. 3rd Edition. Crown 8vo, cloth. 2s.

———— The same. II. Historical Pieces and Tales. 3rd Edition. Crown 8vo, cloth. 2s.

Little Eugène's French Reader. For Beginners. Anecdotes and Tales. Edited, with Notes and a complete Vocabulary, by Leon Delbos, M.A., of King's College. 2nd Edition. Crown 8vo, cloth. 1s. 6d.

Krueger (H.) **Short French Grammar.** **6th Edition.** 180 pp. 12mo, cloth. 2s.

Victor Hugo. Les Misérables, les principaux Episodes. With Life and Notes by J. Boïelle, Senior French Master, Dulwich College. 2 vols. Crown 8vo, cloth. Each **3s. 6d.**

—— **Notre-Dame de Paris.** Adapted for the use of Schools and Colleges, by J. Boïelle, B.A., Senior French Master, Dulwich College. 2 vols. Crown 8vo, cloth. Each 3s.

Boïelle. French **Composition** through Lord Macaulay's English. I. Frederic the Great. Edited, with Notes, Hints, and Introduction, by James Boïelle, B.A. (Univ. Gall.), Senior French Master, Dulwich College, &c. &c. Crown 8vo, cloth. **3s.**

Foa (Mad. Eugen.) Contes Historiques. With Idiomatic Notes by G. A. Neveu. 3rd Edition. Crown 8vo, cloth. 2s.

Larochejacquelein (Madame de) **Scenes from the War in the** Vendée. Edited from her Mémoires in French, with Introduction and Notes, by C. Scudamore, M.A. Oxon, Assistant Master, Forest School, Walthamstow. Crown 8vo, cloth. 2s.

French Classics for English Schools. Edited, with Introduction and Notes, by **Leon Delbos**, M.A., of King's College. Crown 8vo, cloth.

- No. 1. Racine's Les Plaideurs. 1s. **6d.**
- No. 2. Corneille's Horace. 1s. 6d.
- No. 3. Corneille's Cinna. 1s. **6d.**
- No. 4. Molière's Bourgeois **Gentilhomme.** 1s. 6d.
- **No. 5.** Corneille's **Le Cid.** 1s. 6d.
- No. 6. Molière's Précieuses Ridicules. 1s. 6d.
- No. 7. Chateaubriand's Voyage en Amérique. 1s. 6d.
- No. 8. **De Maistre's** Prisonniers du Caucase and Lepreux d'Aoste. 1s. 6d.
- No. 9. **Lafontaine's Fables Choisies.** 1s. 6d.

Lemaistre (J.) French for Beginners. Lessons Systematic, Practical and Etymological. By **J.** Lemaistre. Crown 8vo, cloth. 2s. **6d.**

Roget (F. F.) Introduction **to Old French.** History, Grammar, Chrestomathy, Glossary. 400 pp. **Crown** 8vo, cl. 6s.

Kitchin. Introduction to the Study of Provençal. By **Darcy** B. Kitchin, B.A. [Literature—Grammar—Texts—Glossary.] Crown 8vo, cloth. 4s. 6d.

Tarver. Colloquial French, **for** School and Private Use. By H. Tarver, B.-ès-L., late of Eton College. 328 pp., crown 8vo, **cloth.** 5s.

Ahn's French Vocabulary and Dialogues. 2nd Edition. Crown 8vo, cloth. 1s. 6d.

Delbos **(L.)** French Accidence and Minor Syntax. 2nd Edition. Crown 8vo, cloth. 1s. 6d.

——— Student's French Composition, for the use of Public Schools, on an entirely new Plan. 250 pp. Crown 8vo, cloth. 3s. 6d.

Vinet (A.) Chrestomathie Française ou Choix de Morceaux tirés des meilleurs Ecrivains Français. 11th Edition. 358 pp., cloth. 3s. 6d.

Roussy. **Cours de Versions.** Pieces for Translation into French. With Notes. Crown 8vo. 2s. 6d.

Williams **(T. S.)** and **J. Lafont.** French Commercial Correspondence. A Collection **of** Modern Mercantile Letters in French and English, with their translation on opposite **pages.** 2nd Edition. 12mo, cloth. 4s. 6d.
    For a German Version of the same Letters, vide p. 4.

Fleury's Histoire de France, racontée à la Jeunesse, with **Grammatical** Notes, by Auguste Beljame, Bachelier-ès-lettres. 3rd Edition. 12mo, cloth boards. 3s. 6d.

Mandrou (A.) French Poetry for English **Schools.** Album Poétique de la Jeunesse. By A. Mandrou, M.A. de l'Académie de Paris. 2nd Edition. 12mo, cloth. 2s.

German.

Schlutter's German Class Book. A Course of Instruction based on Becker's System, and so arranged as to exhibit the Self-development of the Language, and its Affinities with the English. By Fr. Schlutter, Royal Military Academy, Woolwich. 5th Edition. 12mo, cloth. (Key, 5s.) 5s.

Möller (A.) A German Reading Book. A Companion to SCHLUTTER's German Class Book. With a complete Vocabulary. 150 pp. 12mo, cloth. 2s.

Ravensberg (A. v.) Practical Grammar of the German Language. Conversational Exercises, Dialogues and Idiomatic Expressions. 3rd Edition. Cloth. (Key, 2s.) 5s.

——— English into German. A Selection of Anecdotes, Stories, &c., with Notes for Translation. Cloth. (Key, 5s.) 4s. 6d.

——— German Reader, Prose and Poetry, with copious Notes for Beginners. 2nd Edition. Crown 8vo, cloth. 3s.

Weisse's Complete Practical Grammar of the German Language, with Exercises in Conversations, Letters, Poems and Treatises, &c. 4th Edition, very much enlarged and improved. 12mo, cloth. 6s.

——— New Conversational Exercises in German Composition, with complete Rules and Directions, with full References to his German Grammar. 2nd Edition. 12mo, cloth. (Key, 5s.) 3s. 6d.

Wittich's German Tales for Beginners, arranged in Progressive Order. 26th Edition. Crown 8vo, cloth. 4s.

——— German for Beginners, or Progressive German Exercises. 8th Edition. 12mo, cloth. (Key, 5s.) 4s.

——— German Grammar. 10th Edition. 12mo, cloth. 4s. 6d.

Hein. German Examination Papers. Comprising a complete Set of German Papers set at the Local Examinations in the four Universities of Scotland. By G. Hein, Aberdeen Grammar School. Crown 8vo, cloth. 2s. 6d.

Schinzel (E.) Child's First German Course; also, A Complete Treatise on German Pronunciation and Reading. Crown 8vo, cloth. 2s. 6d.

——— German Preparatory Course. 12mo, cloth. 2s. 6d.

——— Method of Learning German. (A Sequel to the Preparatory Course.) 12mo, cloth. 3s. 6d.

Apel's Short and Practical German Grammar for Beginners, with copious Examples and Exercises. 3rd Edition. 12mo, cloth. 2s. 6d.

Sonnenschein and Stallybrass. German for the English. Part I. First Reading Book. Easy Poems with interlinear Translations, and illustrated by Notes and Tables, chiefly Etymological. 4th Edition. 12mo, cloth. 4s. 6d.

Williams (**T. S.**) **Modern German and English Conversations** and **Elementary Phrases**, the German revised and **corrected** by A. Kokemueller. 21st enlarged and improved Edition. 12mo, cloth. 3s. 6d.

—————— and C. Cruse. **German and English Commercial Correspondence.** A Collection of Modern Mercantile Letters in German and English, with their Translation on opposite pages. 2nd Edition. 12mo, cloth. 4s. 6d.

    For a French Version of the same Letters, vide p. 2.

Apel (H.) **German Prose Stories** for Beginners (including Lessing's Prose Fables), with an interlinear Translation in the natural order of Construction. 12mo, cloth. 2s. 6d.

—————— **German Prose.** A Collection of the best Specimens of German Prose, chiefly from Modern Authors. 500 pp. Crown 8vo, cloth. 3s.

German **Classics for English Students.** With Notes and Vocabulary. Crown 8vo, cloth.

  Schiller's **Lied von der Glocke** (the Song of the Bell), and other Poems and Ballads. By M. Förster. 2s.
  —————— Maria Stuart. By M. Förster. 2s. 6d.
  —————— Minor Poems and Ballads. By Arthur P. Vernon. 2s.
  Goethe's Iphigenie auf Tauris. By H. Attwell. 2s.
  —————— Hermann und Dorothea. By M. Förster. 2s. 6d.
  —————— Egmont. By H. Apel. 2s. 6d.
  Lessing's Emilia Galotti. By G. Hein. 2s.
  —————— **Minna von** Barnhelm. By J. A. F. Schmidt. 2s. 6d.
  Chamisso's Peter Schlemihl. By M. Förster. 2s.
  Andersen's **Bilderbuch ohne** Bilder. By Alphons Beck. 2s.
  Nieritz. **Die Waise**, a German Tale. By E. C. Otte. 2s. 6d.
  Hauff's **Mærchen.** A Selection. By A. Hoare. 3s. 6d.

Carové (**J. W.**) **Mærchen ohne Ende** (The Story without an End). 12mo, cloth. 2s.

Fouque's Undine, Sintram, Aslauga's Ritter, die beiden Hauptleute. 4 vols. in 1. 8vo, cloth. 7s. 6d.

  Undine. 1s. 6d.; cloth, 2s.   Aslauga. 1s. 6d.; cloth, 2s.
  Sintram. 2s. 6d.; cloth, 3s.   Hauptleute. 1s. 6d.; cloth, 2s.

Latin and Greek.

Cæsar de Bello Gallico. Lib. I. Edited, with Introduction, Notes and Maps, by Alexander M. Bell, M.A., Ball. Coll. Oxon. Crown 8vo, cloth. 2s. 6d.

Euripides' Medea. The Greek Text, with Introduction and Explanatory Notes for Schools, by J. H. Hogan. 8vo, cloth. 3s. 6d.

——— Ion. Greek Text, with Notes for Beginners, Introduction and Questions for Examination, by Dr. Charles Badham, D.D. 2nd Edition. 8vo. 3s. 6d.

Æschylus. Agamemnon. Revised Greek Text, with literal line-for-line Translation on opposite pages, by John F. Davies, B.A. 8vo, cloth. 3s.

Platonis Philebus. With Introduction and Notes by Dr. C. Badham. 2nd Edition, considerably augmented. 8vo, cloth. 4s.

——— Euthydemus et Laches. With Critical Notes and an Epistola critica to the Senate of the Leyden University, by Dr. Ch. Badham, D.D. 8vo, cloth. 4s.

——— Symposium, and Letter to the Master of Trinity, "De Platonis Legibus,"—Platonis Convivium, cum Epistola ad Thompsonum edidit Carolus Badham. 8vo, cloth. 4s.

Sophocles. Electra. The Greek Text critically revised, with the aid of MSS. newly collated and explained. By Rev. H. F. M. Blaydes, M.A., formerly Student of Christ Church, Oxford. 8vo, cloth. 6s.

——— Philoctetes. Edited by the same. 8vo, cloth. 6s.
——— Trachiniæ. Edited by the same. 8vo, cloth. 6s.
——— Ajax. Edited by the same. 8vo, cloth. 6s.

Dr. D. Zompolides. A Course of Modern Greek, or the Greek Language of the Present Day. I. The Elementary Method. Crown 8vo. 5s.

Kiepert's New Atlas Antiquus. Maps of the Ancient World, for Schools and Colleges. 6th Edition. With a complete Geographical Index. Folio, boards. 7s. 6d.

Kampen. 15 Maps to illustrate Cæsar's De Bello Gallico. 15 coloured Maps. 4to, cloth. 3s. 6d.

Italian.

Volpe (Cav. G.) Eton Italian Grammar, for the use of Eton College. Including Exercises and Examples. **New Edition.** Crown 8vo, cloth. 4s. 6d.

———— Key to the Exercises. 1s.

Rossetti. Exercises for securing Idiomatic Italian by means of Literal Translations from the English, by Maria F. Rossetti. 12mo, cloth. 3s. 6d.

———— Aneddoti Italiani. One Hundred Italian Anecdotes, selected from "Il Compagno del Passeggio." Being also a Key to Rossetti's Exercises. 12mo, cloth. 2s. 6d.

Venosta (F.) Raccolta di Poesie tratti dai piu celebri autori antichi e moderni. Crown 8vo, cloth. 5s.

Christison (G.) Racconti Istorici e Novelle Morali. Edited for the use of Italian Students. 12th Edition. 18mo, cloth. 1s. 6d.

Danish—Dutch.

Bojesen (Mad. Marie) The Danish Speaker. Pronunciation of the Danish Language, Vocabulary, Dialogues and Idioms for the use of Students and Travellers in Denmark and Norway. 12mo, cloth. 4s.

Williams and Ludolph. Dutch and English Dialogues, and Elementary Phrases. 12mo. 2s. 6d.

Wall Maps.

Sydow's Wall Maps of Physical Geography for School-rooms, representing the purely physical proportions of the Globe, drawn in a bold manner. An English Edition, the Originals with English Names and Explanations. Mounted on canvas, with rollers :

1. **The** World. 2. Europe. 3. Asia. 4. Africa. 5. America (North and South). 6. Australia and Australasia. Each 10s.

———— Handbook to the Series of Large Physical Maps for School Instruction, edited by J. Tilleard. 8vo. 1s.

Miscellaneous.

De Rheims (H.). Practical Lines in Geometrical Drawing, containing the Use of Mathematical Instruments and the Construction of Scales, the Elements of Practical and Descriptive Geometry, Orthographic and Horizontal Projections, Isometrical Drawing and Perspective. Illustrated with 300 Diagrams, and giving (by analogy) the solution of every Question proposed at the Competitive Examinations for the Army. 8vo, cloth. 9s.

Fyfe (W. T.) First Lessons in Rhetoric. With Exercises. By W. T. Fyfe, M.A., Senior English Master, High School for Girls, Aberdeen. 12mo, sewed. 1s.

Fuerst's Hebrew Lexicon, by Davidson. A Hebrew and Chaldee **Lexicon to the** Old Testament, by Dr. Julius Fuerst. **5th** Edition, improved and enlarged, containing a Grammatical and Analytical Appendix. Translated by Rev. **Dr.** Samuel Davidson. 1600 pp., **royal 8vo,** cloth. 21s.

Strack (W.) Hebrew Grammar. With Exercises, Paradigms, Chrestomathy and Glossary. By Professor **H.** Strack, D.D., of Berlin. Crown 8vo, cloth. 4s. 6d.

Hebrew Texts. Large type. **16mo,** cloth.
Genesis. 1s. 6d. Psalms. 1s. Job. 1s. Isaiah. 1s.

Turpie (Rev. Dr.) Manual of the Chaldee Language: containing Grammar of the Biblical Chaldee and of the Targums, and a Chrestomathy, consisting of Selections from the Targums, with a Vocabulary adapted to the Chrestomathy. 1879. Square 8vo, cloth. 7s.

Socin (A.) Arabic Grammar. Paradigms, **Literature,** Chrestomathy and Glossary. By Dr. A. **Socin,** Professor, Tübingen. Crown 8vo, cloth. 7s. 6d.

Bopp's Comparative Grammar of the Sanscrit, Zend, Greek, **Latin,** Lithuanian, Gothic, German and Slavonic Languages. Translated by E. B. Eastwick. 4th Edition. 3 vols. 8vo, cloth. 31s. 6d.

Nestle (E.) Syriac **Grammar.** Literature, Chrestomathy and Glossary. By Professor E. Nestle, Professor, Tübingen. Translated into English. Crown 8vo, cloth. 9s.

Delitzsch (F.) Assyrian Grammar, with Paradigms, Exercises, Glossary and Bibliography. By Dr. F. Delitzsch. **Translated into** English by Prof. A. R. S. Kennedy, B.D. Crown 8vo, cloth. 15s.

Williams (T. S.) Modern German and English Conversations and Elementary Phrases, the German revised and corrected by A. Kokemueller. 21st enlarged and improved Edition. 12mo. cloth　　　　　　3s

Williams (T. S.) and C. Cruse. German and English Commercial Correspondence. A Collection of Modern Mercantile Letters in German and English, with their Translation on opposite pages. 2nd Edition. 12mo. cloth　　　　　　4s 6d

Apel (H.) German Prose Stories for Beginners (including Lessing's Prose Fables), with an interlinear Translation in the natural order of Construction. 2nd Edition. 12mo. cloth　　　　　　2s 6d

────── **German Prose.** A Collection of the best Specimens of German Prose, chiefly from Modern Authors. A Handbook for Schools and Families. 500 pp. Crown 8vo. cloth　　　　　　3s

German Classics for English Schools, with Notes and Vocabulary. Crown 8vo. cloth.

Schiller's Lied von der Glocke (The Song of the Bell), and other Poems and Ballads, by M. Förster　　2s
────── Minor **Poems.** By Arthur P. Vernon　　2s
────── Maria Stuart, by Moritz Förster　　2s 6d
Goethe's Hermann und Dorothea, by M. Förster　　2s 6d
────── Iphigenie auf Tauris. With **Notes** by H. Attwell.　　2s
────── Egmont. By H. Apel　　2s 6d
Lessing's Minna von Barnhelm, by Schmidt　　2s 6d
────── Emilia Galotti. By G. Hein　　2s
Chamisso's Peter Schlemihl, by M. Förster　　2s
Andersen (H. C.) Bilderbuch ohne Bilder, by Beck　　2s
Nieritz. Die **Waise,** a Tale, by Otte　　2s
Hauff's Mærchen. A Selection, by A. Hoare　　3s 6d

Carové (J. W.) Mæhrchen ohne Ende (The Story without an End). 12mo. cloth　　2s
Fouqué's Undine, Sintram, Aslauga's Ritter, die beiden Hauptleute. 4 vols. in 1. 8vo. cloth　　7s 6d
　Undine. 1s 6d; cloth, 2s.　Aslauga. 1s 6d; cloth, 2s
　Sintram. 2s 6d; cloth, 3s.　Hauptleute. 1s 6d; cloth, 2s

Williams and Norgate's School Books and Maps.

Latin, Greek, etc.

Cæsar de Bello Gallico. Lib. I. Edited with Introduction, Notes and Maps, by ALEXANDER M. BELL, M.A. Ball. Coll., Oxon. Crown 8vo. cloth 2s 6d

Euripides' Medea. The Greek Text, with Introduction and Explanatory Notes for Schools, by J. H. Hogan. 8vo. cloth 3s 6d

—— Ion. Greek Text, with Notes for Beginners, Introduction and Questions for Examination, by the Rev. Charles Badham, D.D. 2nd Edition. 8vo. 3s 6d

Æschylus. **Agamemnon.** Revised Greek Text, with literal line-for-line Translation on opposite pages, by John F. Davies, B.A. 8vo. cloth 3s

Platonis **Philebus.** With Introduction and Notes by Dr. C. Badham. 2nd Edition, considerably augmented. 8vo. cloth 4s

—— Euthydemus et **Laches.** With Critical Notes, by the Rev. Ch. Badham, D.D. 8vo. cloth 4s

—— **Convivium,** cum Epistola ad Thompsonum, "De Platonis Legibus," edidit C. Badham. 8vo. cloth 4s

Dr. D. Zompolides. A Course of **Modern** Greek, or the Greek Language of the Present Day. I. The Elementary Method. Crown 8vo. 5s

---

Kiepert New **Atlas Antiquus.** Maps of the Ancient World, for Schools and Colleges. 6th Edition. With a complete Geographical Index. Folio, boards 7s 6d

Kampen. 15 Maps to illustrate Cæsar's De Bello Gallico. 15 coloured Maps. 4to. cloth 3s 6d

Italian.

Volpe (Cav. G.) Eton Italian Grammar, for the use of Eton College. Including **Exercises** and Examples. New Edition. Crown 8vo. cloth (Key, 1s) 4s 6d

Racconti Istorici e Novelle **Morali.** Edited, for the use of Italian Students, by G. Christison. 12th Edition. 18mo. cloth 1s 6d

Rossetti. Exercises for securing Idiomatic Italian, by means of Literal Translations from the English by Maria F. Rossetti. 12mo. cloth 3s 6d

—— Aneddoti **Italiani.** One Hundred Italian Anecdotes, selected from "Il Compagno del Passeggio."

www.ingramcontent.com/pod-product-compliance
Lightning Source LLC
Chambersburg PA
CBHW032143160426
43197CB00008B/761